JEAN-PHILIPPE SOULÉ

I, TARZAN

AGAINST ALL ODDS

AN INSPIRING REAL-LIFE STORY OF COURAGE, HOPE, AND TRUE RESILIENCE

Advance Praise

"Jean-Philippe's life is like the ultimate ultra-marathon, where hope, perseverance, and grit determine the outcome. I, Tarzan: Against All Odds is his story of redemption and remembrance that inspires and energizes the reader to believe that far-reaching dreams can come true. Jean-Philippe proves that your attitude determines your altitude — and high he climbs in this must-read memoir!"

— Dean Karnazes, ultramarathoner and *NY Times* bestselling author

#

"Marco Polo meets Tom Sawyer, I, Tarzan is the roller-coaster chronicle of Jean-Philippe Soule's early life of challenge and adventure. He skillfully and candidly guides us through his journey of discovery, from the depths of emotional anguish to towering personal achievements. This is a story of success, wrought in the fires of despair and wrapped up in good old-fashioned storytelling."

— Ian Adamson, author and world's most celebrated adventure racer (gold Medalist, 5-sport world champion, 6x world record holder)

A Note from the Author's Sister

I have very few childhood memories, but I know that I called my big brother "Indiana Jones" and my "Tarzan." To me, Jean-Phi was this adventurous hero who lived a thousand and one lives. His book *I, Tarzan* is about resilience, inviting us to follow a little boy struggling to pursue his dreams, to define his own legend, despite his uncooperative family and societal environment.

But how do you move forward when you don't fit the mold, when your family not only refuses to support you but actively stifles your dream of a lifetime?

I, Tarzan is his story: one forged with courage, and heart.

His memoir overwhelmed me in so many ways. Jean-Phi and I are as different as night and day, and although it seemed at times like I was reading about the childhood of a stranger, I often felt that I was also reading about my own life experiences and emotions — that his truth matched my truth. With *I, Tarzan*, he restored for me an historical and emotional integrity, easing my self-doubt.

Throughout my brother's journey, he dared to step out of his comfort zone, against all odds. He dared to leave the smooth and straight easy street to travel winding, diverging, sometimes arduous, sometimes wonderful but always enriching and revealing paths. He dared to listen to the music of his heart.

Of course, one might think that our kinship would make me lack objectivity, but in all honesty I don't think so. I devoured this book with apprehension, anticipation, emotion, and pride.

This book is a gift to anyone looking for hope.

— Karine Lafouge

First Edition

ISBN: 978-0-9843448-5-7 Paperback
ISBN: 978-0-9843448-0-2 e-Book

Published by Native Planet Adventures
www.jeanphilippesoule.com

Dedication

To Jacques Cousteau and all the other great world explorers.
To all the authors who inspired me as a kid.
To all the people who have believed in me since my childhood, for you gave me the strength to become myself.
To all the children with dreams. All those bullied, abused, or neglected. All those who deserve a better life.
To all the people who dare to believe in their dreams and make them a reality.
This book is for all of you, my readers. With *I, Tarzan*, I hope to inspire you to believe in yourself, follow your dreams, and live your own life.

Acknowledgments

My deepest thanks to my editors C. J. Anaya (C.J. Anaya Publishing) and Heather Sangster (Strong Finish Editorial Design) and to my friends Dominique Blachon, Nick Tribe, Jim and Hui-Ying LeSage, and Eddie Dinkins, who provided invaluable editorial feedback throughout the manuscript's various stages.

Contents

Chapter 1

Nothing to Lose

Far outweighing me and much older, he stood a full head taller. He smiled coldly as he looked down at me and moved forward, not bothering to raise his fists in defense, certain he'd knock me out with a single blow.

True, I was just a kid…

I looked like a juvenile junkie — barely standing; reeking of tequila, gin, and tobacco; my fingers brown with nicotine.

Dodging under his first swing, I swept his legs, sending him crashing to the ground, and unleashed my wrath. The fight was over in less than a minute. Only then, covered in his blood, did I return the smile.

Until I turned thirteen, I had dreamed of hiking through jungles, climbing mountains, diving in tropical waters, and exploring the globe. There had been no doubt in my mind that I would become a world adventurer like my favorite explorer, Jacques Cousteau.

In a few short years though, my life had fallen far from those goals, and my hope for a brighter future seemed gloomier every month.

I understood the economics of life, that I'd never be an adventurer. Nobody was paid to just travel the world, a sentiment my parents had drummed into me as fact. I had lived my entire childhood engrossed in a utopian dream, and I was being forced to outgrow it, becoming an empty young teenager.

My life was now all about survival — and the only way I knew how to do that was by fighting. I didn't care whether I lived or died. Dying would come as a relief. In every fight, a part of me hoped to be killed.

I didn't do it to hurt people. I fought because I wanted to be hurt, to *be* hit, to feel something other than numb. My adventurous goals had vanished.

Gangs became the closest thing that felt like family to me, but even with those ties I still experienced profound loneliness. Slipping into a criminal world, lacking guidance and support from my own family, I had lost my soul. I was on the surest path toward self-destruction.

But deep inside my heart, despite the pain and the doubts, there lived a breath of hope: a long-held dream. I can only attribute its endurance to its unfailing strength in my earlier childhood.

It was the only thing that kept me alive.

Chapter 2

Jacques Cousteau

"I am enough of an artist to draw freely upon my imagination. Imagination is more important than knowledge. For knowledge is limited, whereas imagination encircles the world."
— Albert Einstein

My dreams of becoming an adventurer started with my family's first TV.

When I was born in 1966, not all French families owned a television set, and my father was still a poor student at the optometry university of Lille. It was not until 1969, when I was three, that my father finished his studies and moved us to the southwest region of Bordeaux. We rented a modest house and bought our first TV.

I have vivid memories of my father installing it in the living room and turning it on. It was a small, heavy box with a tiny black-and-white screen. It only had three channels, with sporadic programs: some news, a few movies, Walt Disney cartoons, and TV shows.

Having this amazing invention at home was magical. My parents toyed with the two movable antennas, hoping to capture half-decent images with a sound we sometimes barely comprehended. The reception varied from one day to the next: sometimes it was all fuzzy; other times we had a sharp image for a few hours. It was the prehistorical era of TV, and my entire family was hooked.

For us, the greatest show of all was the incredible underwater images filmed by French explorer Commandant Jacques Cousteau. My father never wanted to miss one of those documentaries. Intrigued from an early age, I also watched them. I didn't understand how people could breathe in water and swim with fish. The fuzzy underwater images fascinated me, particularly those of the whales, sharks, and sea lions.

My father stood one meter ninety[1], much taller than most French people, and had broad shoulders and a muscular, athletic figure. He held a black belt in judo; became a good skier; loved sailing, spearfishing, and scuba diving; and played tennis and squash. People looked up to him. He was my hero, and I felt as if our underwater adventures via television brought us closer together. It was how I connected with him.

I shared my dad's excitement every time the show came on, which was rebroadcast all the time because Jacques Cousteau instilled a sense of pride within our nation. The greatest French explorer from the 1940s to the 1960s, he had conquered the sea — not only for himself but for the entire world — by inventing modern diving gear and underwater filming. He was the only filmmaker to ever win the Palme d'or for a documentary, a feat he realized at the 1956 Cannes Film Festival. His footage was unique and incredible for that era, and I wanted nothing more than to travel the world and go on never-ending adventures just like him.

My first adventure began at the bottom of my bathtub amid a raft of sea lions and schools of fish. I'd surface for a few moments, wipe water and bubbles from my face, and catch my breath before diving in again, trying to emulate the divers from Cousteau's films.

There may not have been real fish or sea lions at the bottom of my tub, but imagination has a way of creating hope, a more profound vision of life, and a more ideal reality.

1. six-foot-three

Jacques Cousteau did more than inspire me to attempt a record-breaking freedive in the bathtub. At four, I was already determined to live a life of great exploration and adventure.

Chapter 3

Tarzan

"You can't put a limit on anything. The more you dream, the farther you get."
— Michael Phelps

Cousteau was not my only source of inspiration. I was five years old when I saw the first Tarzan movie, featuring Olympic swimmer Johnny Weissmuller. A man who lived in the jungle, flew like a monkey from one tree to the next, and communicated with animals, Tarzan instantly became my new hero.

Every night, I pestered my parents to let me watch the next episode, not understanding it only came on once a week. I imagined that I was Tarzan, having heroic adventures in the wilds of Africa. I didn't feel that my life's purpose involved school and homework. (In France, we start attending at age three.) Cleaning my room? Merely a waste of time. I was meant to swing from tree to tree while letting out a true Tarzan call. I ruled over my own animal kingdom. I may have only been five, but I'd already figured out my goals.

"There was no doubt in my mind, I was Tarzan, King of the Jungle."

You may think that all kids do the same: they incarnate their superheroes, behaving just like their favorite role models. But I wasn't pretending. I lived every moment *as* Tarzan, from the loud jungle scream to the incessant tree climbing.

Around this time, my dad's first optician store became a success. He was an entrepreneur, with business acumen coursing through his veins. He talked with great confidence and charisma, making himself the center of attention with his group of friends. When he spoke, people listened. He was an awe-inspiring figure. He was also a storyteller and had a good sense of humor that bordered on the dark side.

French humor is particular and can be quite sarcastic and bitter. My father was a master at black humor, something his audience found entertaining. I was too young to understand that this often involved jokes at the expense of others, sometimes to the point of denigration. The more ashamed one could make a friend feel in front of others, the more enjoyable it was for the group. I didn't understand the flaws in this or the damage it caused. I simply saw my father as the guy people looked up to. Again, he was a hero to me.

My dad's success allowed us to move out of our small house in Le Haillan to Saint-Médard-en-Jalles, where my parents purchased a two-acre lot bordered by forest and built a new house.

There was no fence between our backyard and the forest, and this opened up my world, offering me an endless mass of woods I called my jungle. It felt as if the Universe had acknowledged my claim as Tarzan, bequeathing me an entire kingdom to rule as I saw fit.

Climbing trees and swinging from ropes became my life. There was not a single day in which my mom didn't urge me to leave the tops of the trees. She preferred not to watch as I descended, soaring down with my perfected Tarzan scream. She always feared that I would miss a branch or let go of the rope and break my neck from a ten-meter[1] drop.

But how could I? I was Tarzan, the Ape Man.

These were my very first outdoor adventures, the first time I had harbored dreams and saw them come to fruition in reality. Anything was possible, according to my five-year-old way of thinking.

1. thirty-three-foot

Sadly, the *Tarzan* TV series lasted only a few months, but by that time I had memorized the storylines of every episode and continued to live in my own imaginary jungle.

Every day, all day long, I envisioned myself living in an outdoor world where school did not exist, only a life in harmony with nature. I taught my three-year-old brother how to climb trees and add to our treehouse — building cabanas and rudimentary tools and furniture — inspired by a beautifully illustrated book about Robinson Crusoe's adventures.

When evening came, I'd take a break from my explorations, and my mother would prepare a feast fit for the King of the Jungle. Those dinners were happy times as I sat with my family.

Unfortunately, I didn't realize that the happiness of childhood could end so abruptly. I never imagined that my hold on the little joys and pleasures of a carefree life was so tenuous.

I had no idea that dreams could disintegrate just as easily as they were formed.

Chapter 4

Back to Reality

"The true sign of intelligence is not knowledge but imagination."
— Albert Einstein

Living in an imaginary world was no longer easy. My amazing adventures stopped every single time I went to school. Along with the daily dreariness of the classroom, the cruel reality of the schoolyard always caught up to me.

I failed to listen in class. I didn't see any benefit to paying attention because what the teachers said seemed so obvious and simple. Due to utter boredom, I dove straight back into my own kingdom.

While the other kids learned math and grammar, I wrestled crocodiles, fought with gorillas, swung between trees, jumped from high cliffs, and rode atop an elephant's back. There was so much going on in my mind that I was clueless about what was happening in the classroom. This led to trouble, as one would expect. Immersed in my daydreams, I missed new topics my teachers presented.

From my perspective, the other kids were not even real, nor were the teachers, and the classes were so dull and dumb — how could this be reality? To make matters worse, the teachers spoke to us as if we were unable to comprehend the most basic lessons, treating us like unintelligent beings. When I saw the other kids attentively trying to listen, I often wondered if they were even human. What if they were robots being programmed by the robot teacher to behave a certain way? Was I stuck in a robot factory where I didn't belong?

Each time the teacher called me to the board, I was slammed back to reality, standing before the class in a cold sweat, eyes wet as I tried to hold back my tears. I remained speechless, frozen, wondering what the subject was about and unable to answer any of the teacher's questions.

Not only did my lack of focus get me into trouble when called to the board, but it became a problem in other aspects of my schooling. I kept forgetting my schoolbooks, notebooks, supplies, and even clothing. My parents and teachers were bewildered by this behavior, and eventually my grades reflected it too. They were all over the place, from excellent to almost fail, depending on whether the teacher and the subject matter could hold my attention.

Naturally, my habit of needing to escape into imaginary worlds of adventure was ripe for mockery from many students. It made me an easy target for the school bullies.

It also didn't help that I was pathetic at playing soccer, and I never scored a goal, even when the net was without a goalkeeper. At a time when soccer was the only sport we practiced in school, I was considered a stupid, uncoordinated kid, and the very worst of my class.

Nobody at school knew I'd been born with a strong strabismus, which is a divergence of the eyes that leads to double vision. Although my right eye only stared in the wrong direction when I was tired or sleepy, I frequently saw everything doubled. It wasn't a noticeable handicap, but I struggled with this condition. I'd had two eye surgeries at the ages of three and five, but they were complete failures, and I wore glasses that didn't help me much. In fact, I would have needed such powerful prisms to correct the strabismus in my right eye that the glass lens would have been too thick to balance on my face. My left eye offered me perfect vision. Despite this infirmity, my body learned how to compensate for this strabismus. To avoid seeing double, I kept my head slightly tilted to the left.

My brain adapted to my eyesight with my head in this position. I didn't appear completely crooked. Most people failed to notice it at first glance. My head was only tilted by ten degrees, but it was obvious enough that every time I had my picture taken, photographers told me to straighten my posture and the position of my head. I always replied that my head was, in fact, straight. At least for me it was straight; otherwise, I'd get double vision again.

So, I lived with my head tilted. It became natural for me, and was the only thing I could do to see normally, but it didn't completely solve my vision problems. When tired, I would occasionally see double, but the secondary image appeared so far down and to the right of my leading left eye that my brain learned how to dismiss it, only showing me what my left eye saw.

Because of this strabismus and my right eye's amblyopia (lazy eye), I also had a problem with depth perception, particularly at a distance between one and two meters, the exact distance between me and the soccer ball when I tried to kick it.

My physical education teacher, who never knew about my handicap because it wasn't obvious, went so far as to mock me in front of the other kids, which in turn gave them tacit permission to do the same at recess. He thought I was a lost cause or that I purposely tried to miss the ball, kicking incorrectly. I always felt humiliated.

Before the start of each game, the two elected team captains took turns picking their players, selecting the quickest and most skilled boys first, then the other boys, and then the girls. I was always the last kid to get picked, joining a team by default.

Although I couldn't get a full eye correction, my doctor thought it was important for me to wear glasses. It forced my right eye to continue working. The glasses merely added insult to injury, covering my face and further branding me an outcast. It yielded me the nickname *Binocleux*, a pejorative and mean French expression that meant "a stupid boy wearing glasses," similar to the derogatory English "four eyes."

From the age of six, my tilted head, huge glasses, and never-ending disconnect with my surroundings while living in my own world created the perfect storm. I became an easy target for bullies. I had no identity, only a label: Binocleux.

The other kids knew my dad built, adjusted, and sold glasses, so they took great pleasure in hitting me in the face, trying to break mine. Most of the time they succeeded: sometimes the arms would get bent or broken, and often the lenses would blow out of the frame. It didn't matter, Binocleux could always get a new pair.

Time after time, I would return home with broken glasses and bruises. I avoided crying in front of my parents, too proud to admit I was being bullied at school. I would always invent stories to explain how it happened, and it was always easy for them to believe me because I often scratched my face and dropped my glasses while climbing trees in our woods. Plus, by this time, neither one of them paid much attention to me, each caught up in their own lives.

I'm not sure my parents ever noticed or understood the extent of the bullying, how miserable I actually felt at school. While the bruises faded, the emotional injuries remained.

Chapter 5

Slammed Down

"You gain strength, courage and confidence by every experience in which you really stop to look fear in the face. You are able to say to yourself, 'I have lived through this horror. I can take the next thing that comes along.' You must do the thing you think you cannot do."

— Eleanor Roosevelt, *You Learn by Living*, 1983

When I was seven, my dad decided to enroll me in judo. He had a black belt, so perhaps he wanted me to follow in his footsteps — or at least keep me out of the woods where I was always breaking my glasses. Even though the local judo club had a minimum age membership of ten, Dad met with the dojo owner and pressured him into accepting me.

He was a master at imposing his will and wishes on others. Between his physical stature, business success, connections, and eloquent authority, he always managed to get what he wanted from people.

Learning judo could have been a great experience, toughening me up. Unfortunately, there was a reason for the age restriction. The youngest kids were between ten and twelve years old, three to five years my senior. They were too big for me to learn with and practice on. Each time I tried to sweep one of them down with a judo technique, they would use their superior weight and force to counter my poor technique. All they had to do was stand still to prevent me from doing any of the moves.

When it was their turn to practice on me, the results were very different. I flew to the ground so violently that I was often hurt. The kids closest to my age weren't malicious, but they had a hard time practicing with older kids, so they loved partnering with me. They took me down easily enough, even without performing the correct movements or techniques. I got banged up in every possible way, sometimes so hard that I couldn't hold in my tears.

I don't think the instructor appreciated my dad pressuring him into taking me on as he acted like he couldn't have cared less about me. It didn't matter to him whether I learned judo or not, and I suspected he enjoyed seeing the other kids slam me on the floor.

Luckily, there were a few nice teenage boys bearing impressive brown and black belts. They were tall and powerful, and their technique was so good, they had nothing to prove. When I got to practice with one of them, they'd patiently show me the moves and gently put me down, holding me back before I even touched the tatami. I finally learned some fundamentals while working with them. They let me practice all the moves on them, and even though I didn't have the strength to put those guys off balance, they allowed themselves to be thrown to the ground with every move I made. They laughed with me and made me feel good. Even though this only happened on occasion, I really appreciated their mentorship.

Most of the time, though, I was with the younger yellow and orange belts, ensuring that I ended every practice covered in bruises.

I returned home crying more than once, and when the first year ended, I told my mom that I hated judo and didn't want to return. Although that sparked an argument between my parents, it did put an end to my martial arts practice, and it hadn't helped to boost my confidence in the least, nor did it prevent me from being bullied at school.

On the contrary, I had been thrown down on the tatami so forcefully and so swiftly so many times by bigger kids that I truly believed I was weak, never daring to fight back.

When I turned eight, I moved to another school. Once again, my daily daydreams in my imaginary world left me with few friends. My loner status, lack of focus, and four-eyed appearance made me the prime target for harassment: a bully free-for-all, with me as the perfect loser. And the biggest, toughest kid and his gang — two to three years older than me — were master bullies.

They made fun of me, spat on me, and pushed me to the ground, where they continued the torture by kicking me in the stomach. Terrorized by these much bigger kids, I would curl into the fetal position — my head tucked into my arms, protecting my face — to absorb all the kicks and punches. I would wait to cry until after they'd finally had enough and left me lying there battered and broken.

They persecuted me day after day, and the physical pain was nothing compared to the constant humiliation that consumed me.

Luckily, I found my escape every time I returned home. I ran to the woods, where I would build cabanas, climb to the top of the highest trees, and become the invincible Tarzan. I would summon all the animals and confront the school bullies, engaging them in brutal battles and claiming victory again and again. My imaginary world was where all my dreams were fulfilled, all my desires were attainable, and all my strength was found. The weaker I became at school, the stronger I became in my own fantasies. I learned from those very bullies that mercy was for the weak and so, in my perfect world, I showed them absolutely none.

Chapter 6

The Toughest Kid in School

"It is when power is wedded to chronic fear that it becomes formidable."
— Eric Hoffer, *The Passionate State of Mind*, 1954

My new school was *L'École des bois* (School in the Woods), named for its location in the middle of the woods, of course, and for having large recess grounds that included a few wooded areas. It was the perfect playground for a loner like me, who preferred to climb trees rather than play with the other kids. But it would also prove to be excellent turf for bullies, as no teacher could ever keep an eye on all the kids at the same time.

The school was a good distance from my home, and after a few months my parents arranged to carpool with another family from the neighboring village. This was how I met Jean. He and I formed an instant bond, becoming the best of friends. He was six months older than me, but I was slightly taller. Jean was my opposite in many ways. He was very athletic. Not only had he just earned his brown belt in judo at the young age of ten, he could walk on his hands and do endless frontflips and backflips.

Once during recess, we went to play in the forested part of the school grounds when the usual group of bullies took us for prey. The toughest kid at the school was going to kick my butt again, and his three friends were there to help him. All were a head taller than us, and we were too far from the recess supervisor's view to hope for anybody to come to our aid.

Jean immediately understood the situation. I had taken months of beatings, and it showed in my frightened tear-filled eyes.

It requires courage to fight back and defend yourself, and I had none. Each beating had further lowered my self-esteem, destroying every ounce of courage I'd ever possessed. Despite the imaginary justice I dished out in my perfect world in the woods, I didn't believe I could defend myself in the real world, so I never tried.

I knew how much I was going to suffer, both physically and emotionally, and I prepared myself for the inevitable humiliation. I couldn't speak, and I couldn't move — every fiber of my being rooted to the spot as they mocked me, preparing to beat me up.

The four of them laughed as the ringleader said, "Oh, you have a friend now. We're going to beat the crap out of him too."

Little did they know that Jean, although much smaller, had years of judo fighting experience. He moved before anyone else and took the first kid down within seconds, turning immediately to face the other two. I was left to brawl with the giant.

Witnessing Jean attack those bullies — fighting kids much bigger than him — without an ounce of fear did something to me, sparking a flare of hope, making me realize I didn't have to cower in defeat. I didn't have to take this anymore.

When the giant was less than a meter[1] away, I used the adrenaline coursing through my veins to punch his nose with all my strength. Astonished, he drew one step back. His mistake. I swept him down with an *Osotogari*, the very first judo technique I had learned as a white belt. He slammed onto his back, and I took advantage of his vulnerable position, immediately jumping on him.

I kneeled atop his body, attacking him with everything I had. Years of pent-up rage, fear, pain, and humiliation erupted as I pounded this kid in the face over and over again while he covered his head in an attempt

---

1. three feet

to protect himself from the onslaught. I couldn't stop. It was as if a flame had finally lit the powder keg within me, and the results were explosive. His nose and lips were a bloody mess, but I kept punching, and punching, and punching. He suffered for all his crimes against me and for the crimes of past bullies.

I was completely out of control, a wild injured animal, fighting for survival with nothing to lose. I may have only been nine, but my twelve-year-old tormentor couldn't do a thing. I completely overwhelmed him, and his blood flew everywhere. I would have injured this kid far worse if Jean hadn't interrupted my hyper-focused attack.

"Stop. He's done, he's done. You've kicked his butt," he said, pulling me away.

My nemesis stayed down, holding his head and crying in his own blood. He'd never expected me to launch the first attack. His three friends, already beaten by Jean, looked terrified. They stared at me as if I was the Devil himself. After destroying their gang, Jean and I instantly became the toughest kids at school.

We didn't get into too much trouble with the school principal. Rumors had preceded these kids, which meant Jean and I were let off the hook with a few warnings.

That was a huge turning point for me: I learned that to survive and thrive you had to fend for yourself in any way possible. Unfortunately, I also learned that anger and pain had one outlet: violence. At the time, there was no one in my life to tell me otherwise. The old, weak, terrified version of me had been replaced, and things began to change after that. Maybe judo had toughened me up after all, and the daily hours I'd spent climbing trees and swinging on ropes gave me more strength than I had ever thought.

From that day on, I gained a tremendous amount of self-confidence. I realized that fear was not necessarily a hurdle. When we overcome our fears, we can accomplish what seems impossible. I moved forward with an increased belief in my physical abilities that I would eventually channel into other aspects of my life.

I'd found my power, and I was never going to let anyone take it from me again.

My glasses had flown off during the fight, and I could see better without them anyway. My eye doctor wanted me to wear them, to force my right eye to work. But, actually, my right eye often sent a double signal to my brain, creating a second parasitic image that didn't line up with what I was seeing with my good eye, sometimes giving me headaches. Removing my glasses allowed my left eye to be in charge. My spectacles had been the stuff of so much mockery, I decided to abandon them altogether. I told my dad, and Binocleux was no longer!

Chapter 7

Boarding School

"If you don't get out there and define yourself, you'll be quickly and inaccurately defined by others."

— Michelle Obama, *Becoming*, 2018

At the age of ten, I entered my first boarding school — a brand-new experience. In this year of middle school, I was in the youngest class. Jean didn't graduate and had to stay in our previous elementary school for another year. Once again, I was the new kid on the block, alone with no friends.

I had to stand my ground from the beginning and set some rules. I had to gain respect, not only from the kids in my own class but also from the two classes above me since we shared the recess playground and dormitories. I decided not to wait.

I asked around and discovered the identity of the head bully, but I wasn't going to be stupid and start a fight. I waited for him to make his move on a kid who couldn't defend himself. When he attacked a boy my age, two years his junior, I jumped on him. Even though I was the younger and smaller defender of the poor boy, the beating I gave that bully shocked all those kids.

I possessed a crazy rage within me that would unleash with incredible speed and violence. After suffering years of bullying and physical abuse from other kids, I had toughened up, and I didn't fear anybody or anything. I never started a fight. I never attacked the defenseless, but I challenged the biggest guys and prompted them to throw the first punch. I begged for the attention I never received at home, gaining my own recognition with my fists.

I became the alpha boy and the ace troublemaker. Jean joined me a year later in the same boarding school. We were already too much trouble individually. Together, we became a real handful. We did *Les 400 Coups* (we raised hell, pulling every trick in the book) until we both got kicked out and our parents separated us, putting us in different schools. But deep inside we weren't mean, bad kids. We were just fighting our demons, each of us carrying strong burdens.

Jean had been abandoned by his mother and left in an orphanage at an age when he remembered it. No matter the love he received from his adoptive parents, he lived with that memory of being abandoned by his birth parents, and he felt worthless. Serendipitously, his wonderful adoptive parents filled a big hole in my heart that my parents couldn't.

I needed to feel loved, recognized, and to be given some guidance, but my early burden was about to get heavier.

Chapter 8

Dad's Imaginary World

> *"…humor that belittles can be extremely damaging within the family. Children take sarcasm and humorous exaggeration at face value. They are not worldly enough to understand that a parent is joking."*
>
> — Susan Forward, *Toxic Parents*, 2010

Aside from the troubles I dealt with at school, my home life and my relationship with my parents contributed to many of my self-esteem issues and insecurities. I wasn't the only person in my family who lived in his own world — I definitely got that gene from my father. Our imaginary worlds were probably very different, though. His was most likely driven by business and financial thoughts. But nobody ever picked on him, and he never paid for his daydreaming the way I did. My younger brother, sister, and I were his casualties. He never meant to harm us, but he often forgot about us, leaving us in dire situations for our age, and the emotional backlash for us kids was tremendous.

For example, when I was three, I used to ride up the ski lifts inside a backpack on my dad's shoulders. I would ski down with him, first between his legs, and then proudly on my own next to him. He would take the beginner's lift two to three times to descend with me, then ask me to wait somewhere while he did a run or two — or many more.

Once, the ski-lift operator found me crying. I was freezing, my hands and toes numb with the cold. I told him that my dad had asked me to wait, but he hadn't come back. The lift operator took me to his shelter, sat me next to the heater, and made me a hot drink. I stayed with him for a few hours until Mom finally arrived. Dad had forgotten about me. After spending hours skiing on his own, he had returned to the apartment rental alone, where she promptly asked him about me. Under the assault of my mother's screams, it always took him a while to remember where he had left me.

When I was six, I had an evening appointment at the eye doctor, whose office was located above my dad's optician store. That evening Dad didn't have any clients, so he closed up early and went home — home being in another town a half-hour-drive away. On occasion, he would close his store to do some shopping and then return to reopen it. At first, I thought this was the case, so I just sat down in front of the door and waited. Minutes became an hour, an hour turned into two. As I continued to wait, I began to realize that Dad had forgotten me once again.

It was a chilly winter night. I was alone and freezing, crying in front of my dad's store, waiting for him to pick me up. Mobile phones didn't exist back then, and I didn't see a single person in the streets. It was only after Dad had returned home — probably after stopping in at a friend's place — that Mom, horrified again, asked him where he'd left me. She instantly knew that he had forgotten me after my eye appointment. They both jumped in the car and raced back, finding me shivering.

When I was eight years old, we returned late from sailing, which was another of Dad's hobbies. My three-year-old sister, six-year-old brother, and I were sleeping in the back of the car. When we arrived home, Mom carried my sister to her bedroom and asked Dad to carry me and my brother to bed.

At daybreak, I woke up in my room, freaking out when I heard knocking on the exterior wooden blinds of my window. I thought it was a burglar trying to break in. I ran to my parents' room, screaming, "There is someone in the garden. They're knocking on my window."

My dad jumped out of bed and grabbed a fighting stick, running outside toward the main entrance to confront the burglar. Meanwhile, someone came knocking on the outside door of my parents' room. We heard a small voice saying, "Maman." It was my brother, Olivier. He had spent the entire night outside.

After taking me to bed, Dad had forgotten to return to the car to get Olivier. He'd locked the house and gone to sleep. When my brother woke up, he didn't dare rouse my parents. We had often been scolded if we played too loudly after waking up early in the morning and didn't let them sleep. So Olivier got out of the car, unleashed our German shepherd, and went with him to the forested part of our garden.

He climbed into the treehouse, but the dog couldn't follow him up the tree. Olivier quickly became cold. Instead of staying there on his own, he descended and laid down with our dog, sleeping at the base of the tree. At daybreak, he was chilled and thought it would be okay to enter the house, but he still didn't want to wake our parents, so he knocked on my window first.

Dad forgot us everywhere, time after time. Once, when he took my sister, Karine, to kindergarten, he drove to my brother's school instead and left her there on the front sidewalk. Not recognizing the location, Karine cried until a lady stopped and asked her what had happened. When my sister said that her dad had made a mistake and dropped her off at the wrong school, the lady took Karine to the nearby kindergarten. The school called my mom, asking her to explain why a three-year-old girl had been left by herself on the street ten blocks from her school.

The number of times he forgot us in various places meant we kids had to grow up quickly and learn to adjust to each scenario, which likely helped me forge the survival mindset I would need in future expeditions. We also had to adjust to his nonchalant attitude. His forgetting about us was never a big deal to him; he never showed regret — sometimes we'd get a small hug or a pat on the back, which was somewhat comforting. He never apologized.

My dad's greatest love was sailing. He first bought a small cabin sailboat when I was six, Olivier four, and Karine an infant, and the family sailed and fished together. Nothing at all adventurous, in my opinion, and the only person enthusiastic about sailing and fishing at that time was Dad. We hated getting stuck on a cramped sailboat for hours, but we enjoyed stopping for a swim, catching crabs, and eating wild oysters off the shell.

As we got a little older, Olivier and I started to love sailing too, and it represented perfectly the relationship we had with our dad as young kids. When Hobie Cat catamarans started appearing on the water, the speed at which they flew by us fascinated my dad. When I was nine, he sold his slow sailing bathtub and bought his first Hobie Cat.

The eighteen-foot Hobie Cat was made for two people, although Dad made it work with two kids and him as the captain. He entered races with it, often partnering with another experienced adult. (He eventually set the speed crossing record for Carcans Lake and later for the Bassin d'Arcachon, a bay on the southwest coast of France. He loved challenging every sailboat that crossed his path.)

He also purchased a Laser dinghy so my brother and I could learn, practice, and race on our own. But he didn't always have an adult crew to join him, or sometimes when the wind wasn't strong, it was advantageous to partner with a very lightweight crew, like a kid. Olivier and I would take turns crewing with him on the sporty Hobie Cat and sailing on our own with the Laser.

Dad never understood that we were still small kids. He would quickly give us some pointers on how to operate the boat, and then we were left to learn while practicing. He had no patience. We needed to catch on to things immediately. When we raced with him on the Hobie Cat, or even while we were training, if we didn't master a maneuver or weren't fast enough to pull on the ropes and jump on the trapeze, he would scream at us (things like "Putain, merde! You're stupid or what?" or "Merde, bouge ton cul!" *Fuck, move your ass!*) because we were slowing the boat's momentum, making him lose precious seconds and any advantageous positioning he'd had over the other boats. He would be furious one moment, and then all excited to race back toward the lead a minute later, joking and laughing with us.

Even though it was routine to us, his screaming always affected me. It made me feel that I was unworthy, that I just sucked at a sport I enjoyed. I never met his expectations. Yet, I much preferred to race on the Hobie Cat with my dad than being on my own in the Laser. It was a fun and sporty boat, but the much faster Hobie Cat was the real deal. Though I hated being screamed at when I always did my best, I loved the adrenaline, and Dad's competitive attitude was addictive. The Hobie Cat was for the grown-ups, and that's where I wanted to be.

Both Olivier and I were gifted with athletic abilities — we were competitive and fast learners — but it was never enough for my dad. It was always "keep up or stay home with your sister," whether it was sailing or any other outdoor activity. (He stopped taking us skiing until we were good enough and fast enough to descend any slope without him having to wait for us.) We shared the joys of our sailing victories, but not without moments of feeling unworthy during both regattas and training. But as Dad would say, the captain is always right and needs to be strict with his crew to make split-second decisions. Screaming was part of it; "it's the fire of the action," as he used to say. We didn't know any better, and just assumed it was the same way in every crew.

But as Olivier would later understand when he was the teenage crew for the Tahitian world champion, a good captain never screams. He learned so much from his mentor that he quickly left Dad and his domineering approach behind. While my brother and I pursued different interests from each other as young adults, as captain of his own boat, Olivier would claim the title of regional Hobie Cat champion, compete in nationals, and even be sponsored to race with the famous professional teams in big waves and storms around La Reunion Island off the African coast. (Today in his early fifties, he continues to be an accomplished sailor, competing on larger sport sailboats, regularly winning regional and national regattas, and still breaking speed records.)

Around the time my dad started sailing Hobie Cats, he also learned to windsurf. When I was twelve, he decided to teach me. As with sailing, windsurfing was easy to get the hang of. I learned how to lift the sail out of the water, hold it straight, grab the mast to place my hands on the boom, and throw the sail into the wind, gliding over the water. Dad sailed on the Hobie Cat next to me, telling me to follow him and his sailing partner. We had a three-fourth tailwind that became stronger the farther we went from the beach. I flew behind the Hobie Cat. It was a great feeling for my very first day. I did well, and I rarely fell off the board despite the strong wind. When I fell, I could quickly pick it back up and resume traveling at high speeds over the water.

When we were in the middle of the lake, kilometers from the shore, a Tornado catamaran flew by us and passed my dad. The Tornado was a newer model that had even more sailing power than the eighteen-foot Hobie Cat, theoretically faster. Dad immediately adjusted his boat and went racing after it, leaving me there in the middle of the lake. I couldn't keep up with him, losing sight of him and his friend as they continued toward the end of the lake. He caught up to the Tornado and passed it but never came back for me.

I decided to turn around and return to our base camp. That was when things became complicated. The wind had strengthened significantly, and I fought it head on, constantly tacking against it. Even though I moved fast, I didn't make much progress, and any progression I did make created too much of a zigzag. I couldn't move forward enough, I could only sail sideways. The wind became violent with sudden gusts. I could no longer hold the sail, which was too big for my size and weight. I kept falling into the lake, exhausting myself by lifting the sail out of the water time after time. I no longer made any progress, and there was no shore in sight.

I knew that Dad wouldn't be coming back. Even if he wanted, he couldn't possibly find me. After two hours of fighting the wind, I knew I'd never be able to go back to shore, at least not by sailing. It would take me forever to hand paddle the kilometers I had sailed so rapidly before, but there was no alternative.

At sunset, I folded the sail and the mast, rolled them up on the board, laid flat on my stomach, and started hand paddling toward my destination. Luckily, I was good with navigation. I paddled until my shoulders and triceps were so sore, I could barely lift my arms. I propelled myself toward shore until the skin under my ribs turned raw and felt bruised. In pain, I kept paddling, harder and harder as night fell. Then I continued into the night. I could see the lights of our base camp, and I knew if I kept moving, I'd get there in an hour, maybe two, but I would succeed.

When I finally reached the shore, I was so exhausted I couldn't stand up or sit on the board. I let myself roll into the water and held on to it, floating, waiting to recover enough to stand and walk onto the beach. I dragged the board with me and stored it next to my dad's car. I went back to find him relaxing with his friends next to their trailer. It was almost midnight, and when he saw me, he became furious and screamed at me.

"Where the hell were you? We've been looking for you everywhere. We ate dinner without you."

I stood speechless. My words wouldn't come. After everything I had done to reach the shore, after being left behind, he had the nerve to blame me for it! I turned around and, without a word, went straight to the tent I shared with my brother.

Exhausted, I fell asleep as soon as my head hit the pillow.

As was so often the case, my dad, clueless to the situation, had forgotten all about me. He thought I'd returned before him and had played somewhere with friends. I could have drowned, but he didn't even realize he'd abandoned me nautical miles from the shore against a strong headwind on the very first day I'd learned how to windsurf. I was only twelve but already so used to these types of situations that it didn't surprise me.

"Walk or die" could have been his motto, although I don't believe he was ever conscious of it. He never understood that we might have some limitations as kids. Sometimes we were scared but never fully aware of the real dangers we were facing. But I suppose Dad was even less aware of the risks we were willing to take just to enjoy these activities with him.

That was how he operated, and there was nothing I could do about it.

Mom once told me that my dad, in response to her criticism, said, "If they are my kids, they'll survive. If they don't, it's better they die as kids than live a weak, miserable life."

I would later understand that my mom's version of events and the things she claimed others had said were unreliable, never to be trusted. In fact, Dad may have said something as simple as, "It's not a big deal. It will toughen them up." But I had no reason to doubt her at that time.

I never had the desire to try windsurfing again, but as my dad might have said, it had been an experience that strengthened me, one I have never forgotten. It may have even helped me forge the fighting spirit I would need to survive future sea expeditions.

My father was easy to read. He was very primal, governed by basic animal instincts. His centers of interest were money, women, food, and fun. He got his fun from practicing casual sports, which was also a good way to show off his success and meet women.

Apart from politics, and talking about himself, his only other subjects of conversation were business and sailing. He loved talking about business success stories and ideas on making money. He also discussed real estate and later, when we were teens, the stock market. His daily conversations revolved around how much money he had made or lost on any given day. Other subjects that were not about these specifics, or about him, were of no interest. That included anything having to do with his kids.

I think he loved us in his own way, although I didn't feel or understand it then. At least, he never claimed the Superdad title.

Despite all I had endured as a boy, I really loved my dad until I became a teenager. Then his behavior and complete lack of interest in us grew progressively worse, and my resentment, not to mention my ability to notice these things, increased as well.

His painfully mean, sarcastic, or mocking statements and black humor were often directed at me and hurt me deeply. I couldn't take it. Yet, I loved him, and for years I kept trying to impress him with my physical abilities, but I never received any of the recognition I always craved from him. So, I found it in the schoolyard, fighting for those who couldn't fight for themselves. One would think that I could have turned to my mother for the attention I needed. One would be wrong.

Chapter 9

Mom's Reality

"What children want and need from us is thoughtful attention. They want us to notice them and pay some kind of attention to what they do, to take them seriously, to trust and respect them as human beings."
— John Holt, *Learning All the Time*, 1968

Inversely to my memories of my dad, my memories of my mom from when I was a small child are scarce. She often protected us when Dad forgot us somewhere, ensuring that we would get picked up and brought home. But I only have a few specific memories of her that marked my early childhood.

For example, when I was five years old, I remember Mom passing out. She was rushed to the emergency room by ambulance as Dad, my baby brother, and I raced behind in the family car. She survived, and Dad explained that she was sick.

This was the first of many incidents that I can vividly remember. It was only much later that I understood half of these cases to be suicide attempts. The other half were the result of deep depressive states during which she would spend days bedridden without eating.

Mom was generally very sweet, but occasionally her temper flared. Her mood swings could change from one day to the next, and those moods were most influenced by the state of her relationship with Dad, something

I didn't understand for many years until the same situation happened with her future partners.

My parents fought constantly, verbally at first, at least in front of me. Dad would leave the house, seeking refuge at his store, in one of his many recreational activities, with his friends, or with other women. Mom stayed home, depressed, crying, and bedridden. At other times, she became aggressive, scolding me for no apparent reason that I can remember. Sometimes the intensity of her chastisement was completely disproportionate to the little things my siblings and I may have done. Other times, when depressed, she'd tell us our father was a monster in a subtle, manipulative way, which made it all the more convincing.

Neither Dad nor Mom ever helped us with our homework. Dad was always too busy. He did work late into the evening, when he was not playing squash or out scuba diving, so he was rarely home to assist us.

Mom always claimed that she couldn't help because she hadn't finished high school, preferring to go to an art school. She was an artist, and her work was truly exceptional, especially her oil paintings. She was, indeed, a master, eventually winning awards for being the best oil painter in Europe, but she used it as an excuse whenever we asked for help. She always said that she didn't have the intelligence to immerse herself into her kids' homework. In fact, she easily admitted she understood nothing. But, how could she? She never opened one of our textbooks, never even tried to see what we studied or how she might be able to help.

My younger brother, Olivier, was the only one who got some help with reading (because of his dyslexia), but Mom left me to fend for myself. We had hours of homework assigned to us by our teachers, during which we were confined to our rooms. I kept a textbook on my desk that I never opened. I rarely did my homework. Instead, I devoured books, many books. I read all the real-life adventure stories I could get from the library, transporting myself into imaginary worlds where life was so much better. After a couple of hours had gone by, I would claim I had done all my homework and go play outside. Since my mother never bothered to check, she never knew.

For someone who claimed no intelligence, Mom excelled at twisting facts and other people's words. She crafted the wildest stories, doing it so naturally that we always believed everything she said. Her two prime targets were my dad and my grandmother. Yes, her very own mother.

She specialized in taking words out of context, interpreting them according to her own point of view. Or she'd often change quotes and facts to suit her manipulative goals. She did that with any conversation she'd had or any book she'd read. Mom controlled the narrative to suit her own purposes, expertly guiding it to affect perceptions and opinions in a way that benefited her most. She did it with all her friends. She did it with her own kids.

As a ten-year-old, I didn't understand her modus operandi. To me, she'd always been my dad's victim. Dad was strong and powerful. Mom's physical abilities often switched from that of a very joyous and healthy woman who loved to garden all day, practice delicate embroidery, and paint marvelous pieces of art to that of a sick, crying, and depressed bedridden mother. I was too young to understand. I assumed that my dad was the only cause of my mom's misery, depression, and regular suicide attempts. He was no longer my hero.

Though my mother may have truly been depressed, her frequently botched suicide attempts were another way to position herself as the victim. She used it to influence the minds of her friends, family, and particularly her children. She even believed her own lies, placing the blame on my dad and us. Since I was the eldest, I received the brunt of it.

I pitied her, and was tormented trying to figure out what I had done that was so horrible that she preferred death. When she told me that I was an insensitive, egotistical monster like my dad, part of me denied it, but it profoundly affected me, leaving me to doubt my worth. I didn't think I was a monster, but maybe I was; otherwise, my mom wouldn't have claimed I drove her to suicide.

The relationship between my parents devolved from occasional quarrels to frequent verbal and physical fights. I was seven years old the first time I begged them to stop fighting. I didn't understand the situation then and blamed Dad for everything. It would take twenty years for me to finally see the situation for what it had been. My dad wasn't the monster, nor was my mom the victim she'd depicted.

They were both to blame, not only for the fights they waged against each other — right in front of us — but for the total lack of care for their three children. They became so centered on themselves that they didn't truly see us anymore.

I urged them to get a divorce, and they finally did. The physical fights stopped, but their hatred for each other consumed us all. They continued quarreling in court and through us. I felt miserable and couldn't bear to stay home. It seemed like I was always the one they blamed for their problems, or the one they tried to pull to their side, pitting me against the other. I had become the currency they used to hurt each other, a mere weapon. This was the main reason I begged them to send me away to boarding school, the only escape for a ten-year-old.

After my parents separated, Mom continued to struggle with men, always playing the victim, never in the wrong. Over the next eight years, a half-dozen men moved in and out of our home, one after the other. The relationships kept to a specific pattern, starting on a super high where my mom was happy, a veritable bomb of enthusiasm. During that time, she treated us with kindness.

In some ways, my mother was quite the opposite of my father. In her high moments, she loved to take on the Supermom role, particularly when her friends or others noticed. She wanted everyone to think she was a model mother, and I have to recognize that there were times when she treated us with love and behaved like a nurturing parent.

But it never lasted. When her partners no longer served her hand and foot, treating her like a queen, her moods gradually darkened, depression set in, and the relationship deteriorated. A victim yet again, men were nothing but liars and cheaters; yet she was the one who broke each one of them. Nobody could withstand her mood swings and manipulative tricks, but I always defended her, believing she was right. All men, including me and my father, were mean, egoistical creatures.

As a kid and a young teenager, I didn't see the act she put on, didn't recognize the farce she played at being a good mother. And when she wasn't a good mother, I always gave her the benefit of the doubt, feeling miserable because of my dad. He was guilty, and she was only the victim. How could she be a good mother when all she wanted to do was to die?

I felt that I bore responsibility as well. Hadn't she also blamed me for her suicide attempts? She kept telling me I was too much like my father, and that thought sickened me. Decades later, I would finally understand that my mom suffered from bipolar disorder. To this day, she refuses to admit her mental health issue, nor will she get treated for it. Instead, she continues to blame others for her depression. As a kid, the guilt I felt devoured me.

The family situation affected us kids differently. Olivier was smart, but he suffered from severe dyslexia, which caused him great difficulties in school. He was the only one Mom helped when it came to reading, teaching him when he reversed his words. She claimed that Dad was to blame for my brother's dyslexia and sensitivity. Olivier became quite her favorite, often receiving special treatment. She always said he was a strong kid with a very good heart and a great sense of humor. I was envious of him, as she never gave me such compliments. My little sister, Karine, who almost died of kidney failure, had one removed at the age of two. Because she wasn't physically strong as a young child, she also received more protection from my mother. Often this was more attention than my mother could manage to give at one time, leading me to believe that she didn't care for me as much as she did them.

I was the tough, hardened kid; the bad boy. I could take a lot of abuse. My skin was so thick, nothing affected me. I never openly cried. They believed I was impervious to hurt. My parents never understood how much I suffered inside. That I had developed this defense mechanism because of the emotional pain they inflicted upon me. I was fragile and suffered from low self-esteem. I felt unhappy all the time. Beneath my seemingly resilient façade, I harbored deep emotional wounds.

Physically, I looked like my father. I believe this was also one of the reasons my mother resented me. My appearance was a trigger for her.

Granted, I was not the easiest boy and certainly deserved occasional rebukes. My mom would proudly tell her friends, even as I stood next to them, that spanking me hurt her hands too much. She happily told everybody that when I needed correcting, she'd take the horsewhip and lash me on the legs, arms, or ribs. That way, I could feel the pain without her injuring herself.

This form of punishment wasn't frequent, and it felt like no more than a big spanking, almost not worth mentioning here. But it wasn't the physical impact of the whipping that hurt me; it was the emotional pain and the shame I felt when she joyfully told her friends or oil painting students about it. Behind my tough-boy persona, I was extremely sensitive, and that humiliation hurt deeply. And I didn't understand how she felt no shame for her actions. How could a mother boast to her friends that she horsewhipped her kid, even if that were true?

When I was on the receiving end, I tried not to show any sign of pain, further infuriating her. My best defense involved smiling, which probably reinforced her idea of me: that I was a tough, mean little creature.

I learned that crying was a sign of weakness. Whether it was a punishment from my mother, a fight at school, or a tackle on the rugby field, you never showed your pain. You never cried. I vowed that no physical pain would ever make me cry again. No matter what.

Chapter 10

Summers in Ardèche

"The purpose of life, after all, is to live it, to taste experience to the utmost, to reach out eagerly and without fear for a newer and richer experience."

— Eleanor Roosevelt, *You Learn by Living*, 1960

Part genius, part crazy, he was a passionate and inspiring naturalist. He practiced taxidermy (stuffing of animals) and was a famous entomologist and herpetologist (insects and reptile specialist), as well as a paleontologist. My mother's youngest brother, Uncle Philippe, could be the subject of an entire book of his own. One of my greatest pleasures as a kid was spending one month with him in the southern region of Ardèche — away from the tensions of my family and boarding school. From age ten, I went there every summer.

With him, my summers would turn into colorful adventures that brightened my otherwise dark existence. Under his guidance, my cousins and I practiced spelunking, exploring the deepest caves to excavate fossils. We collected skulls, teeth, and bones from prehistorical cavern bears and lions, and an incredible variety of plants and animals that had lived millions of years ago.

We also hunted local wildlife. I learned to grab scorpions and catch snakes with my bare hands. We set traps to attract a multitude of nocturnal and diurnal insects. In his home, he had a mini-zoo, where he exhibited fossils and minerals in one room and live local and exotic wild animals in the next. There were also two deep pits filled with all the local species of snakes.

As we learned a great deal about nature from my uncle, he received free labor in return as we guided the visits of his little exhibits. Satisfied visitors gave us tips, and we mastered the best way to secure those.

My cousins and I loved talking about the fossils and minerals we had excavated, and we enjoyed showing people the snakes and other animals. The snake pit was two meters wide and a meter-fifty deep, with fences on top. There were two pits, each hosting two dozen snakes of five local species. We would explain how to catch and manipulate the snakes, to differentiate between the various species, and to recognize the dangerous ones. We would show the difference between the smaller viper and the longer colubridae species. The slanted eyes and smaller scales on the heads were characteristic of these venomous but rarely aggressive snakes.

For the highlight of the show, we caught a *couleuvre à échelon* (ladder snake), a harmless but highly aggressive snake. We got it to bite us on the hand or arm under the flashes of the cameras. It always ensured a great harvest of tips.

The snake that attracted the most attention was the superb two-and-a-half-meter[1] green *couleuvre d'Esculape* (Aesculapian snake). It was a master climber. We kept it inside a fully enclosed terrarium to prevent it from escaping. This snake took its name from Asclepius, the god of medicine and of the healing arts in ancient Greek mythology who carried around a staff wrapped by a snake. Many legends merge together to agree that today's Aesculapian are the serpents represented on the current symbol of medicine.

The Aesculapian was also nonvenomous, but its bite was much more painful and drew blood every time. That snake bit me nonstop as I showed it off to audiences while telling its story. It was another method that promised good tips at the end of the visit.

1. eight-foot

We also played with the giant Teraphose tarantulas from Mexico, letting them run all over our arms. And we did the same thing with the scorpions. Over the years, I became cocky in my endeavors to earn even more tips. I started putting a scorpion on my tongue and then inside my mouth, closing it entirely while all the people screamed with a mixture of fear, disgust, and awe. I would reopen my mouth and stick my tongue out to remove the scorpion.

When one of the visitors shared this with my uncle, he became upset. I had done it for a full season without him knowing, and he was right to be mad. A week later, I got stung on the tongue, and it swelled so much I could no longer talk clearly. Luckily, we had a black stone from Africa. It sucked most of the venom out of my tongue, leaving me with a mild fever and the inability to talk for twenty-four hours.

Despite how much I loved my time with my uncle, he suffered from huge self-esteem problems that affected his behavior. Uncle Philippe was an amazing man, but he felt the need to rally the strongest person around him to make fun of the easiest prey. It was another example of bad French humor. Sometimes we, his young nephews, were his easiest targets. When he had an audience, family or friends, he mastered the art of making us feel terrible by lowering us in every way. In some ways, it was so over the top that it wasn't as effective, or as painful, as my father's more subtle and devastating words. Yet, when we were alone with our uncle, he would share amazing secrets about nature. He would take us to the most incredible places, teach us more than we could ever learn in books or in school. He was a real living encyclopedia and one of the most interesting people I had ever met, even to this day over forty years later.

Philippe was a genius, but a lazy one. He would only work when he was passionate about something. He barely survived financially. My grandmother partly subsidized his living, even paying for our food and the cost for us to stay at his place in the summer. Philippe liked to have my cousins and I come at different times so we could be guides for the entire summer while he napped or went out drinking with friends. But there were always overlap days, which was a great way for me to spend time with my cousins without our parents present.

My uncle also loved to shock people with stupid things. In many ways, he was even more of a kid than we were.

During my first summer in Ardèche, Philippe told one of my cousins and me how to make surprise chocolates for our relatives. Little did he know that we'd put his lesson to good use at the following family Christmas gathering. We followed his recipe to the letter. We grabbed some fresh goat droppings from my aunt's farm, melted some chocolate, quickly dipped the small round balls of droppings into a thin layer of almost liquid chocolate, and, when still hot, we rolled them into a thin coat of ice sugar powder. We then wrapped a handful of them into a fairly new handkerchief and tied it with a small ribbon. We made one for each of our adult family members who had gathered to celebrate Christmas. That included my grandparents, my mother, my two uncles, two aunts, and their spouses.

Nobody will ever forget that Christmas.

When my Uncle Yves tasted a few homemade chocolates, Philippe immediately laughed so hard that both my grandparents and all his siblings realized he had something to do with it. And everyone knew if Uncle Philippe was involved, it couldn't be a good thing.

Yves, who was Philippe's brother-in-law, didn't understand the trick. The chocolate and sugarcoated layers covered the mild taste that came from the goat shit. My mother immediately told him to stop eating it and turned to Philippe, asking him what stupid trick had he taught us.

When he told them it was goat shit, Yves rushed to the toilet to try spitting it out, nearly gagging, while a couple of adults screamed at Philippe, "You're disgusting." The others cried with laughter, and so did my cousin and I.

We didn't get scolded, but we were warned against ever listening to and carrying out Philippe's tricks. But how could we not? He was so exuberant, not always funny to adults but so funny to us kids. We loved him.

Philippe often behaved more like a big brother than an uncle, even though he had two boys five and six years younger than me. The fun we had rarely came with any rules attached. He took pleasure in breaking all the taboos. I owed him a great deal, for I never felt more freedom as a kid than I did with him.

To my greatest regret, he eventually became an alcoholic. After drinking liters of beer, our wonderful and mesmerizing uncle would often turn into a mean and dark character. The more he drank, the meaner he behaved. His wife eventually left him, taking his two boys with her. His alcohol problem worsened over the years as he started drinking before eating breakfast, remaining in an almost permanent drunk state.

When drunk, his passion for life disappeared entirely, only to leave space for a mean and abusive man who targeted the weakest in his circle. His comments and actions were denigrating. There was nothing funny about them. He was just a drunk man, unable to control his words and behaviors, being mean and stupid. Even though I was never his victim, I couldn't bear to see him metamorphose like this. Uncle Philippe had always been one of my heroes, but he had transformed from an Indiana Jones–like naturalist I idealized into a disgusting drunk.

Eventually, I could no longer stand spending time with him. For five years, I had enjoyed every summer at his place, but his drinking made it impossible to continue. I still have fond memories of all the wonderful experiences I had, learning the secrets of animals, plants, and nature. My summers with him had been a much-needed break from my own personal hell at home and at school, but my uncle was no longer the same person, and my place of refuge was no longer an option.

Chapter 11

Destiny

"What makes great journeys so marvelous is that their magic begins even before they start. You open the Atlas and begin to dream over the maps, rolling round your tongue the splendid names of towns you've never been to."

— Joseph Kessel, *La vallée des rubis*, 1955

Adventure, exploration, nature, and my own imaginary worlds remained the source of my escape and my place of refuge throughout my life. Since the age of three, I never missed watching the Cousteau documentaries, remaining in awe of the *Calypso* ship of Commandant Cousteau as they continued to explore the oceans and most remote places on Earth.

When I was ten, I watched his collection of movies on Antarctica that made me dream of polar expeditions, and a few years later I consumed the full documentary series on the entire Amazon. A small team traveled with Cousteau's son to descend the glacier source of the Peruvian Mountains. They kayaked down rapids that quickly grew to a large river, continuing their navigation toward the Brazilian border. As they made their way downstream, Cousteau and his crew, aboard the *Calypso*, navigated upriver from the Atlantic Ocean. They simultaneously filmed and documented the Amazon from both expeditions until the two teams met.

I was obsessed. The Amazon seemed so daunting and yet so intimate. It called my name, whispering words of true escape, the opportunity to leave all my troubles and worries behind.

The Tarzan I had imagined myself to be had evolved and was still tangible for me.

Upon watching the Amazon documentary, I dreamed again of becoming an explorer. I'd read several books from the greatest explorers, but seeing the Amazon through the eyes of Cousteau and his crew made the idea of becoming one possible. Tarzan may have been part of my imaginary world, but Cousteau confirmed it as reality. He was my grand inspiration, but he wasn't my only role model. I read everything I could about mountaineering, the jungle, the ocean, the Arctic, and any other locations where expeditions had been done. From *The Iliad* to Marco Polo, from Jack London to Hemingway, and countless epic stories. I sucked in all the adventure I could find.

At home, I dove into maps. Mom purchased my first map for me when I was eight. Naturally influenced by my interest in Tarzan, I grabbed a map of the African continent, which featured all the mountains and jungles marked with different colors. I devoured the pictures of the animals that lived all over the continent. I spent hours imagining myself atop every mountain and exploring every jungle the map had to offer.

Many maps followed; I was addicted to them. When I was ten, I learned how to read and calculate the elevation curves. I could now see all my 2D maps in 3D, visualizing the landscape by watching the curve lines. By the age of twelve, I was a skilled map reader. I could imagine exactly how a place looked just by studying it. I could even hand-draw rough profiles of the terrain by looking at the map elevation curves.

My mother probably wondered what I wanted to do with them. Little did she know, I was planning expeditions to every place in the world, from Antarctica to the remotest jungles. I didn't study in school, but I did study my maps, envisioning my future career upon the *Calypso* alongside Cousteau and his crew. My imaginary world had extended to encompass every natural environment.

I also dreamed of being a pilot. The Cousteau crew explored the entire world aboard his ship, but they also had a small submarine and a seaplane they used on many expeditions. The idea of exploring via plane fascinated me.

I read tons of books on aviation exploration from Saint-Exupéry — not only *The Little Prince* — and all his travel and pilot experiences found in *Terre des Hommes (Wind, Sand and Stars)*, *Night Flight*, and *Flight to Arras*. I then read *Mes Vols*, the work of Jean Mermoz, another influential pilot.

All this reading inspired me. Engrossed by Jack London's *Call of the Wild* and Beth Day's *Glacier Pilot*, I wanted to become a small-plane bush pilot. Alaska sat high on my dream list. There, I imagined flying over uncharted territories populated only by herds of wild caribou, visiting and sharing the lives of the Inuit and meeting real mountain men, joining them on their grizzly hunts. I wanted to land my wings in the remotest places on Earth. Yes, I'd be a bush pilot, that was certain.

My parents killed that dream as soon as I told them about it. They explained that pilots needed perfect vision in both eyes, with no correction. My strabismus and lazy eye had doomed me. It crushed me to learn that I could never be a pilot, but I had to accept this fate. It wouldn't be the last time my dreams were shattered, but my intense calling for epic adventures soon compelled me forward, switching my focus onto other pursuits.

Chapter 12

My Love of Sports

"The biggest adventure you can take is to live the life of your dreams."
— Oprah Winfrey

For as long as I could remember, I'd been a huge fan of the Olympics. The achievements of those athletes amazed me. I admired how they had forged their bodies to conquer the most incredible records, how they set their minds to win against all odds. I watched the Olympic Games the same way I read *The Iliad* and *The Odyssey*, cheering both Olympians and demi-gods in their quests.

And it was definitely another dream of mine — I often imagined I would be an Olympian myself, competing to win the gold, honoring my national flag in front of a cheering crowd — but I hadn't found the one sport I best excelled at.

I had skied as a little kid. I had been sailing on my own since I was ten years old. Although my first year of judo wasn't to my liking, I had a growing interest in practicing martial arts. And I loved being in the water, body-surfing in the powerful Atlantic waves; holding my breath to dive as deep, and stay under as long, as I could in the lakes. Of course, I couldn't stay away from climbing trees and swinging off ropes on the few weekends I returned home from school. I had even set up a Tyrolean traverse to jump from the top of the tallest tree to the ground. Though I was mature enough to know I wouldn't be another Tarzan, I loved that feeling of speed, the adrenaline rush of freedom. I relished pushing my body and mind to achieve what nobody thought could be achieved. Sometimes I even surprised myself.

I also practiced several sports at boarding school. Apart from gymnastics, I started to excel at any activity that required speed, strength, and endurance. When I was twelve, our physical education teacher introduced us to rugby. Up until then, I had been terrible at any ball sports, but when I had that oval ball in my hands, nobody could take it away from me. I was fast and quick, strong and fearless, and I loved the contact. I immediately joined the school's team.

A couple of months after my first rugby game, I became the regional champion in discus and javelin throwing. I didn't choose to throw the discus — frankly, it didn't interest me. I only started because our physical education teacher demonstrated the technique and had us mimic him. We tried the slow-motion movement until we understood the basics. The teacher then stood on the soccer field a third of the distance away. From there, he could see all the students' techniques and throws, moving toward us to measure the distance. He usually stood three meters[1] farther than the longest throws. After most of my classmates had done their best, it was my turn. The discus flew well above his head to land five meters behind him.

All we heard was "Fuck!"

He stood speechless for a few seconds. Then he walked over to the discus and measured my throw. He turned back toward us and said, "You're going to compete."

I was instantly drafted into the regional championship, which I won. I took the gold in discus and the bronze in javelin. I decided not to continue to the nationals because I had no interest in it, and it required missing out on my rugby games, which I enjoyed much more. I had potential, but the discus and javelin were sports I didn't want to pursue.

1. ten feet

I was also drafted into the triple jump because I easily broke the school record, and I competed in the 100m sprint. I participated in all four disciplines on the same competition day, but I did so without passion. I knew I wanted something else, but I just wasn't sure what that might be. I needed to try out different types of sports to discover the perfect match.

Outside of school, I returned to martial arts. I had convinced my mother to pay for Aikido classes, saying that I had to channel my energy and better control myself. Unlike the judo classes of my earlier childhood, I was of similar size and strength as my classmates and I learned quickly. Although I enjoyed the martial arts, they still weren't what I was looking for.

Competing in the Olympics was another dream of mine that I shared with my parents, whose response was less than enthusiastic, but I remained hopeful that one day they'd take me seriously and recognize my physical potential and determination. I firmly believed my Olympic dream could become a reality if I trained with the greats — and there was only one place I could do that.

Chapter 13

The Only Way

"Failure I can live with; not trying is what I can't handle."

— Sanya Richards-Ross, Rio de Janeiro Olympic Games, 2016

After the disastrous performance of France at the 1960 and 1964 Olympics, the French government created the Sport-Étude academic program. It had one goal: recruit the best young athletes in France and train them to become Olympic and World champions in all Olympic sports. The program spanned from sixth to twelfth grade, with students spending one half of the day learning a condensed academic curriculum and the other half of the day training in the sport of their choosing. In the early years, athletes were introduced to various sports until they found the discipline that best matched their skills and desires. They then focused on that sport exclusively, training for the Olympics under the expert guidance of the nation's best coaches, attending additional instructional camps, and competing in national and international competitions.

Students could join a Sport-Étude program anytime between the sixth and tenth grade. Only the nation's youth with the most potential were granted the exception to join as late as eleventh grade. But the younger you mastered your sport, the higher your chances were to join the national team.

Not all graduating athletes would succeed, but the great majority of national team athletes and French Olympians graduated from a Sport-Étude.

As a young teenager, I wanted nothing more than to enter a Sport-Étude program.

These schools were slightly more expensive than those I attended, but it was the best way to achieve my dreams of becoming an Olympian. From seventh grade on, I never stopped asking my mother to send me to a Sport-Étude. She would always respond with the opinion that physically and intellectually I wasn't good enough.

She would then lecture me on how sports were not important in life and bad for one's health, coming to this conclusion after hearing that people were sometimes injured when participating in extreme sports. Each time I talked about a Sport-Étude, she would find a way to make me feel terrible about it — as if I were stupid to even want to do it and foolish to think I could ever be selected. She didn't understand my physical abilities, mental strength, and passion for sports, and she never encouraged me. She didn't understand that my academic grades were just average because I never tried, not because I was stupid. I simply lacked the motivation. If I had been working toward something like a Sport-Étude, I would have put my studies first. She made me feel so awful about my dream of being in the Olympics that I stopped talking about my athletic pursuits entirely. I did much of my training without her knowledge.

My father had used sports as an excuse to be away from home. It was also his playing field for meeting women. Mom associated all these physical activities with my father; therefore, she refused to hear anything more from me on the subject. She often said if I was involved in sports, then I was a clone of my father and clearly no better.

Dad wasn't much more supportive. When I was younger, I thought he loved sports with a passion. He was definitely strong, athletic, and competitive, but he never tapped deep into his physical potential. He couldn't bear any type of pain. Training had to be fun, and the fun stopped as soon as pain was involved.

He was also an adventurous dreamer, but he never really challenged himself. Even though he watched all the movies and documentaries about the famous sailing races and four-wheel-driving expeditions around the world and bought all the equipment to follow in the footsteps of the greats, he never dared to take action, never had the courage to try, outside his small circle.

He would boast that one day he would race the Paris-Dakar, a four-wheel drive odyssey across the Sahara, but he never even attempted to participate. He always had a lame excuse: he couldn't take time off work (yet he could leisure travel with friends for an entire month), he didn't have the right car (even though he could afford to buy one), or it was too expensive (even though he could easily pay the $10,000 entry fee). As he grew older, he finally had a valid reason — he was too old.

His whole life he talked about one day sailing around the world. He bought many boats over the years (he shopped around a lot, taking us with him) but never one for transatlantic sailing: they were either too big, too small, too old, or too expensive. The truth was, he was secretly terrified of the adventures he was dreaming about. He had good sailing technique but was too afraid of encountering storms or other problems at sea. Despite his big talk, he always played it safe. He only went out on the ocean to race, when the usual regatta safety teams were in place to help any boat in trouble. On his own, he sailed the lakes or the inside sea of Arcachon, within sight of the shore. All his adventures were limited to the daytime, where he had some control over the weather forecast and the option to bail out and quickly retreat to comfort and safety.

As I later learned, he only enjoyed sports as leisure activities; they were just hobbies. They made it possible for him to show off to others. You could buy fancy gear, wear great clothing, and parade around, proud as a peacock, racing against other peacocks.

My dad's motto about sports, which he repeated time after time, summed him up perfectly: "If we're not the best, at least let's be the most elegant."

As far as he was concerned, sports wasn't a profession, and he wanted me to become an optician like him, working for him. After a few years of following in his footsteps, I would even be able to open up my own store. One day, I would have the money to practice all the sports I liked. According to my father, a Sport-Étude wasn't something for me. Neither was the Olympics.

Without a Sport-Étude to hope for and help fulfill my dream, my existence started to feel empty and meaningless. I was heartbroken that my parents never took me, my achievements, and my dreams seriously, and yet I couldn't stop yearning for their recognition.

Chapter 14

From Dreams to Hell

"The end of hope is the beginning of death."
— Charles De Gaulle

In my early teens, disillusioned by my parents' lack of support, I drifted away from sports and started to spend all my time drinking, smoking, and brawling just to feel alive ... just to feel anything other than despair. My dreams had become a list of distant wishes that would never happen anyway. They had not entirely vanished, but I realized I had lived my childhood in a utopian world that would never materialize. I now lived in darkness, trying to drown my demons with alcohol.

My father never recognized how much he'd hurt me. How much I hated his humor and sarcasm. How much I despised it when he praised other people's kids and failed to ever praise me about anything. Above all, I hated that he never noticed my physical abilities, never considered my wishes, and constantly put me down, making me feel worthless.

I was miserable. All I wanted was for my parents to love me, something I didn't know how to express. Affection seemed difficult to share on both sides. After the age of seven, I don't remember telling my parents I loved them either. I didn't feel loved, so why express it? I was left with permanent feelings of loneliness and anger.

And now I was a drunk — not like some teenagers, who occasionally got shit-faced at a party and eventually passed out in their own vomit and piss in the streets. I had reached that level of inebriation a couple of nights a week for months when I was twelve. At that time, I competed with my friends at boarding school, downing an entire bottle of tequila, gin, or vodka as fast as possible. When I didn't have money to get booze, I would occasionally make my own by mixing pharmaceutical 90% proof disinfecting alcohol with Coca-Cola. I would drink until I puked my guts out.

But at thirteen, as I was fighting bigger guys outside of school, I realized that even though I could out-drink many of the boys I shared bottles with, I didn't enjoy that stage of total drunkenness. It was important for me to stay in control, to be ready to fight and win. I never drank to that point again, but I drank close to it.

I loved alcohol. I drank every night until my head spun, until I felt the booze rushing into my bloodstream, until it transported me to that secondary state where I was no longer on Earth. It tasted good, and it felt good. I loved that moment just before it affected my vision, before nausea set in. It was the perfect balance between drinking enough to be buzzed without losing my ability to fight. That drunk stage was the only time I didn't feel lonely.

I was drunk every night, rebelling in a self-destructive way: a broken teenage boy with no more hopes and dreams. And the only time I truly felt good was when I was physical, when I brawled, gaining respect from my peers, being known as the tough guy.

I stayed true to my code, though. I never started a fight and swore to never bully anyone. But fighting quickly became my new escape, my outlet, my way of handling the years of neglect from my parents and the early bullying at school. I had to establish who was king of the block. After all, if I couldn't be king of the jungle, I supposed the block was the next best thing.

I also loved music, listening mostly to rock and pop at the time: anything from The Beatles and Simon and Garfunkel to Pink Floyd and The Police. But I was even more interested in classical music. My mother listened to classical and opera all day long, and I loved it. Beethoven, Rachmaninov, Schumann, Mozart, and Chopin were at least as important to me as Johnny Hallyday (a legendary French rock singer), Jean-Jacques Goldman (a famous French pop star), and The Eagles.

But how was I to tell my teenage friends that my favorite music varied between Beethoven's 5th and 9th Symphony and Chopin's Nocturne, depending on my mood? Would I dare say I preferred the voices of Gundula Janowitz and Maria Callas over those of Elton John and David Bowie? How could I enter a trance-like state when I listened to Beethoven's Moonlight Sonata and still be a tough guy?

I never admitted that it was this type of music that transported me to another world when my friends were fans of AC/DC. It would have revealed my sensitivity, that my tough-guy persona was fake.

At thirteen, I had taken down all the local big boys, and there weren't many other opportunities for me to fight within the confines of school. So I took my aggression to the streets. Tall and muscular, I looked two years older than I was and hung out with older teenage delinquents and young adults. I'd go to bars (they never checked ID then), get drunk, and piss people off until they would start a fight. I would bait them a bit, prompting them to throw the first punch, and then unleash my wrath.

I was fearless when challenging much bigger guys because I hated life. I had a death wish, with literally nothing to lose. I wasn't someone who ever considered committing suicide, though. I'd had enough of my mother doing so repeatedly. I thought it was weak and appalling, and I didn't want anybody to ever think that I was weak.

My young age offered me the advantage of surprise. My opponents always underestimated me. As soon as the fight started, my rage took over, shocking my often stronger combatants with the fearless violence that inhabited me.

I wasn't necessarily the strongest, as I was often challenging kids three years my senior, kids much bigger than me. But as soon as the fight started, I released my fury with so much speed and intensity that I ended it before my opponent could give me more than a couple of punches. Upon victory,

I finally found the calm I needed, feeling a great sense of satisfaction and peace. I loved that feeling, but it was temporary, which meant I was always fighting, chasing that high.

I was addicted to it. The rush. The adrenaline. The approval of those who watched me fight.

I loved the prelude to the fight, I loved the actual fight, and I loved the experience after the fight when my audience, who thought I didn't have a chance in hell of winning, watched me with surprise, impressed by the young boy who had won a brawl that seemed very unfair from the start. I thrived on being the underdog, and I enjoyed it when spectators cheered me on. This eventually led me to hanging out with gangs.

At that time, our small gangs were made up of teenagers and young adults; the average age was eighteen. At fourteen, I was by far the youngest member. We were not true thugs, at least not yet. We simply lived with no purpose: we were just fighting for the pleasure of it. We were drunk every day, but we didn't deal drugs. We weren't thieves, just low-level gangs of brawling bums, wandering the streets at night and hopping from bar to bar.

I continued reading outdoor adventure books and never stopped dreaming about it, but I had lost all illusions as to whether or not I could make that happen. I would never have the money to travel anyway. In the back of my mind, I still harbored all these desires, but they remained that way: the types of dreams that, in a different world, you wish would miraculously materialize without effort on your part. The way most people dream, thinking, *That'd be nice, but that's not me.* After being made to feel worthless too many times, my metamorphosis was complete. I had transitioned from an idealistic, hopeful boy to a self-loathing doubter. I had stopped believing in myself.

I would never go to a Sport-Étude or compete in the Olympics. I would never climb mountains. I would never fly planes like Saint-Exupéry or scuba dive like Cousteau. I would probably never travel very far either.

I was no longer living for my dreams; I was living in hell.

Chapter 15

A Free Pass to Nature

"Today for Show and Tell, I've brought a tiny marvel of nature: a single snowflake. I think we might all learn a lesson from how this utterly unique and exquisite crystal turns into an ordinary, boring molecule of water, just like every other one, when you bring it in the classroom. And now, while the analogy sinks in, I'll be leaving you drips and going outside."

— Calvin, in Bill Watterson's *Homicidal Psycho Jungle Cat: A Calvin and Hobbes Collection*, 1994

I never liked school but not because I wasn't smart. My teachers over the years had all agreed on one thing: I could have been one of the best students if only I had listened. But I was constantly bored, either escaping into my own world or skipping class entirely. At that young age, I didn't understand how studies could lead me to live my dreams. School was merely a forced track toward a future I didn't want.

I hated physics in particular because I didn't like to study formulas — I couldn't see the point. Even though I didn't like math, I understood that I could apply some of it daily, but I couldn't understand how physics applied to anything practical in my life. Little did I know that I would later need it.

Chemistry was a mixed bag of boring formulas and exciting moments of discovery watching how components reacted together to form something different. I was not big on quotes, but French chemist Antoine Lavoisier's words — "*Rien ne se perd, rien ne se crée: tout se transforme*" (Nothing is lost, nothing is created, everything is transformed) — made a great impact on me. This quote proved to be true inside and outside of chemistry.

I also despised history, especially because we had to remember stupid dates of events that made no sense, events I cared very little about. But sometimes a few good teachers were able to bring life into their class, making us live the subject instead of memorizing useless data or regurgitating boring facts.

As a sophomore at my new Jesuit-run boarding school, I had a good teacher who brought history to life, actually fostering my interest in something I thought I hated. He helped us visualize and feel what it would be like to live during a specific time period. He helped us understand the cause of the wars and other major political events. The most diligent students who took notes on the entire textbook tended to fail, whereas I, who could never remember a single history date, excelled in tests and essays. That teacher helped me tap back into my imagination. History became my favorite subject, something I continued to be interested in my entire life thereafter, proving that a good teacher can motivate a student to be the best in anything.

Maybe with the right teacher, I might have loved physics, math, and French literature too.

Geography was another class I liked — it fit right in with my dreams of travel and living in the outdoors — but there was one subject I had always adored: biology. My early love for the animal kingdom as Tarzan, my deep understanding of marine biology instilled by Jacques Cousteau and hundreds of hours of documentary-watching, and my summers learning from the living encyclopedia that was my Uncle Philippe ensured that I always led biology classes without ever needing to study a lesson. I had already read in-depth research on my own. Some biology teachers even felt intimidated by my knowledge concerning their specialty, rarely appreciating my input.

I was also blessed that year to meet an open-minded biology teacher. Thanks to all my summers in Ardèche with my Uncle Philippe, I knew nature in a practical way that even our instructor didn't fully understand. I was already his ace student, and he was intrigued by the experience I'd gained from Uncle Philippe.

The first time I released a green whip snake into the class, I wanted to have a good laugh by scaring everybody, and it worked — especially since the snake was almost two meters long and nearly too thick to wrap my thumb and index finger around. Not only did the girls scream, but the boys were pretty terrified as well, standing on top of their school desks.

Our biology teacher, unfazed, smiled and said, "Jean-Philippe, why don't you catch your snake before someone falls from their desk. Come here and tell us about it." Other teachers would have kicked me out of the class and sent me to the principal's office. But not Tonton.

Tony was his first name, but later, after we had broken through the teacher-student boundary, I called him Tonton, which means "uncle."

Tonton was impressed with the stories I told about this snake and its environment. He prompted the other students to ask me questions. One of them asked how long I'd had my pet snake and they all freaked out when I told them that I had caught it twenty minutes ago during recess.

My teacher noticed how my participation with a live snake animated the entire class. Students weren't napping on their desks, nor were they passing notes or otherwise misbehaving. They took part in the Q&A. Some wanted to touch the snake's tail. Others wanted to stay away from it. But everyone was engrossed in the subject matter for the entire time.

At the end of the class, Tonton called me forward and asked if I wanted to be the leader of a small biology club. The school allowed for groups of five to fifteen students to form an activity lab under the auspices of a teacher. We would collect various animals and keep them in terrariums for other students to learn about the wildlife of our surrounding ecosystem. Tonton would get authorization from the principal allowing all club members to venture out of the school boundaries to catch insects, forty-centimeter-long[1] fluorescent-green lizards, and other unspecified small creatures.

I loved the idea and immediately chose my two best friends, Frédéric and François, to be my first disciples in the bio club. Unlike me, the two had never been in a fight; but like me, they loved sports and were good athletes. Together, we escaped to run in the woods all afternoon every Wednesday and every other weekend when we stayed at the boarding school. A free pass to leave school without having to sneak out and dodge the always vigilant principal was something we couldn't refuse.

We took advantage of this opportunity, enjoying much more freedom than the pass granted us. We would have amazing picnic feasts, each of us bringing plenty of food and booze. Our other two club members, Christophe and Bertrand, were from farming families, so their contributions of farm-fresh food and homemade spirits were especially delicious.

Tonton lived on a farm four kilometers[2] from the school. One Sunday, the bio club decided to visit him. Surprised that we had showed up on his doorstep, he invited us in and we shared lunch together. We had so much fun that we made our visit into a biweekly event, at which time his nickname stuck.

The times spent with Tonton and my bio club friends were my only nondestructive escapes, but they weren't enough — I continued to drink, smoke, fight, and skip classes I didn't like. Except for Tonton and my history teacher, all the other academic teachers hated me as much as I hated them. It didn't take long for my rebellious attitude to bring troubles upon me at my new school. My already doomed future took an even deeper dive.

1. fifteen-inch-long
2. two-and-half miles

Chapter 16

Jesuit School

"Abused children have a caldron of rage bubbling inside them. You can't be battered, humiliated, terrified, denigrated, and blamed for your own pain without getting angry."

— Susan Forward

I was the one who pushed a cow up the staircase into the school director's bedroom one night. The uncooperative bovine spread a nice carpet of near-liquid poop all over the stairs and almost gave me up when it mooed as soon as I closed the door behind it. This wasn't only an irresistible dare from my friends but also a chance to flex my nonconformist muscle, letting all the students know that even the greatest (and most feared) authority — the school director and his extreme rigor — was vulnerable. (The cow was easy enough to "borrow." Along with the standard high school curriculum that I was enrolled in, our school offered an agronomy and farming specialty, supported by a working farm run by the Jesuits on school grounds.)

On a day that we didn't want to take a test, my friends François, Frédéric and I released all the farm's pigs onto the soccer field. We laughed our hearts out along with all the other students, watching as the Jesuit brothers ran, forcing all the teachers to chase after the squealing piglets. They even ordered our French teacher, in her dress and high heels, to run after them in the mud. It was hilarious and one of the best days us students ever had in school.

I also dumped some methylene blue (a benign organic chloride salt used as intravenous dye marker in various treatments) into the water reserve for the showers. When I spotted the substance during a chemistry lab, I thought it would be a fun joke, an idea I got from Uncle Philippe the summer before. It turned the first three kids who showered that morning into blue Schtroumpfs (Smurfs) for days.

None of these was the likely reason that the strict Jesuit order wanted to kick me out of their school halfway through the academic year. It had nothing to do with my reputation as a rule breaker, or because I was suspected of escaping from school at night to look for trouble. These were mere rumors. I was never caught.

The real untold reason for them kicking me out: from day one, I had broken a tradition that this school — which took great pride in being one of the most traditional in France — had managed to preserve for over a century.

It didn't seem like a big deal to me, but this was one of the few schools that still required students to wear a uniform. It wasn't a typical one, or even nice. It was just an ugly lightweight button-up jacket (like a lab coat): mouse gray for the boys and sky blue for the girls — a jacket I swore I would never wear and refused to even purchase.

When I attended class without my uniform, at first I was grounded to the detention hall, with forced studies during recess for a week. As I continued my protest, I was grounded continuously. I had to stay in and study under the surveillance of a Jesuit brother instead of hanging out with my friends.

I held strong with the firm conviction that I wouldn't wear that ugly jacket. I felt that it stole everybody's identity. I was not a pawn, and nothing could convince my nonconformist mind otherwise. After a couple of weeks, my friends decided to join me, throwing their jackets away and staying with me in detention. Eventually, all three sophomore classes refused to wear their uniforms, and it didn't take long for the junior and senior classes to follow. I had started a revolution: in less than three months I had destroyed the century-long tradition the school so proudly upheld.

That I was guilty of, and they knew it. Even though the Jesuits never came right out and said it, that uniform was the real reason I was being kicked out. Little did I know, I had someone in my corner.

My fifteen-year-old power, speed, and fighting spirit quickly earned me the position of captain of the school's rugby team, despite me being the new kid that year. As with fighting, on the field I enjoyed seeing the fear in my opponents' faces when I charged with the ball and the respect I gained from my teammates when I scored.

Accolades asides, I lacked the guidance to express my physical abilities in a positive way. Being kicked out of another school early in my sophomore year meant the certain end of my formal education. No other school would ever accept me. I didn't care much about it since I wasn't going to a Sport-Étude anyway, and I had no interest in studying other things. Luckily, though, someone else cared.

When my rugby coach, who was also the physical education teacher, learned that I was going to be expelled, he talked to the school director. He was a retired pro-rugby player: a two-meter-tall[1] giant with wide shoulders and a hundred and ten kilos[2] of muscle. He looked like Atlas himself, and his stature impressed people. He asked the director not to expel me, explaining that I was the best athlete he'd ever had the chance to coach and he could help me tap into my potential.

The director didn't care. The rugby team only played small games with other local schools, and one talented kid was not going to make a difference.

Scanning all the old trophies displayed in the director's office, my rugby coach pivoted. The school had long ago lost its dominant edge in the regional cross-country run, so he made the director another offer: "If he wins the regional cross-country run this year, will you keep him in the school?"

1. six-foot-seven

2. two hundred and forty-five pounds

At the time, my coach only shared with me that he'd struck a deal with the director: I win the race, I stay in school. I can only imagine that the rest of the negotiation went something like this:

After the director finished laughing, he said, "Come on, the kid is a fighter. He smokes cigarettes and escapes from school every night to look for trouble. He's aggressive on the field, I give you that, but he can't run more than the length of a rugby field. He'll never even finish the race. He's just trouble."

My coach didn't give up on me though. He somehow convinced the director to keep me in the school if I won the regional cross-country competition. The director probably didn't care about the race — he was only making peace with my coach, certain that I would fail.

Chapter 17

Awakening

"Not till we are lost … do we begin to find ourselves…"
— Henry David Thoreau, *Walden*, 1854

Along with my biology and history teachers, my physical education teacher/rugby coach was the only other person I respected in the school. When he called me into his office to discuss the deal he'd made with the director, I laughed, telling him I was not a girly-boy, willing to dress in Lycra and run around in the woods.

Grasping me by the shirt collar, he lifted me up in the air with one hand. He held my face a half arm's length above his and said, "I put my neck out for you, so you're going to win this cross-country run or the next person you fight will be me."

I'm not sure what I was thinking at the time. I never would have allowed someone to confront me like that without fighting back, even if he was a giant I couldn't defeat. I wasn't afraid of anybody, no matter their age or size, but he was the only one who'd ever encouraged me, and I respected him. He was my coach and my hero. I realized in that moment that he cared about me, something I'd rarely felt from my parents. He was firmly convinced that I was meant to be much more than a gang fighter, that I had potential. Suspended in the air, speechless, I nodded.

The first thing he did was put the kibosh on my drinking and smoking, and he asked my friends and teammates to make sure I complied. I didn't stop smoking entirely — I hid it from the others — but I did cut back by more than half. I met my coach early every morning for a training run before school. For the first week, he ran a few laps with me daily, but as my speed increased, he preferred to stand on the sidelines with the stopwatch, offering motivation. It was the first time I had been coached one-on-one. Although I was grateful he was saving me from expulsion, it took me decades to realize the power he was giving me by boosting my confidence as an athlete. It took me even longer to fully appreciate what he had done for me — he had put his trust in me while asking me to trust him in return.

Three months later, I won the regional race and became the school's star. It was an amazing feeling. All the teachers, the Jesuit director, and the principal, who I thought hated me, congratulated me with enthusiasm. Compliments never stopped, even from the other students. I had never in my life felt that good. I received the entire school's recognition without having to fight anybody.

I came to realize that my teachers, who I thought were evil, never really hated me. I had hated them unfairly. I was the nonconformist kid who never listened or studied. I hid behind my bad-boy, tough-kid attitude. I projected my anger and feelings of misery onto everybody else, assuming they either despised me or only respected me out of fear.

Winning that small cross-country run was a deliverance, giving me a self-confidence boost and the recognition that I desperately needed. It broke my bad-boy shell and touched my heart, inspiring me to progressively start believing in my dreams again. It gave me hope. I would later learn that self-recognition is far more important than any accolade bestowed on me.

At the time, I was too young and immature to understand and fully appreciate what my physical education teacher had done for me. He had believed in me and given me a chance to prove myself. It's amazing that forty years later, I don't even remember his name, but I'll never forget that I owe him. I started to see my future in a very different light.

He likely saved my life.

Chapter 18

Endurance

"In overstepping our limitations, in touching the extreme boundaries of man's world, we have come to know something of its true splendor."
— Maurice Herzog, *Annapurna*, 1951

I got hooked on that girly-boy sport, feeling more alive when I ran than I had in any of my fights. I cut back even further on my drinking and smoking, and I quit fighting entirely. I loved running above all, and I ran all the time.

I wasn't built to be a long-distance runner, though. My upper body was quite muscular, due partly to my dad's genes and partly to my daily push-ups, pull-ups, and ab workouts.

At twelve years old, when I joined my first rugby team — and to increase my strength for fights — I designed my own morning routine, which I'd performed daily for the past three years. The first thing I did when I got up was five sets of twenty push-ups, thirty pull-ups, and two hundred ab crunches. I was quite a sight for all my dormmates. I'm sure some thought I was crazy. At the same time, it also sent the message that I was the alpha boy of the dormitory.

My routine only took a few minutes, but I could feel my strength increasing by the week. The stronger I became, the more I upped the repetitions. I didn't look like a bulky bodybuilder, but I had powerful shoulders, pectorals, biceps, triceps, and abs. Even though I had minimal body fat, I was not a skinny, lightweight runner…

Nevertheless, running became an addiction. A few months later, just as I turned sixteen, I entered my first marathon, completing it in three hours and ten minutes. More than ever, I wanted to do a Sport-Étude, and I kept begging my parents to let me try, to no avail.

When I started running marathons, it gave my entire body a rush, a feeling similar to drinking but much better. The sensation I enjoyed from the alcohol flooding my system, the lightheaded spin, the feeling of being transported into another dimension … I felt it exponentially stronger when I ran.

I'm not sure whether it was an endorphin high without loss of consciousness, a meditative state, a feeling of physical invincibility, or a combination of everything, but I no longer needed to drink booze. I didn't quit instantly, but I quickly realized that the next day after drinking, I couldn't run as well, and alcohol never made me feel as good as running.

I had been a drunk for three long years, but for me quitting happened naturally and effortlessly over the first couple of months of training. Although some people may not consider running for hours every day to be effortless, for me it felt that way. It was my new drug. My new addiction — and a much healthier one. At sixteen, I was a recovered alcoholic, but I never felt like it. I had simply moved on, discovering that I was made for endurance sports.

During that time, I barely saw my father. Whenever I mentioned professional sports or going to a Sport-Étude, he made fun of me, thinking it was simply a joke. I don't think he realized how much he tore me down.

He was probably trying to protect me. He was a businessman after all, and money mattered more than anything. It was his way of bringing me back to Planet Earth and steering me toward a real job. Because he was totally unable to push himself physically to reach a goal that wasn't related to business, he just put me in the same boat, thinking that I could never become an athlete if he couldn't.

I had never found my limits, and I didn't believe I had any. My father could take neither rigor nor pain, but I loved the rigor and pain required to train and push myself. People called me a masochist, but the physical pain I felt while running ultra-distances and pushing myself to my extreme limits was a joy and relief from my emotional pain. Another way to escape.

I remained at boarding school every other weekend, only returning home twice a month, and I only saw my mother and my siblings.

Regardless of the emotional torment my mother inflicted, at that point I still thought she was the victim in her relationship with my father and that her consistent depression was the result of her miserable life, raising kids with no money and no support. (I was unaware of the amount of child support my father was paying at the time.) After Dad had left, we lived a frugal existence. When I turned fourteen, in an effort to make and save some money, my mom moved us to a much smaller and cheaper house while she rented out our own house for a year.

I felt sorry for my mother as her significant others abandoned her time after time, always leaving her in more misery. For a few years, we were so poor that all she could afford to feed us were eggs and mashed potatoes. There was no meat, no cheese, and no desserts. To reduce utility expenses, when I returned home during holidays, we could only take a bath or a shower once a week. Mostly, we washed ourselves using a small sink filled with water and a washcloth. (As an adult, I learned that although we were living below the poverty line those few years, my father was paying more than reasonable monthly support, which my mother put away as savings, worried about her future.)

She was poor. She was abandoned. She was sick. She was depressed, and I always felt very guilty. But despite the number of times she told me that she was sick because of me, despite the hurt and the worthless feelings her words always generated, and no matter how miserable I felt, I always forgave her.

I never felt good going back home, even though I had stopped fighting and was no longer the bad kid of my early teens. Mom made me feel like I was Forrest Gump, running like an idiot with no purpose. She repeated again and again that it had been proven that sports were bad for your health and that people doing endurance sports specifically ended up destroying their bodies.

As usual, anything she heard became something she would exaggerate exponentially. She may have learned somewhere that overtraining could lead to injury, but in her warped way of thinking, that meant that all sports were hazardous, health-destroying activities. I tried talking sense into her, but I would have had more success conversing with a tombstone.

From that time on, I significantly increased my amount of training and decided to never share it with my parents. The less they knew about me and my training, the less opportunity for mocking me: the running idiot. I ran in as many marathons as I could, whether I registered for them or not. If I couldn't afford the fee, I simply raced without a bib number. I was lucky that age restrictions were not enforced. A decade later, I wouldn't have been allowed to enter events like these at such a young age.

With each race, I increased my speed and lowered my time. To my parents, these races and tests of endurance were leading nowhere, but I soon discovered that they brought me to exactly where I needed to be.

Chapter 19

Reaching New Heights

"On this proud and beautiful mountain we have lived hours of fraternal, warm and exalting nobility. Here for a few days we have ceased to be slaves and have really been men. It is hard to return to servitude."

— Lionel Terray, *American Alpine Journal*, 1964

On clear days, from school I could see the entire Pyrenees mountain chain, glistening white with snow in the winter and turning from apple green in the late spring to golden brown in the fall. The contrast of these ever-changing mountain peaks against a crisp blue sky mesmerized me. I couldn't stop looking at them. I kept thinking that one day I'd go there and climb them all. They were calling my name.

The more I trained for marathons, the more I stared at the mountains. Instead of watching the asphalt bouncing under my shoes, I imagined taking giant steps up those snow-covered summits. I remembered all the books I'd read a few years earlier, and they came back to haunt my thoughts.

My fantasy world hadn't been one of dragons, fairy tales, or science fiction. It had centered solely on being the hero of all the true adventures I'd read.

I had pored over those books, transporting me to other worlds where I could travel and live the excitement myself. *Le lion* was one of Joseph

Kessel's masterpieces, a book we were assigned to read in school when I was ten years old. This had been the only homework I ever felt passionate about, finishing it before the deadline. I read Kessel's other remarkable adventure stories too, *La vallée des rubis* and *Les cavaliers*, discovering other cultures and lifestyles so different from mine. I continued on to read many of his World War and French Resistance books.

I don't know why I hadn't read any mountaineering books until the age of twelve, but when I stumbled upon *Premier de cordée* (First on the Rope), Roger Frison-Roche's first book, my imagination was captured for months. Suddenly, Tarzan's jungles had lost their allure in the shadow of mountain expeditions. I also delved into all the great classics from Gaston Rébuffat. He was a climber on the first successful Annapurna expedition, and I read his *Annapurna* book in a single night. And I couldn't read Rébuffat without reading a different account of the same adventure by expedition leader Herzog. Lionel Terray made me travel even more with *Conquérants de l'inutile* and his other books, sharing his adventures on all continents. *Nanga Parbat* by Hermann Buhl was added to my list.

It was a time before the modern mountaineering climbs masterfully described by Jon Krakauer and Joe Simpson. It was a time when Heinrich Harrer's books were not yet translated into French. It was a time when large-scale commercial climbing had not yet become the norm. It was a time when mountaineering defined the essence of adventure.

I couldn't stop reading about it. Even though I never had the chance to climb, I was climbing daily in my imaginary world.

Before losing my soul to alcohol at thirteen, I had always believed that when school was a distant memory, I would realize all my dreams. Money was the least of my worries, and I didn't think about the cost attached to these expeditions and adventures. As far as I was concerned, the only things preventing me from living them as a kid were my parents, my school, and French society. But one day I'd break free from it all. Nothing would stop me from climbing mountains, diving into oceans, crossing jungles, living with Indigenous peoples, and going on these adventures that were so real and present in my mind.

Mountain climbing had once been at the top of my dream list, and it wasn't until I started running marathons that this particular dream was reawakened. The more that I studied the Pyrenees in the distance while I ran, the more I dreamed about scaling those peaks.

My paternal grandfather was from the Pyrenees, and I had gone there on holidays. I'd done ski trips and family outings but never trekked, let alone climbed, any of these mountains.

One day at school, I told my friend Frédéric how I dreamed of climbing them. He smiled and told me he knew all about them, discussing the mountains in great detail. His father was an avid mountain climber, and Frédéric had been climbing with him since he had learned to walk. During all our bio club lab outings and school recesses, I kept pestering Frédéric to tell more stories about his Pyrenees climbs.

In May, on the way back from Tonton's farm, Frédéric said to François and me, "Why don't you two come with us to the mountains this summer? I'll ask my father if you can join."

François and I stared at each other. We'd never dared to ask, but we took no time to answer: "Oh, yes!"

The following week, we met Frédéric, who delivered the great news. His parents had approved. François and I secured the authorization from our parents. My mom easily gave in when I promised to buy all the equipment on my own. We couldn't wait for the summer holiday to head to the mountains together.

In early June, Frédéric came back to the boarding school with the news that his father had to work in July and couldn't guide us. We were disheartened. For the first time in my life, I was about to realize one of my dreams — I was already living it in my own thoughts all the time. Within seconds, all my visions of mountaineering vanished. I was devastated.

"But," Frédéric said, smiling, "my father told me that if we don't do technical climbs, I can guide you without him."

François and I couldn't talk. We must have stayed mute for half a minute, staring at him, wondering if we'd heard correctly.

François and I were sixteen years old, and Frédéric was only fifteen, but his father had that much trust in him. Frédéric had even gone mountaineering on his own on multiple occasions. He knew the mountains, their beauty and their dangers. He understood how to plot a route on a map and how to navigate his way even without visibility. His father also knew his son's capabilities and was reassured that we were the school's best athletes. And as his own father had trusted him decades ago, he thought that Frédéric was ready to guide. It would be an incredible experience for him to be responsible to lead us.

The toughest thing would be to get new approval from our own parents. Would they let three teenage boys go on a two-week Pyrenees mountain trekking expedition on their own? We never even told them we'd be climbing. We left it at trekking, with some walking on the snow. My mom would have never agreed otherwise.

Both François and I understood that the easiest and safest way to ensure that we would enjoy this adventure was to not tell our parents. They had already given their consent about the trip and didn't need to know that Frédéric's father would not be with us, or that our lives would be in the hands of a fifteen-year-old.

And this was how François and I prepared for our very first mountaineering expedition under the expert guidance of our best friend.

Physically, I was ready. I had upped my running distance from a marathon to a 100km. But I had never held an ice ax and never walked with crampons. I knew nothing about ropes. My knowledge about mountaineering came from what I'd read. These books were filled with amazing adventures, but they also had their fair share of drama, not to mention mortality. I had already climbed dozens of mountains, but only in my imagination. I would have to rely entirely on my guide.

Frédéric drafted an amazing route. He brought a map to show us, and while I could see that François was excited, he didn't pay too much attention to the map. I thoroughly examined every curve line. I had a perfect mental image of the walls we would scale. I saw the difference between the trekking and climbing sections. It was so exciting to contemplate that during my training runs I would visualize the map and imagine I was already there climbing.

We needed to buy gear, and I used all my savings and borrowed money from my mom to purchase it. I had a one-month job lined up in August to work in my uncle's textile factory, and I would reimburse her with my full wages.

On the eve of our departure, François and I arrived at Frédéric's home with heavy-loaded packs. His parents welcomed us as we proudly displayed our new backpacks, mountaineering shoes, and climbing gear.

Frédéric looked at us and laughed, saying, "What do you have in your bags? You're not going to carry all this. It's way too heavy."

And so we unloaded our twenty-kilo[1] bags in his room, filling up every space. We covered his bed, his desk, and the entire floor with mountains of clothing and food. Frédéric kept shaking his head and laughing. An hour later, his mom opened the door to call us for dinner. She stared at the gear, smiling.

We spent three hours packing, unpacking, and repacking our bags. We kept less than half of the clothing and food we'd brought and added the climbing ropes, harnesses, webbings, and carabiners. When finished, Frédéric showed us how to set and adjust the crampons on our shoes. He also taught us how to attach them with the ice ax and pad them with the sleeping mat. We had to prevent injuries from the sharp metal in case of a fall if the rubber protections came loose. After five hours of intensive preparation, we were ready and went to bed but couldn't sleep for the longest time. We were too excited.

After an early breakfast, Frédéric's mother drove us to the UNESCO World Heritage mountain site of Gavarnie. His father would come to pick us up in that same village two weeks later.

It was an immense feeling of freedom. The cirque of Gavarnie stood before us: a natural amphitheater made by thousand-meter limestone cliffs from which sprinkled dozens of waterfalls. Europe's tallest waterfall

1. fifty-five pound

dropped a final four hundred meters,[2] billowing out mist hundreds of meters away. It was breathtaking before even taking a single step.

I remembered how Victor Hugo described it in his poem "Dieu": *"It's both a mountain and a wall; the most mysterious building by the most mysterious architects; it's the colosseum of nature: it's Gavarnie."* Here, in front of me, Hugo's words suddenly came to life.

This succession of three-thousand-meter[3] mountain peaks defined the border between France and Spain. They all bore mythic names: Petit Astazou, pic du Marboré, pic Brulle, pic de la Cascade, Épaule, Tour, and Casque du Marboré had been the playground of the greatest mountaineers.

Behind them, hidden from our sight a few hundred meters into Spain, stood the tallest mountain of the region, El Monte-Perdido. It means The Lost Mountain, named after its remote and hard-to-reach location. We planned to climb them all, and I was ready to experience my most amazing adventure.

Two full weeks in the mountains with no adults. Two weeks to push physical limits. Two weeks to fight our fears. Two weeks reaching new heights. Two weeks of intense friendship. Two weeks of mimicking the greatest mountaineers whose books had inspired me for years. These were two revealing weeks.

Each time I reached a mountaintop, with my heart pounding, I discovered a landscape of peaks that I hadn't been able to see from the lower valleys. Reaching each summit was like being on top of the world — a feeling of freedom I had never experienced, a physical exhaustion that felt better than any run I'd ever done.

It was both sport and adventure, the combination of all my dreams, and a revelation. I was hooked on mountain climbing. I had found MY SPORT.

For the past three years, I had stopped believing in my imaginary world and forgotten about my dreams because I thought — and had been told repeatedly by my parents — that they would never happen. But after

2. thirteen hundred feet
3. ten-thousand-foot

spending two weeks climbing the Pyrenees with my friends, my new passion for mountaineering reignited all my adventurous aspirations. Tarzan, Cousteau, Robinson Crusoe, Saint-Exupéry, Frison-Roche, Herzog, Rébuffat, and Terray came back to life to inspire me.

I would become a mountain guide and travel the world to live all these dreams. I needed two more years to finish high school, and I simply had to spend eleventh and twelfth grade in a Sport-Étude. Nothing else could prepare me to climb mountains. I had a taste for it, and I would not settle for anything else. All I had to do was convince my mom.

Of course, harsh reality returned to bite me. Once again, my mother would not allow me to do a Sport-Étude. Her refusal shattered all my hopes to make a living as a mountain guide. What was I to do?

Chapter 20

An Open Door

"It's the possibility that keeps me going, not the guarantee."

— Nicholas Sparks, *The Notebook*, 2011

Until 1996, France imposed a mandatory twelve-month-minimum military service on all men aged eighteen to twenty years unless they were enrolled in university studies, which meant they could wait to serve until the age of twenty-four. From their eighteenth birthday, however, most men were drafted as soon as they finished their studies.

France relied on a small number of professional militaries complemented by a large contingent of drafted citizens. Most draftees would then constitute the reserve and were at risk of being deployed until age fifty in case of a conflict.

Young drafted recruits were dispatched to army, navy, and air force corps all over France, with little say in what they did.

Doctors, nurses, and medical students in their final years of study always served in the medical fields. For others, it didn't always match. A mechanic could end up as an assistant nurse, an electrician as a cook, and a mathematician in an infantry battalion. But most people became simple privates — pawns in a random fighting battalion.

I wasn't an anti-militarist, but I was a nonconformist. Doing my military service was a drag, something I definitely hadn't looked forward to.

Then Frédéric told me that it was possible to do our mandatory service in the elite Mountain Commandos. They climbed mountains all day long. The selection process was extremely hard. His father had done it thirty years earlier.

From that time on, I researched information about this unique group. I didn't envision my life in the military, but if I could spend my full mandatory service climbing mountains, maybe that would help me later pursue a career in sports or as a mountain guide. At least it would give me the time to live my dreams and climb mountains while I reassessed what I really wanted to do, or *could* do, in life.

I discovered that the elite Mountain Commandos — one of the world's best Special Forces — were among the most coveted specialties in the military corps and the toughest to join. They spent all their time climbing and training in the mountains. Being selected as a member was considered to be virtually impossible, even for the greatest athletes.

Joining one of these Mountain Commando units was my only goal. I became obsessed with it.

In that unit, I could push my physical limits with some of the best athletes. It would never replace the Sport-Étude that I had been denied, but it would be the next best thing. And it was also a prestigious group who received much respect from the people of France.

There were only six mountain battalions in France, each with their own commando units called SR (*section de renseignement*), or Recon Team. Five out of the six were located in the Alps.

To even be able to compete to enter one of these elite mountain recon units, you would first have to be drafted into one of the six mountain battalions.

The first problem: People were often drafted to serve one year without a say in the region or the corps where they would serve. Often it would be in the region where they lived, but sometimes it could be on the other side of the country, where they needed more people. The mountain battalions, in general, were in the highest demand, and they always gave priority to people who lived in the Alps.

Both my parents lived near Bordeaux. When the time came, I would most likely be drafted in that region. Around Bordeaux, there were three regiments: navy, infantry, or, if I was lucky, a paratrooper battalion.

Expecting to be drafted in a specific battalion was like hoping to win the lottery without purchasing a ticket.

This was one of the few high hurdles, and my friend Jean gave me the solution to leap over that first one.

Chapter 21

Improving the Odds

"Opportunities are not offered. They must be wrested and worked for. And this calls for perseverance ... and courage."
— Indira Gandhi

While I was running my heart out dreaming of mountains, Jean followed an entirely different schooling system, where he learned a practical job as a mechanic.

He told me that when he turned eighteen, he wanted to serve his military duty as a mechanic in the air force. That service time would teach him precious skills to get a better job when he returned to civilian life. To do so, he registered for Military Preparation, which would allow him to choose to be assigned to the Merignac Air Force, next to Bordeaux.

He recommended that I also attend Military Preparation. This training was spread over twelve Saturdays, followed by a period of five days. It could be done from age sixteen to twenty as long as we were students.

I didn't know when I would finish school, or when I would do my mandatory service, but I knew how I wanted to do it: to choose one of the Mountain Battalions, I had to attend Military Preparation. It also yielded another benefit. After just one of these training sessions, we would start our mandatory military duty with the rank of private first class instead of a second class.

At barely seventeen, I registered for Military Preparation close to home with the paratroopers of the 13th RDP (*13e régiment de dragons parachutistes*), which would take up most of my weekends and part of my Easter holiday.

In that group, there were thirty of us between the ages of seventeen and nineteen, all there for different reasons. Some just wanted to avoid being drafted far from home, some wanted to have a career in the army. I wanted to choose to be drafted into a mountain battalion.

We started our very first day with an eight-kilometer[1] run on a well-marked set course that was mostly, but not entirely, flat. Parts of it were on hard or asphalt surfaces; other parts were on grass or gravel trails. A twenty-one-year-old paratrooper sergeant led us, setting the pace.

From the start, I took the sergeant's wake, running so close behind him I had to be careful not to kick his heels. The first kilometer's pace was gentle, yet we had already dropped half of the group. I moved to run beside the sergeant, and he increased the pace slightly to stay ahead of me. I matched his pace to remain on his right side. We kept speeding up progressively every few hundred meters until halfway through the course we were only a group of three.

My heartbeat remained low, and I felt comfortable. I hadn't pushed myself yet. When I realized both the sergeant and the other trainee were breathing hard, I knew it was time to accelerate. I progressively upped the pace until I could no longer hear their breathing or their steps. I continued running at a comfortable pace, and then I put the hammer down. I was no longer competing against them; I had already dropped them. I wanted to run for myself. I pushed until my chest and thighs burned and I could taste the blood in my throat.

I finished the run a full minute before the sergeant and kilometers ahead of most of the guys. The sergeant needed to catch his breath and, without a word, came to tap me on the shoulder. He couldn't talk for two minutes — until the second trainee arrived.

He finally said, "That's good, guys. Well done!"

1. five-mile

And then we waited, and waited, and waited. We stood there for more than half an hour for the last guy to show up, painfully walking and almost crying. His dream of having a career with the paratroopers probably died on this very first day of training. He was absent the next weekend. He had quit, along with three other guys.

Luckily, I had shown my worth on the run because the next exercise proved to be impossible for me: we had to learn how to parade, which required walking as a synchronized group. We lined up in a few columns and had to keep the same speed, moving our legs and arms at the same time. It seemed simple, but it wasn't for me.

During the first hour, my inability wasn't noticeable as everybody was off. But as the guys improved, I didn't. The sergeant gave the rhythm, and I was always off the beat. It felt so artificial, walking with these big steps, raising our arms so high. I couldn't get the coordination between my arms and legs. But it was no big deal. It was our first day, and we were not yet in the army. Most of us were still teenagers, and the sergeant was easygoing.

In the afternoon, he introduced us to the obstacle course. Each battalion had their own. We didn't run the full course on day one. We spent time learning the techniques to overcome each obstacle. I easily passed through them all. It was fun, at least for me. Some guys got stuck in the pit, unable to get out of it for the longest time, and most never made it over the horizontal board. They didn't have the upper-body strength or the drive to lift themselves. They had the same problems with all the rope climbs and anything that involved any type of pull-up. While they suffered, I couldn't wait to do the full course at speed.

I only had one goal: to crush the sergeant's time. But I'd have to wait another weekend, as our first training ended when each of us had finally managed to go through all the obstacles minus the board.

We finished day one with some classroom time, learning about the different military battalions and all their specialties. All this training had two purposes: to groom potential future corporals (graduates starting their mandatory services with a "private first class" grade were fast-tracked) and, more importantly for the army, to try to recruit career soldiers. Each weekend, someone gave us a presentation about a different army corps. We even had a warrant officer from this paratrooper base tell us about their own commando unit, sharing information about their training and missions. I listened with great interest, applying this to the Mountain Commando unit I wanted to join.

For people doing their mandatory service, there was a huge benefit in starting the army as a private first class instead of second class. A first class would always be given the priority over a second class to assist a corporal or a sergeant in leading the men for an exercise, and thus hone their skills. The best of them could eventually become a corporal. Although there were no guarantees, a successful Military Preparation was the fastest route to reaching that status before the end of military service. There was also a small financial benefit. Although the wage difference between first class and second class was meager, at the end of the month it could pay for a couple more beers. And the wage of a drafted corporal was even higher.

I finished Military Preparation after crushing all the other trainees in all the physical exercises. I didn't succeed at beating the sergeant's time on my first obstacle run, but it only took two other tries to do so. I remained pathetic at marching in the ranks, though. And with my eye problem, shooting wasn't my forte, but I still finished the training in pole position.

I had done it. When the time would come for me to be drafted for military duties, I would be able to enter my battalion of choice. And even though there was no guarantee that once there I could make the selection for any of the six mountain Special Forces units, at least I'd be drafted into one of the best battalions with a chance to try for the extremely competitive recon team selection.

I no longer needed a lottery ticket. It would now be entirely up to me.

Chapter 22

Falling Apart

"Run when you can, walk if you have to, crawl if you must; just never give up."

— Dean Karnazes, *Ultramarathon Man: Confessions of an All-Night Runner*, 2006

At age seventeen, I was a true addict. Not a drug addict — I was no longer a bad boy — but a running addict, craving the endorphins that my body would secrete while traveling long distances, yearning for the speed and the wind on my face, and needing the liberation I felt when I ran. And running was the best way I could train daily to climb mountains in the future: the hillier the route, the better.

I realized that marathons did not offer the best distance for me. They were too short. My fastest time was 2h51', and I was still more than 30' off from the world's best times. That was an impossible gap to bridge, especially with my more muscular physique.

The longer I ran, the faster I became compared to others. Before turning seventeen, I entered my first 100km[1] and finished in just a little over nine hours. I loved that distance, at least for a few months, as my time to cover it kept decreasing. Eventually, I decided that it wasn't enough either. I had heard of an ultra-race, where people ran for an entire twenty-four

1. This event is usually referred to as a 100K race, which is a sixty-two-mile distance.

hours, trying to cover the greatest distance possible. That became my new goal. I'd run at least 240 kilometers[2] in that timeframe. This distance would guarantee me a podium place, and maybe even the victory, something that could never be possible with a marathon.

Unfortunately, there weren't enough hours in the day for me to train while in school.

Since the age of sixteen, I'd continued my practice of escaping the dormitory at night by climbing over the roof of the two-story building and lowering myself down to the ground via the water pipe. But I was no longer heading to the town's bars. I had not been in a single fight in almost two years. Instead, I spent many nights running two or three hours in the countryside hills around the school.

To move from 100km to a twenty-four-hour goal, I needed to significantly increase my training. So, I ran every night, all night long. Luckily, I didn't need too much sleep, but each day I couldn't help drowsing, sometimes falling asleep at my desk during an academic class.

One of the problems I faced while running so frequently was the wear and tear on my shoes. The more I ran, the faster I destroyed them. I didn't even have real running shoes. I had general sports shoes, which kind of looked similar to running shoes. They were adequate for light jogging, but they were not made for long-distance runs.

Running shoes were too expensive for my mother to afford. The more I ran, the more quickly we needed to replace them, and the cheaper the shoes my mom allowed me to purchase. It was a Catch-22 that led me to entirely destroy a pair of shoes in less than six weeks. Mom was pulling her hair out, thinking I kept destroying them on purpose.

Her wallet wasn't the only thing suffering. The lower the quality, the less support they offered. I did multiple 100km runs every week with the ambition to win a twenty-four-hour event. My shoes never held up, and one day my knees didn't either. I was able to withstand a lot of physical pain, so even when my knees started bothering me, I always thought it was normal, and I just kept running until both my knees had doubled in

2. one hundred and fifty miles

volume. They were so inflamed that I could barely walk. It was time for me to see a doctor.

My general practitioner referred me to a sports doctor, who administered shots of corticoids to reduce the pain and swelling and sent me for a six-month treatment in kinesitherapy (similar to physical therapy).

To better understand my problem, the kinesitherapist wanted to see my running shoes. I shocked him when I told him they were the ones I was wearing.

"These are not running shoes!" he said. "Did you run marathons with these?"

I replied, "Yes, and I know, but running shoes cost seven to ten times more, and my mom won't buy them."

The treatment combined electro pads to send a specific frequency of electricity through my knees. We would alternate with cold compresses and anti-inflammatory gel massage. This was also combined with leg exercises to isolate and strengthen specific muscles. But the verdict was categoric: no sports! He forbade me to run for at least six months. And both the therapist and doctor told me that I might never be able to run long distance anymore, not even a half-marathon.

Once again, it gave my mom a good reason for not having sent me to a Sport-Étude. It confirmed that I was crazy and sports were bad for one's health.

This period was stressful. Running provided me a sense of freedom. Every time I ran, be it on asphalt or in the forest, I imagined myself running up mountains. I traveled into a world that wasn't part of my daily surroundings. I escaped from school and from my family situation. I was alive.

When I had to stop all sports, it was a multiple-edged sword that wounded me physically and psychologically. I couldn't fathom that I'd never be able to run ultras again. That also meant I couldn't climb mountains anymore. I had done Military Preparation for nothing. My dreams had been shattered again. I was devastated once more.

During the therapy treatments, I did all the muscle reinforcement exercises with great fervor. In fact, I always did twice what the therapist asked but without telling him. During these exercises, I focused on a full recovery so I could do mountaineering.

I found myself diving back into my mountaineering books. I had read many stories of people fighting adversities and accomplishing what everybody said to be impossible. I had dreams, and I thought that both the doctors and the therapist were wrong. I'd recover, and I'd run and climb mountains again.

After two weeks stuck without being able to run, my body was in serious endorphin withdrawal. I could feel my anger building. I had given up fighting entirely. It wasn't something I'd resort to again, but I had to find a way to control the steam that threatened to burst from my body. I had to assuage my mind.

The best solution I found was to significantly increase my reps of push-ups, pull-ups, and ab crunches. I progressively doubled my morning sets, and anytime I had a few minutes, regardless of where I was during the day, I'd just do a set or two, or more. When my chest, shoulders, triceps, biceps, and abs burned, it helped, giving me another outlet and making me feel good.

The inflammation in my knees went down in a few weeks, and the knee pain progressively disappeared in two months, but my therapist remained resolute with his strict interdiction of running. He understood that with the pain gone, I was never going to hold still and patiently wait for another four months. He was right, for I had already started jogging lightly, testing to see if I could go further without any pain. I told myself that I would run until I started to feel a light twinge, and then I would stop immediately and walk, but I couldn't cheat the therapist. Every week he saw how much I had used my shoes.

After a treatment session, the therapist told my mom which pair of shoes she should purchase. He explained that although they were more expensive, these would last ten times longer and cost less over the long-term.

My therapist warned me that until we finished another four months of treatment, I should limit my running to no more than ten kilometers.

I really tried not to run more than a marathon's distance during my last three months of treatment, but how could I? I had new marathon shoes, no more pain, and I felt like I was flying.

Chapter 23

No Guidance

"I do not live for what the world thinks of me, but for what I think of myself."

— Jack London, Letter to Charles Warren Stoddard, August 21, 1903

When I recovered from my knee injuries in the early months of 1985, I had turned eighteen and my father, whom I had barely started visiting again after two years of estrangement, had asked me to sign an official document transferring legal guardianship from my mother to him.

"You're an adult now," he told me. "And I'm not going to keep up child support payments to your mother for your cost of living. Sign this paper if you want me to continue paying for your studies."

I didn't. I couldn't.

My mother had recently remarried, and when my baby sister Aurelie came into our lives, my brother, harassed by our new stepfather, moved in with Dad, who took over his custody. I was still legally living with my mother. This meant that with my two sisters and me, she had custody of three children. My parents had never stopped fighting over custody. For my mom, with her low income, the number of children she had custody over impacted the amount of government social aid she received and there was a significant increase in aid for the three children in her care. For my dad, each child he had custody over meant an additional portion he could deduct from his income taxes.

I thought that Mom couldn't afford losing the social aid from my fiscal part, particularly if it went to Dad, who didn't seem to be in any financial duress. It still shocks me to have been treated as a mere currency in their fight.

Not only had my family situation not improved, but I had zero motivation regarding my last year of studies. What good would physics bring me in the jungle? How would memorizing poetry help me in the mountains? Why do I need art classes to dive with sea lions?

In spite of the fact that they lacked interest in helping me with my homework or in inquiring after my studies, my parents did care about my final grades. Only good grades would ensure advancement in the French school system. By forcing me to follow a standard school system, it had only fueled my aversion to it though, as had been evident throughout my whole time in school. All I saw was a system I despised that molded kids into brainwashed robots, telling them how to think and feel, forcing them into whichever career society mandated. There was no room for marginals who didn't fit into that system.

I was stubborn, intent on following my own dreams because my parents said I couldn't and shouldn't, and because they never encouraged me. The more they tried to kill my hopes, the more they hurt me and left me with doubts, the more I recovered from their blows and believed there could be no other life for me than to pursue my dreams.

School prepared kids to be doctors, teachers, or salespeople. I wanted none of that. Maybe this was their life, but not mine. If I couldn't live my dreams, then what was the purpose of living.

In all this emotional turmoil, even at age eighteen I didn't understand that school could actually provide me with the best tools to live my life, that it was the surest path to realizing my dreams. The truth was, many fields of study could have steered me in the right direction.

I could have been a marine biologist, navigating around the world on large-scale research missions.

I could have been an anthropologist, documenting the culture of Indigenous peoples.

I could have been a journalist, writing about Everest and other mountain expeditions for adventure magazines.

I could have been paid to live my dreams. All I needed was some motivation and interest and mentorship to help me understand that there were academic paths that would allow me to accomplish my dreams. Without guidance, however, I saw school leading me toward a life I didn't want.

So, at the time, the best solution seemed to be that I should quit the school system, be rid of the entire burdensome environment of my childhood. This would come with dire consequences I would have to accept.

In French society, it meant that I would never get a good job.

I would never receive a decent salary.

People would never respect me. Nobody respects a high school dropout.

As I struggled to reach a decision, I remembered this quote:

> *"If one advances confidently in the direction of one's dreams, and endeavors to live the life which one has imagined, one will meet with a success unexpected in common hours."*
>
> — Henry David Thoreau

I became convinced that I couldn't live the life my parents had chosen for me, or the one they or others around me were living.

Being a high school dropout only meant that I would start life with a very poor hand of cards. But I had a few things going for me. I had dreams. I had passion. I had drive. Even though a diploma would have helped me tremendously, it was only a tool. And life gives us plenty of other tools and means to move forward.

It was time to take my life into my own hands.

I was ready to move on, even if that meant carrying the heavy burden and social stigma of being a dropout.

I'd felt lonely my entire life, and my only joy came from believing in what was left of my childhood dreams. I would never be a world adventurer, but maybe I could climb mountains. My goal was to make the elite Mountain Commando team, an impossibly tight selection process that would only recruit the best athletes in France. I was convinced I'd make the cut.

At that point, I couldn't imagine any other life. I just had to try it.

Chapter 24

Without Endorsements

"People will always try to stop you from doing the right thing if it is unconventional."

— Warren Buffett, *TIME*, 2008

A year from graduation, when I told them I had quit school, planning to join the elite Mountain Commandos, my parents were furious and said I'd never make it through the selection process. That I was still living in my infantile imaginary world and my decision was ridiculous. They wanted me to start an apprenticeship and learn a manual job because I had been too stupid to make it into university.

I expected this reaction, but it still disheartened me. Like so many of my other dreams, I didn't talk with them about it any longer. I immediately went to the paratrooper military base where I had attended Military Preparation and told them I wanted to start my military service and join the mountain battalion as soon as possible.

I felt certain my paternal grandfather would understand. He was someone for whom I had the greatest respect and esteem. He was a judge. As a young man, he had served as an officer in the prestigious Cadre Noir de Saumur. He then fought in World War II. He was captured twice by the Nazis, escaping both times after spending over two years in concentration camps. He was, for me, a hero of courage and rightness.

With his background as a judge, he was intelligent and talked with eloquence. He led his life by example. A devout Catholic who had never missed church in his life except during the war, he only saw the good in people. I didn't share his religious beliefs, but I respected him more than anybody else. He had the greatest esteem for the military, and I thought he'd encourage me in my goal to join the elite Mountain Commandos.

To my dismay, all I received was negativity.

"You'll never make it into the elite Mountain Commandos. They've trained and lived in the mountains since they were kids, and nothing could prepare you for it. You'll serve all your time as a low-rank private in the Mountain Infantry. It will bring you nothing."

He continued, "You like sports, so it's a good idea for you to join the army, but it's the worst thing to enter it from the low ranks. It was a terrible mistake for you to quit school. You should finish high school and apply to enter the St-Cyr military academy. When you graduate as an officer, you'll have many opportunities to serve in the specialty you wish. And you'll be able to move up the ladder to a higher command position. Go back to school."

My grandfather's thoughts were logical and well-founded, and he meant well. He wanted me to succeed and have a good life according to most people's aspirations — but those standards didn't appeal to an outlier like me. He didn't understand my reasoning. With such limited contact, seeing each other only at Christmas or Easter, he didn't know what I had gone through for the past ten years. He had no idea how miserable I had been.

I felt like the entire world was against me. Everyone had the lowest opinion of me. My grandfather's non-endorsement was a big blow, but I was still not going back to school.

I had the sheer determination to be among the sixty people who would join the select ranks of the Mountain Commandos. It was my last chance in life.

There were just a few problems. A few thousand of the nation's best young athletes thought the exact same thing. And I had two huge handicaps, each that could get me eliminated before I'd even be allowed to compete against them.

The army had already sent me a drafting notice, and all I could do was hope that I'd made the right decision and everybody else was wrong.

Chapter 25

27th BCA

"Never was so much owed by so many to so few."
— Winston Churchill, 20 August 1940

My Military Preparation had earned me the rank of private first class and granted me the right to choose the battalion where I'd serve. After some research, my top pick became obvious.

Six BCA (*bataillon de chasseurs alpins*) mountain battalions operated across France's mountain regions. The 27th BCA caught my attention for a number of reasons: they had led important operations during both world wars, with their greatest achievement being in World War II after the French Army had capitulated and signed the Armistice. The 27th BCA refused to give up their weapons and became the local *Armée Secrète* (underground army), beginning a guerrilla warfare campaign that targeted German and Italian troops as well as the collaborationist French Militia. They found shelter on the Plateau des Glières, a high plateau of the Alps, surrounded by mountains where the British Royal Air Force could parachute in weapons and equipment. They held their position for months, during which they inflicted much loss on the invaders and their collaborators.

These 460 men keeping German and Italian soldiers at bay boosted the morale of the French and their British allies. In 1944, they adopted the motto "*Vivre libre ou mourir*" (Live Free or Die), first coined during the French Revolution (and subsequently used by the US state of New Hampshire in 1945). Fueled by this principle, their commando operations and their incredible resistance caused serious problems for the Germans. Fighters from the Plateau des Glières inspired the French Resistance that formed across the country.

It became a priority for Germany to neutralize the resistance movement initiated by the 27th BCA. In 1944, after extensive bombing, the German Army launched a major attack, killing the 425 remaining resistance fighters. Today, an annual commemoration still remembers them as some of the greatest heroes of World War II.

At that time, a unit within the 27th BCA called the SES (*section d'éclaireurs skieurs*) was the closest thing to a modern Special Forces. They served as the inspiration for the founding of the 27th BCA SR Special Forces: one of the very first modern Mountain Commando Units, which has spawned many of today's Special Forces units.

Starting in the 1980s, the 27th BCA took part in several external missions under the aegis of the UN and NATO, particularly in Lebanon, the Balkans, and Africa. They added "Always Ready" to their "Live Free or Die" motto.

Later, in March 2009 in the Alasai Valley, the battalion would defeat the Taliban severely, receiving a presidential commendation recognizing their success and bravery at the highest level.

Among the many famous people who have served in the 27th BCA are Maurice Herzog, the first man to climb Annapurna and whose book inspired future generations of mountaineers, and Nicolas Le Nen, who until recently was the chief commander of the French DGSE (*direction générale de la sécurité extérieure*), which is one of the main branches of the French Secret Intelligence.

Recognized as one of the leading commando training corps for both France and the allied countries, the 27th BCA was my natural choice for my mandatory service. It came with no guarantee that I'd ever make the Special Forces.

Chapter 26

The Very Best

"Be selective about whom you take on as friends, colleagues, and neighbors. The world is full of agreeable and talented folk. The key is to keep company only with people who uplift you, whose presence calls forth your best."

— Epictetus

In 1985, when I was drafted, the 27th BCA was composed of 2,500 mountain infantry personnel divided into six companies, each comprising approximately 400 people. There was one admin-logistic-command operation, four fighting companies, and one reserve company.

There was also a highly specialized group of twenty-four people who weren't part of these companies and operated as a self-sufficient squad. The SR (*section de renseignement*), or Recon Mountain Commando Team, was the best Special Forces unit of the French Army. Each of the six BCA had its own SR.

SR men were described as having extraordinary capacities in the high mountains, earning them the nickname "The Invisibles" for their intelligence work.

SR commandos were trained to operate in units of three men up to a small platoon of twenty-four. However, they worked best in squads of six or fewer. Most missions they did were special and black operations, highly secret, and executed with precision and swiftness.

SR squads were kept voluntarily small to be light, fast, and able to easily infiltrate and exfiltrate the world's toughest environments.

"Infiltrate, Recon, Sting and Disappear" was the SR's motto.

Infiltrate and Recon: Infiltrate enemy lines to spy on strategic operations.

Sting: Once the recon work is achieved, the sting becomes a demolition or sabotage operation, the killing of specific targets, or even a hostage rescue mission.

Disappear: The toughest part of any mission is to escape enemy lines once the operation is accomplished and after the enemy sends all its troops to catch the commandos. That's where the art of disappearing is most vital.

The French government facilitated media coverage of its larger commando platoons such as the Paratroopers and the Foreign Legion to exhibit the involvement of the French forces on foreign territories. They are the nonsecretive vitrine of French operations that the world knows about and that have been represented in movies.

But it purposely protected the SR Special Forces from the media, keeping it as low profile as possible to utilize these highly specialized and small elite commando units in the most vital black operations and conflict zones.

Later, in 1997, the SR evolved and was renamed GCM (*groupement de commandos de montagne*). Today, CGM remains the first Special Forces Unit sent on special and black operations.

A Mountain Commando unit was composed of a lieutenant as a commanding officer, a warrant officer or chief warrant officer, two truck drivers, two professional cooks, and eighteen operational commandos.

The Mountain Special Forces units of these six battalions are very prestigious and highly respected. At the 27th BCA, a blue star on a piece of fabric was appended to the left shoulder of the uniform to distinguish members of the Special Forces. Bearing one on your shoulder yielded the utmost respect from all others in the battalion, including higher-ranked officers.

The biggest SR distinction could be seen on the annual July 14 military parade for the national Bastille Day celebration on the Champs-Élysées, where the French military paraded in their dark uniforms under the eyes of the French president and the world's televisions. Only members of the six *section de renseignement* stood out from the dozens of thousands of other militaries. Wearing the entirely white parade uniforms of the elite Mountain Commandos, this select group of over a hundred men led the march in front of the rest.

Naturally, many young men dreamed of entering one of these units. It guaranteed a distinction from any other soldier.

It was an extremely tight selection with fierce competition. Every year, thousands of prospects wished to be among the select group of 108 active commandos who made up the operational commandos of these six Special Forces units. Around half of these positions were opened each year.

I had only one goal: make the selection to enter one of these six prestigious elite Mountain Commando units, preferably the one attached to the 27th Battalion.

The Mountain Commandos didn't waste time doing petty chores. They were always in the field, training to remain among the world's best. Most important to me, a large part of that training was done in the mountains and included almost daily mountain climbing and mountaineering.

SR units even had their own mountain chalet. Instead of staying all year in the barracks of the battalions with thousands of other soldiers, they had their own private lodging located in higher mountain villages and ski towns. It allowed them to easily access high and technical mountains for training purposes.

For me, no other conceivable choice existed.

The fighting companies spent much more time training like a regular army infantry. Granted, they did so in a mountainous environment, but they spent less time climbing mountains and more time doing chores, parades, and guard duties.

The last thing I wanted was to be drafted into an administrative position or, even worse, a fighting company. I dreaded the idea of being stuck in barracks with hundreds of other soldiers, spending all day carrying a rifle, practicing a marching parade, guarding a gate, and doing the stupidest of chores only to be compelled to unconditionally obey authorities.

I couldn't stand the idea of being treated like a small robot, following meaningless orders. No, that was not for me. I hated discipline and ridiculous rules. I had spent all my years in school breaking them. I couldn't contemplate the idea of being stuck in this situation for twelve never-ending months. A lowly pawn in a large infantry platoon.

I had to make it onto an SR Mountain Commando team.

Chapter 27

Filtering Process

"We must walk consciously only part way toward our goal, and then leap in the dark to our success."
— Henry David Thoreau, *Journal*, 1859

The vision problem in my right eye was the first big hurdle. I worried it would prevent me from even participating in the selection process.

Before entering the army, all young men were called to a military base nearest their home to spend an entire day taking tests. For many, the majority of these tests yielded only two results of importance: *Apte* or *Réformé*. Most people were Apte if generally healthy and suffering from zero psychological troubles. Getting the lowest rating in all the fields wasn't enough to fail. It took a real disability to receive a *Réformé* stamp and return home without ever being drafted.

For me, this basic testing day (now called SIGYCOP) was epically important. We were all rated from one to six in seven different fields, with the lowest number being the best. These fields included upper-body strength, lower-body strength, general health, vision, color recognition, hearing, and psychological tests. To even be eligible to compete for the Special Forces, people had to have no less than a one in every field except vision, color recognition, and hearing, where a two was the lowest rating allowed.

I only worried about the vision. Would I pass the minimum requirement? Would they base their rating on general sight with both eyes open, or would they attach more importance to the vision of each independent eye?

Apparently, the vision in my left eye was exceptional, probably because it had been compensating for my right eye since birth. On the physical test day, we were hundreds going through one test after another. They didn't notice my slightly tilted head or that I suffered from strabismus.

When they asked me if I wore glasses, I replied I didn't. They asked me to read the third line from the bottom of their chart, and I told them I could perfectly see the last line, which was barely visible for most people. I read it, and because I had no problem without glasses, they didn't test each eye individually. Fortunately for me, they didn't do their job thoroughly before sending me to the next physical test.

I later learned that if they had checked my right eye (with its vision of 3/10) like they were supposed to, I would have received a rating of three, rendering me ineligible to even try for the SR selection. And that's supposing they hadn't discovered my strabismus. The strabismus alone would have disqualified me.

I had secured a perfect rating in all other fields and felt relieved to have passed my first potential elimination test.

My second potential problem: the required experience. The elite Mountain Commandos operated in high terrain. They wanted the best mountain athletes.

Because the SR practiced skiing the entire winter, the desire to join it had spiked in popularity over the past ten years. As a result, more stringent requirements had been put in place. I figured they were meant to weed out people from the physical selection.

That year, all candidates for the Mountain Special Forces had to be certified mountain guides, climbing instructors, and downhill or cross-country ski instructors. They could also have national-level training in one of the mountain outdoor sports or be a national champion in other outdoor or combat sports. Graduating from a Sport-Étude would have also qualified me, but all candidates needed to be excellent skiers.

I had none of the required mountain experience. My urgent goal was to clear this filter and take the physical tests.

I knew I'd go through the selection tests in a few months at most, which would be in the summer, during a time when they could test me on many of the mountain skills except skiing. I had done some research. A ski instructor license required a long training period — usually done over three years — and a final exam. I plain lied and said I had done the full skiing instructor training program but had injured myself just before the final exam. I was going to retake it this coming winter.

The corporal holding my file was satisfied enough with this explanation. He didn't seem to care in the slightest. After all, the tests would be tough enough to filter me out. He wrote *ski instructor* in my file and cleared me to take all the tests once drafted.

I knew it was a lie, but I didn't care. I figured it didn't matter. I would be among the candidates to participate in all the selection tests, and that was all I cared about at the time.

Before being released, I had an interview with a sergeant.

The minimum mandatory service was twelve months but could be voluntarily extended to eighteen or twenty-four months. For most people, the goal was to serve the least time possible. Sometimes, volunteering to extend your service time gave drafted people more choices. For example, a private could petition to be sent to an outside French territory such as the South Pacific Islands of New Caledonia. It also yielded double the sixty-dollar monthly wage from the regularly drafted private second class soldiers.

The sergeant asked me if I wanted to do a long service of eighteen or twenty-four months, but I wasn't sure. If I knew I would be selected by the elite commandos, I would probably sign up for the extension. With my first class rank, it would increase my monthly wage to nearly $150. But if I wasn't selected, that'd be a long period of wasting time.

I said no.

The sergeant said, "But you want to enter a commando unit?"

"Yes," I replied.

"So, you need to sign up for eighteen months."

I didn't think twice about it and said okay. I signed up for eighteen months. I later learned that it was bullshit. I would have had the same opportunities with a mandatory twelve-month contract. The sergeant's duty involved enlisting as many guys as possible. I'm not sure if he just knew nothing or if he played me to reach his quota. But I was enlisted for eighteen months. I didn't worry too much about it because I believed I'd make one of the SR teams. And if I made it, I'd sign up for twenty-four months to make the most out of it. If successful, I would even consider enlisting for a fifteen-year career.

It was the only thing I had left in life. My only reason of being. My only hope. But what if I didn't succeed?

Chapter 28

The Squealing Pig

"Extreme hopes are born from extreme misery."
— Bertrand Russell, *Unpopular Essays*, 1950

Nothing can prepare young men for the psychological challenge of Basic Training.

In September 1985, after a twelve-hour night train with a connection in Paris, I arrived the following morning in Annecy, where I walked to the 27th BCA. I remember crossing the tall gates of the battalion after showing my summons. The guard sent me to an open field in front of a building where dozens of young civilians were already gathered. I joined the group, and we waited until our numbers grew to over two hundred young men. Then we waited, waited, and waited some more.

We were all dressed in civvies, with clothing spanning every color of the rainbow and every hairstyle imaginable. It was quite a contrast to all the short-haired, clean-shaven, uniform-wearing soldiers we encountered.

There were people from all backgrounds and social classes. Tall, small, skinny, fat, with or without glasses, tattooed guys, punks, guys wearing three-piece Italian suits, sweatpants, or cowboy boots. We probably represented a good sample of the entire population. Before even talking to each other, we all stuck out as being hugely different, but that changed drastically on this very first day.

Two sergeants appeared, but only one did the talking. After his brief speech, we lined up to receive our gear: a large military duffel bag, a backpack, a sleeping bag, a blue sport tracksuit, a pair of military boots, a pair of mountain shoes, military trousers, summer and winter jackets, a gear belt, a water bottle, a folding shovel, a long knife, and other military paraphernalia.

With our gear in hand, we were instructed to run across the field, the sergeant ordering us to stop in front of what would be our barracks for the next two months of Basic Training.

The drill sergeants gave us five minutes to climb the stairs, pick a bunk bed, change into our blue tracksuits, stuff our bags in our closet, and return to line up in front of them. We understood that we'd better be back within the five-minute deadline. As soon as one sergeant blew his whistle, we ran up the stairs while he screamed, "Faster, faster, faster! What do you think you're doing?"

Entering a barrack with all the bunk beds lined in a row didn't shock me in the least. It was like a boarding school dormitory, only much larger. I chose the first top bed available, changed, and left my bag and all my clothes on the bed without stuffing my things in the closet. I knew there wouldn't be time for that. I raced back and lined up.

Less than half the guys were back down within the five-minute limit. Some were a few seconds late, and the stragglers took as much as seven minutes to return. That's when we started to understand what a drill sergeant was.

He called everybody to attention. His face turned red as he screamed and swore louder than a bleeding pig, letting out an explosion of saliva.

"Where the fuck do you think you are? You're all a bunch of retarded, filthy-looking animals. I'm here to teach you to be soldiers."

He paused a second to catch his breath before spraying another stream of spittle. "When I say five minutes, it's not five minutes and two seconds, and definitely not seven minutes."

He paused again and screamed, "Each time a single one of you is late, you'll all suffer the consequences. After that, you're allowed to beat the crap outta the guy who was late!"

The way he delivered those words made us feel like a bunch of animals.

I was suddenly transported to my childhood, reminded of all the bullying I'd endured. My troubled teenage years and all my self-doubt came flooding back. In mere minutes, I'd been stripped of my confidence. I not only felt humiliated, but I experienced a horrifying moment of insecurity, wondering if I'd made a serious mistake. This was not what I'd dreamed about. My grandfather had been right. I probably should have stayed in school.

Could I have been wrong all along?

I had lived most of my life with low self-esteem brought on by more than a decade of degradation, hiding it with my physical abilities. Humiliation from bullies, from teachers, and, worst of all, a lack of recognition from my parents.

And now? I'd suddenly landed in a confined environment where the tone had just been set. We were going to live out the next few months — or maybe even a year and half for me — neck deep in total humiliation. Chills rippled along the full length of my spine.

Where did I land? What did I set myself up for? Can I even make it to the Special Forces? And if I do, will I even enjoy it?

My thoughts were promptly interrupted.

Still screaming, the drill sergeant ordered us to run to another barrack, where we lined up like a herd of sheep waiting to be sheared. It took less than two minutes per recruit for the four drafted soldiers to shave our heads.

We then gathered outside the barracks, waiting for the drill sergeant. I already had very short hair, and yet I felt naked. I could only imagine the shock experienced by those with long hair and the two punks who had lost their purple mohawks with the tall gelled spikes.

While waiting a couple of hours earlier, a few of us had been talking, still feeling very civilian. Now I could no longer recognize who I'd been conversing with. We all looked alike, with our scalps shining through the three millimeters of hair we had left, wearing the same tracksuits. In less than thirty minutes, we had lost our identities.

The drill sergeant called us to attention and gave us a ridiculously short amount of time to run back to the barracks, change into our military outfit, and race back, lining up in front of him. No matter how fast we ran and changed, the timing was impossible to meet for even one athlete. It was just ridiculous to expect that from a full platoon of trainees. He clearly intended to stress us out and punish us from the start.

It became evident that the drill sergeant was unable to talk without screaming, showering anyone unfortunate enough to be standing within a meter of his face. I never understood how he managed to scream all day long without losing his voice. But I assumed having bulletproof vocal cords was his only forte. Otherwise, after fifteen years of service, he would have reached a higher rank than sergeant, with more impressive duties than stressing out newbies.

We had randomly chosen our barracks and bunk beds. All the newbies were split into two groups, each to be trained by one of the two drill sergeants. I wanted to shoot myself in the foot for not choosing the other barrack. I'd inherited the squealing, spitting pig.

We ended up having to do twenty push-ups for being late. To my surprise, one-third of the guys weren't even able to do them. To my dismay, the drill sergeant kicked a dozen of them in the stomach, leaving them sprawled on the ground, panting for air. I thought it counterproductive. It didn't help those guys finish their push-ups.

He kicked someone next to me, bringing him to tears, plunging me back into memories belonging to a past life — never forgotten but buried deep. Years of feeling defenseless against physical aggressors. The gut-wrenching shame. The experiences that destroyed my self-confidence as a child. The psychological pain that forced me to forge an iron shield and prompted me to war against all tormentors.

Today, the bully became my very own nation, my own government, paying a brainless minion hiding behind a uniform to collectively abuse hundreds of people. A horrible tactic used to break as many young men as possible, hoping to make soldiers out of them.

I wasn't worried about the physical challenges or punishments we might encounter in Basic Training. I wasn't worried about being kicked, but I did feel as humiliated as my poor neighbor, an emotion extremely triggering for me and for which I had nearly reached an overdose. I dreaded it. As a whole, we felt denied any basic human rights.

It was a great relief for us all when lunchtime arrived. That was when we discovered the cantina. We lined up with our aluminum trays, waiting to be served some food that instantly made all my boarding school meals look delicious. After sampling, I determined it was edible, not as bad as it looked, but not much better either. Eating this daily was going to require some getting used to, and it wasn't like I could afford to supplement my diet with the meager mandatory service wage I was receiving.

We didn't have a lot of time to eat, which meant very little time to talk before we had to line up again.

Our first afternoon exercise involved learning how to march. Even though I had already practiced that many times during my Military Preparation, I was as pathetic as those who had never done it. I hated marching. It felt unnatural, reducing us to brainless robotic movements.

The first chance we had to get to know each other was at dinner. It bewildered me to discover that within our group of thirty, four guys didn't know how to read and write. Not even the most basic of words. In all my life, I had only met one adult who couldn't write, and now I was sitting at a table where 10% of the recruits had never been to school. I was shocked.

For the first week, each day that followed was more of the same. We did far more marching within the ranks than we did sports. We were ordered to change clothes at least ten times a day, ten times too many. It was always within a timeframe we couldn't possibly meet. We had to pay for it with sets of push-ups. Worst of all, the drill sergeant never stopped screaming. It was hell for me, and I was one of the fittest. Some guys cried, others retched during the various physical exercises. And the squealing pig would often randomly beat up a few recruits.

He punched or kicked someone in the stomach dozens of times each day. We weren't even sure it was legal or sanctioned by the army. But who would be the newbie willing to risk reporting it to one of the officers? We never even saw any officers. Until we finished the two months of Basic Training, the drill sergeant was in charge of us; and until we joined their platoon, the officers couldn't have cared less.

Many recruits cracked physically, others psychologically. Several guys thought of every possible way to get thrown out of the army. Some deliberately injured themselves. A few even tried to convince the infirmary doctor they were crazy, and others attempted suicide. Only a very few managed to glide through the military net and receive a dismissal from the army for serious psychological problems. Something that would be printed in their file for life and prevent them from working as a police officer, firefighter, public school teacher, or other position in any of the government institutions.

I wasn't that desperate, but I couldn't imagine enduring this for two months. I kept hoping the squealing pig wouldn't touch me. I felt the pressure building in me daily, a mixture of fear and anger. Luckily for me, in less than two weeks, I was going to start the selection tests to make it into the Special Forces unit. I would get out of this stupid and meaningless training, I was sure.

During our first shooting practice, I was lying down with my rifle along with nine other recruits. The targets were set at fifty yards, which was a very close distance. The drill sergeant stood next to me. We were shooting with a FAMAS, a precise assault rifle with a twenty-five-round magazine. Shooting ten bullets, I wasn't able to touch the target even once.

Furious, thinking I was doing it on purpose, the drill sergeant kicked me hard in the stomach. I didn't see it coming and it knocked the wind out of me. It took me a full minute to resume breathing normally. I couldn't see the target with my right eye and shot using my left, but no matter how hard I tried, I couldn't hit it. I couldn't even tell from which side I was shooting. I did my best, but it wasn't something I'd ever be able to do.

Luckily, I redeemed myself in the other physical activities, but I feared the next shooting practice, and my fear was justified. Three days later, the target had been moved to one hundred meters, and the asshole kicked me in the ribs, bruising me so badly, I felt certain if he kept this treatment up, I would be too injured to compete in the selection process. All my hopes for being in prime condition to make it into the SR unit were slowly disintegrating.

Chapter 29

Bullseye

"Before success comes to most people, they are sure to meet with much temporary defeat, and perhaps some failure. When faced with defeat, the easiest and most logical thing to do is to quit. That is exactly what the majority of people do."

— Napoleon Hill, *Think and Grow Rich*, 2005

Two days later, extreme anxiety plagued me as we ran in a pack toward the shooting range for our third practice. I had only ten days until the start of the Special Forces selection, and I worried I wouldn't get out of this exercise without the squealing pig injuring me, ruining my chances of joining the SR.

A lieutenant greeted us at the entrance. The drill sergeant seemed intimidated. He was no longer in charge, no longer screaming. The lieutenant managed the shooting range for this practice, taking the time to offer some tips to a few guys ahead of me.

When it was my turn to shoot along with nine other guys, the sergeant and the lieutenant stood right above me, their legs almost touching mine. As I started to shoot, the first four bullets missed my target. I braced myself, waiting to get kicked. The lieutenant ordered everybody to cease-fire.

The drill sergeant didn't waste any time, telling the lieutenant I was an asshole and a desperate case, swearing he had done all he could to teach me, but I was purposely not trying. The lieutenant ignored him and called me forward. I immediately stood and saluted him, wondering what my punishment would be.

He asked me to cover my right eye and grab the finger he held in front of me. I caught his finger immediately and precisely. He then asked me to cover my left eye and grab his finger. I missed it by more than twenty centimeters.[1]

He said, "You have a left driving eye, and you've been using a right-handed rifle. To line up your eye, you were holding your rifle at a diagonal. You can't possibly touch your target."

He took my rifle, grabbed a new one, and put it in my hands, saying, "This here is a left-handed rifle. The bullet casing will eject on the opposite side. You have to hold it as if you were left-handed."

He made me lie down, putting the rifle in my hands in the correct position. It felt very odd and uncomfortable. I was right-handed, not left-handed.

Then he said, "Now, look inside that visor with your left eye and line it up with the front visor, then line it up with the center of the target. Keep your rifle straight. Start your aim a few centimeters higher, hold your breath, and very slowly lower your aim. When you're on target, delicately pull the trigger."

The full range was quiet, with all eyes on me, as if time had been suspended. Even lying down, my heart pounded. Sweat dripped along my forehead as I followed the instructions. It felt so odd to have my left index finger on the trigger as I remembered the words of the lieutenant: *delicately pull the trigger.*

How can I be delicate with my left hand?

I felt the sweat build upon my brow, and I worried it would enter my eye and blur my vision. I held my breath and shot.

The bullet pierced the target's bullseye.

"Very good," said the lieutenant. "Now try to shoot the remaining twenty-four bullets using the same technique. Take your time."

1. eight inches

And so I did, shooting repeatedly under the gaze of my entire platoon.

The lieutenant went to check my target. All twenty-five bullets had hit dead center, creating the circumference of a golf ball.

"What's your name?" he asked.

I saluted him again and replied, "First Class Soulé, mon lieutenant!"

"At ease, First Class Soulé. Tomorrow, you'll start your sniper training."

And this was how, along with three other guys, I was recruited to start a one-week sniper training. The drill sergeant was speechless. I'm not even sure he understood how dumb he had been.

I couldn't have been more pleased. Not only was I ecstatic about what I'd just accomplished, as I really thought I was useless with a gun, but I got to escape this stupid Basic Training for a full week. The other selected guys and I rejoiced at not having to see the drill sergeant for a week.

In sniper training, we learned great shooting techniques, the importance of good positioning and concentration, and how to control our respiration, holding our breath for three seconds and exhaling before shooting. We learned how to softly pull the trigger without any lateral movement, something that seems easy but may be the hardest aspect of shooting.

We learned the importance of constancy, which is to group all the bullets into the same small space, and how to estimate distance with the naked eye and calculate it with specific equipment. We also learned bullet trajectory and the importance of precision, which is a combination of shooting techniques with correct rifle adjustments. We learned how to take into consideration the wind in different places between the shooter and the target, the atmospheric pressure, the temperature, the humidity, and the light.

We shot with all kinds of rifles, with and without a scope, first at distances of up to six hundred meters. After a few days of training, we were given a chance to shoot the FR-F2 sniper rifle at silhouette targets set at a distance of eight hundred meters.

When I asked the instructor if I should shoot at the head or the chest, he asked, "Can you seriously distinguish the head from the chest?"

"Yes, perfectly clear, mon lieutenant."

He said, "At eight hundred meters with this scope, you should only be able to see the silhouette of the target, not the difference in shade between the body and head. If you think you can, shoot the head."

And so I did, and to my instructor's great surprise, all ten bullets were perfectly grouped in the head. My eye doctors had all told me that the vision in my left eye was superior; I guess they weren't wrong. The officer said I was the deadliest sniper trainee he had ever coached, and if I wanted to be an elite sniper, I might be able to take a two-month advanced class.

I became very good in the prone position. I was not bad while kneeling, but I still had a difficult time holding my rifle as a left-handed shooter while standing. I wasn't bad, but most of the trainees who couldn't match me on the longest ranges while prone were better than me while standing. It would take me some time to get used to the left handling. My instructor told me it was normal and would soon feel natural. The advanced sniper training sounded interesting, but I didn't want to be a sniper or carry an FR-F2 in the mountains. I wanted to be an Operative Mountain Commando.

At the end of the training, the four of us graduated and received two printed pages. One was a proposition to sign up to serve in New Caledonia and the other one to serve in Lebanon. Each required a minimum of eighteen months duty, for which I'd already enlisted.

We would later learn that everybody would receive the same papers a couple of weeks prior to finishing Basic Training, but they encouraged snipers to enlist with higher wages. The wages were actually two times higher for any private enlisting in one of these destinations. Wages were even better for those having graduated from sniper training.

I immediately assumed that the reason we were offered higher wages was because eventually, as a sniper, we'd have to kill someone.

I wasn't quite sure what the situation was in New Caledonia. It was considered a French territory but not a French region. It was a large island in the middle of the South Pacific Ocean, with tropical weather. The French government annexed that territory for geopolitical and strategic reasons to have one more military base in the South Pacific. Some of the

Kanaks, the native people of New Caledonia, were revolting, requesting their independence, or, more precisely, to be freed from the French invaders.

We had heard on national news that a few Kanak terrorists had attacked government officials. I didn't know more than that, but I certainly had no intention of being the sniper who shot a native indigene because he was, and maybe rightly so, unhappy that France stole his island.

As for the situation in Lebanon, we had a full double-spread handout summarizing it, and frankly, I didn't understand much about that conflict either. It was a small Asian country bordered by Syria to the north and east and Israel to the south, with a coastal region on the Mediterranean Sea. After the collapse of the Ottoman Empire following World War I, Lebanon went under French Mandate before becoming independent in 1943. Shortly after, it joined the United Nations. A civil war broke out in 1975, followed by Syria invading parts of the country and then Israel invading another part, and US, French, and Italian troops were sent as peacekeepers.

This seemed to be too complicated of a geopolitical mess for me to comprehend from the top of my eighteen years, even though I had heard the news about many incidents happening in Beirut. I didn't quite grasp who the good and bad guys were or who I would eventually have to shoot with my sniper gun. Despite the lower wages, I was much more interested in making it to the SR and climbing mountains all day long.

Two of the privates I did the sniper training with signed up for *Outremer*,[2] going to either New Caledonia or Lebanon. I was surprised. They knew nothing about these two destinations, not even enough to be able to choose between the two. They just wanted the experience of doing a longer service in a foreign land while receiving three times the meager regular wage — a choice I didn't understand. I could never fathom killing someone for a reason I couldn't comprehend, on the simple basis that it was an order. And to me, it seemed that signing up to one of these destinations as a sniper was exactly that.

2. French territories outside of mainland France

I later learned that snipers were paid much better than others because their main duty was to protect convoys from attacks. To do so, they always sat next to the driver inside the first trucks, and they were the first targets of the enemy's snipers. They were positioned like sitting ducks, taking fire before they even realized they were being attacked. It was the absolute most dangerous position to be in. The army failed to print that information in their almost vacation-brochure-like handouts.

My training over, and with the sniper specialty under my belt, I returned to Basic Training, and I dreaded it. During the sniper training, we understood that other military leaders could be human beings, which was not the case with our drill sergeant. Luckily, I was only going to endure another couple of days with him before starting the selection tests for the Special Forces.

Chapter 30

Ultimate Selection

"People are always blaming their circumstances for what they are. I don't believe in circumstances. The people who get on in this world are the people who get up and look for the circumstances they want, and if they can't find them, make them."

— George Bernard Shaw, *Mrs. Warren's Profession*, 1907

Before doing the first selection test, we had a cardio medical check. With a resting heart rate of thirty-four and a recently tested VO2 Max of eighty-six, I wasn't worried. VO2 Max is the maximum rate of oxygen consumption measured that reflects cardiorespiratory fitness and endurance capacity. The average for young men was between forty-two and forty-six. Above fifty-six was considered excellent for athletes. World-class marathon runners, cycling winners of the Tour de France, and Olympic cross-country skiers had exceptional VO2 Max that ranged between eighty and ninety. I was within that range, more proof that I was made for endurance sports and another reason I couldn't forgive my parents for not sending me to a Sport-Étude.

The first selection test was rope-climbing. We started on a five-meter[1] vertical rope. We had to climb it with hands only, touch the top bar, descend to the floor, and climb again (this time using our legs to help) to

1. sixteen-foot

touch the top bar in less than two minutes. Those who couldn't were eliminated.

Since I had participated in that exercise in my Military Preparation with the Paratroopers, I had practiced it at least weekly at school for the past eighteen months. I had timed myself frequently and could successively speed-climb that rope without legs six times in a row. I did the full exercise without using my legs, which would have only slowed me down.

The next exercise was the obstacle course. I had also done this in my Military Preparation. I managed to get the fastest time during Basic Training. I wasn't worried about it. I made my best time to easily qualify, but I ended the course with a knee pain. I didn't feel anything while on the course. Maybe I banged my knee on one of the obstacles or slightly twisted it on the reception of a jump.

The final exercise for the day was a Cooper test, which required running as far as possible within a twelve-minute timeframe. The qualifying distance was three thousand meters.[2] Achieving thirty-five hundred meters[3] running at a pace of 5'31" per mile ensured me a top position, but one guy crushed me by an incredible three hundred meters.

A mild knee pain had started after the obstacle course. It increased a little after the Cooper test, but it wasn't a big deal until late afternoon when the pain continued to grow and my knee became swollen. The timing couldn't have been worse. We had finished all the qualification tests. Those of us who remained would compete against one another, racing on a mountain course. Anxious, I went to the infirmary. The doctor gave me ibuprofen and an ice compress. I told him I was doing the SR competition the next day and asked for the maximum dosage I could take.

I slept with my leg elevated on top of my bag all night. When I woke up, the swelling had gone, and the pain had almost, but not entirely, disappeared. My knee was much better but not fully healed. I worried about the mountain climb, but I was determined to give it my all no matter the

2. almost two miles
3. just over two miles

pain I'd suffer. I was not going to let my knee fail me. My only limits would either be the cardio or my thighs, but certainly not knee pain.

The rule of the competition was simple. Dressed in the mountain uniform with the big, heavy mountaineering boots, we carried a thirty-kilo[4] backpack. We had to climb and descend two mountains in a row, for a total elevation gain of twenty-six hundred meters.[5]

A strong trekker carrying a five-kilo backpack would do this full course in around seven hours. Most strong trekkers wouldn't even be able to complete the full course in a day with a thirty-kilo backpack.

The weight of the bag alone was more than twice what most army units carried on a "commando run," which was usually done on flat terrain. The trail was steep and technical in some areas. There was no rock climbing involved, but use of the hands was sometimes necessary on the steeper rocky pitches. One section had a cliff where we had to grab on to an anchored chain.

Those who had passed all the tests from every contingent were there for the final competition. We were over three hundred of the best athletes in France to have made it this far. All had achieved incredible times on the obstacle and running tests. The competition would be fierce to be among the top sixty to enter any of the six units. That was my minimal goal. I absolutely had to be in the top sixty. That was the top 20%. Before my knee injury, I was aiming for much higher. A top-ten position or top 3% was what I needed to make the SR of the 27th BCA.

Unfortunately, it wasn't a mass start. They let one athlete begin every thirty seconds, which made it impossible to know our position compared to the others. It would even be feasible to start in the one hundredth position, never get passed by any other soldiers, outrun thirty guys, and yet fail to make the top sixty. There was no way to know how we would fare in the entire race.

Instead of it being a race against others, it would have to be a race against myself. Although I competed against three hundred other recruits,

4. sixty-six pounds
5. eighty-five hundred feet

I couldn't know where I would stand compared to them. I really had to concentrate on myself and going as fast as possible. Without a bag, I had run up mountains at a climbing pace of sixteen hundred meters[6] per hour when I was sixteen, before blowing my knees. But that was with a very light pack.

I had never raced up mountains with a thirty-kilo backpack. The heaviest weight I'd ever had was a little over fifteen kilos, and not in the mountains, just on hills next to my school. But I thought the heavy weight would work in my favor. At one meter eighty-three, eighty kilos,[7] and 9% body fat, I was one of the biggest and heaviest guys at the start.

Although body weight was a big drag on mountain climbs, particularly on the steepest trails, I figured that proportionally, carrying heavy packs, I probably had more power for that extra weight than a small skinny guy. Perhaps someone who may be faster than me on the same course without a bag could actually be slower on the same course with a heavy bag. At least I hoped it to be true. It didn't prevent the knots turning my stomach. I was probably one of the guys with the least amount of mountain experience. The longer I waited for my turn to start, the more I felt my gut tightening up. This was the most important race of my life.

The ibuprofen seemed to work. At least at the start, I didn't feel any knee pain. I really hoped my knees would hold. The heavy pack might later take its toll, particularly in the long, steep descent where it would destroy the legs.

Queuing up to get in line for the start, every thirty seconds I stared at the guys rushing up the hill. The first hill didn't seem too steep, and yet they all quickly walked it. Nobody ran. The bags were heavy and the race long.

When the guy in front of me began his turn, I moved to the starting line, a rush of adrenaline filling my entire body. The countdown began, and as soon as the bell rang, I rushed out like a lion freed from its cage.

6. fifty-two hundred feet

7. six-foot-tall, one hundred and seventy-six pounds

I ran up the first section as if I were on a 100m sprint and passed the guy ahead of me in the first two minutes. He probably thought I was crazy, doomed to collapse within the hour. Maybe so, but I had the confidence and the cardio to back it up. I just hoped that with the heavy pack, my legs would follow and not tetanize or cramp up halfway through the course.

Three minutes later, I caught another guy. The trail was too narrow to pass. I had to jump to the side to overtake him, wasting energy doing so. He was really too slow for me to wait for an opening. When I passed him, I realized he'd been the third guy ahead of me. This meant there was a fast guy who had already passed him.

My goal was not to drop the slowest guys but beat the fastest guys, and I didn't know where they were on the course.

On 20% pitches, I had to stop running to walk at a high pace. But as soon as the slope went below a 10% grade, I resumed running as fast I could. I ran all flat and gradual sections. When forced to walk up the steep slopes, I pressed my hands on my thighs to increase my pace. We were not allowed to use ski poles.

I visualized my legs as powerful pistons mounted on giant springs, and I tried to jump up and forward on every step, imagining my backpack empty. I thought about how it would feel to run this course without a bag and tried to run it the same way.

I kept telling myself, *This weight works to my advantage. I don't feel it. It's very light. Focus on each step. Jump out of every step as if you had springs instead of feet.*

My lungs and legs were burning. I knew that letting the pain slow me down would mean not qualifying.

I quickly passed a dozen guys, but I kept telling myself, Three hundred guys have passed all the tests. Three hundred. That's a lot of people for sixty spots.

And then I remembered that I had enlisted for eighteen months, not twelve.

Not making the cut would mean spending eighteen months in a fighting company. If being in a fighting company involved doing even a fraction of the stupid chores we did in Basic Training, I'd go crazy. I didn't think I could bear it. I couldn't envision myself guarding a gate for eighteen months, receiving stupid orders from someone like the squealing pig. That would be hell. I had enlisted for eighteen months, and now I was here, competing against invisible people. It was the race of my life.

I continued on, passing a new person every few minutes. I kept imagining faster guys coming from behind and catching me. No, I wouldn't let this happen. I was in pain, my thighs were screaming, but I had to move faster. I could take pain. It was only temporary. A few hours. If I didn't make the cut, I'd be in severe psychological pain for eighteen months.

Go faster, I kept telling myself. This is who you are. This is what you've always wanted to do. Go faster.

And then I thought about my father and grandfather telling me I'd never be able to do it. My mother claiming that sports were not important in life. They were so wrong, and today I had to prove it. My only chance.

Go faster. Push harder. This is not pain you feel. It's pure pleasure. Come on, you can go even faster.

I ran the entire descent like a madman, keeping my cardio maxed out even going downhill. I jumped over roots and rocks, risking a twisted ankle on every step, even though I tried to carefully choose the landing for each one. I jumped as much as I ran down. I tried to land as softly as possible, but I couldn't slow down. The momentum of the bag pushed me forward, yet I didn't want to put any resistance on my legs to slow myself. I had to use my weight to my advantage in the descent. I had to run faster.

Luckily, my knee held, but my thighs caused me extreme pain. The second ascent almost came as a relief. I could finally stop running for a steep stretch of trail and switch to a fast walk. As soon as the slope became gradual, I resumed running. I kept pushing. I kept digging deeper and deeper. I reached a level of muscular pain I had never experienced in my life. But I couldn't let myself focus on it.

It's the mind that will win or lose today. It's all in the head.

I felt like I was doing well, at least; I was doing my absolute best. I raced at the limit of my threshold (my cardio and muscle aerobic limit) the entire time. But I was clueless about the other top athletes, and I wouldn't know until I crossed the finish line.

I never slowed down until the end, running more than half of the climbs and all the descents. After three hours and twenty-six minutes of agonizing effort, I collapsed upon reaching the finish line. Lying down, I threw my bag away from my body to better breathe. There were no cheering supporters, no food stop. This was not an organized ultramarathon. It had been a race up and down to hell.

I was surrounded by guys crying, coughing, or cramping. They all looked like they had been pushing and suffering as much as I had. How did they do? How did I do? After sitting down for five minutes, I was barely able to stand back up. I abandoned my backpack to go talk to the guys monitoring the finish line. I didn't worry about anybody taking it and running away. I hoped to get an idea as to my current position.

"The results won't be in until next week," they said.

My tests were over, and I went back to my barrack. The next day, I'd return to Basic Training. Back in my bunk bed, friends asked me how it went. I was unable to reply. I didn't know. I couldn't sleep that night. I kept turning in my bed, wondering how I had done compared to the rest. Did I succeed? Could I have gone faster?

No, I couldn't. I had felt great during the race. I'd pushed myself to the limit the entire way. I ran the perfect race. If I didn't make it, I wasn't cut out for it, and my parents would be right. I'd be a loser. There'd be no other chance anyway. I sank into some serious doubts.

Chapter 31

Back with the Squealing Pig

"The only man who never makes a mistake is the man who never does anything."

— Theodore Roosevelt, 1900

I resumed Basic Training with legs so sore that getting out of bed felt like someone had stabbed my thighs and calves with knives. I walked like a robot with no knee joints. As if my legs were one stiff block from my hips all the way to my feet. There was a single-story level to descend, but I couldn't handle the stairs. I put all my weight on the handrail and tried to fold one of my thighs enough to lower my opposite leg down. I repeated this step after step.

Halfway down, after only ten steps, I stopped, looked around, and laughed. Two other guys were shadowing me. We looked at one another and couldn't stop laughing. We were quite a sight. When we finally lined up in front of the drill sergeant, he called everybody to attention. He rattled off my name and a few others. Twenty-three people in total. I wondered what would come next.

He screamed, "You pathetic pieces of shit. You want to be commandos and you can't even fucking walk after a small mountain climb. Go to the infirmary. You'll resume Basic Training tomorrow."

I'm not sure if these were directives from higher command. Probably, as he had all our names at the ready, and he didn't have our names memorized. For once, he screamed without spitting.

Did he try to give us a compliment? I wondered. Maybe he even tried to be nice.

And so, we went to the infirmary. We spent the entire day relaxing while applying cold compresses on our legs and keeping our feet up. We exchanged war stories. The first question we asked each other was our times. Among the twenty-three of us who were doing Basic Training together, I had taken the second-best time. The only guy who beat me did it by eleven minutes. He was the skinny guy who had crushed me on the Cooper test. He was one meter seventy-eight,[1] and thirteen kilos[2] lighter than me.

I wondered how he managed to go so fast with such a heavy pack. That wasn't normal. That guy was a real freak, and I hoped there were not too many like him among the three hundred. Based on our infirmary group, statistically I had already failed to make the top ten. Not all was lost, for statistically I should make it to the top sixty. But who knew? If other groups of our size had two or more freaks like that skinny guy, I was out.

Our time at the infirmary was fantastic, but the next day our legs felt even worse. We took forever to descend the damn stairs from our barrack, and yet we couldn't stop laughing. We hoped the drill sergeant would give us another day at the infirmary, but it didn't happen. We had to practice the march, and that was excruciating. Our legs were so stiff, our facial expressions showed the level of pain we were in. We stuck out of the crowd.

The drill sergeant never stopped screaming at the entire platoon. But when he looked at some of us, a sadistic grin lit up his face. We had never seen him smile before. He enjoyed our suffering. I wondered if he had ever pushed himself that hard in his life. Of course he hadn't; otherwise, he wouldn't be stuck as a drill sergeant for the past fifteen years.

1. five-foot-ten
2. twenty-nine pounds

Three days later, we returned from the shooting range late in the evening. As usual, we had spent four hours cleaning the rifles after shooting. In reality, the last rifle had been perfectly cleaned in less than an hour and a half, but the drill sergeant would randomly check a rifle with a white cotton glove, sticking his fingers in the barrel and in the smallest of cracks of every gun. If his gloves came out immaculate, he'd take another rifle and do it again.

The first trace of grime or grease on his gloves was enough for him to scream, spraying the poor gun trainee in the face. He'd order us to disassemble our rifles, clean them, and reassemble them. Then he would go to sleep for another hour. An hour later, he'd do the same thing again, just dragging it on forever. Some of the guys were so dumb, the fastest of us had to help them clean their rifles. No matter how much we cleaned, it was nearly impossible to get everything. Inevitably, there were tiny traces on the drill sergeant's white cotton glove from at least one of the firearms.

It reminded me of the first week of Basic Training. One morning, he had selected a few guys in the ranks and told them they had not shaved their faces clean. They had, we all had. He took some cotton balls and rubbed their cheeks against the grain, showing the cotton sticking to them.

"You see, filthy bastard? You haven't shaved clean."

He would send us all back to the barracks after doing twenty push-ups. We all had to shave again in record time and return to lineup. Of course, as usual, the timeframe was impossible to meet, and many cut their faces. And again we were down on our hands to push twenty.

We all loved him.

In the middle of the night, when he finally cleared us to return the rifles, we were exhausted, lining up in the hallway in front of the armory. It took at least an hour to check in the rifles one by one. The guy working the night shift at the armory was a drafted corporal. He had to check each gun to ensure all were clean and undamaged. The squealing pig stood in front of him behind the grill. During this time, a few guys in the back started chatting.

When he heard them, furious, the sergeant came out and screamed, "Shut the fuck up."

At the same time, he landed a kick in the shin of a random guy, who screamed in pain, dropping to the floor and holding his tibia in his hands. He couldn't stand back up. The sergeant always randomly chose his victims. He was mad and out of control. As he walked back toward the armory's corporal, some guys whispered complaints about him.

He had just passed by my side when he heard the whisper. He turned around and punched me in the stomach. I didn't have time to think. I contracted my abdominal muscles before I even felt the full force of his punch and elbowed the sergeant on his cheekbone. He dropped to his belly, knocked out cold. As he remained there, his body a lump on the tile floor, all the guys screamed happily and cheered me on. I hadn't even had time to process. It was a reflex, but I was in serious trouble.

The armory's corporal hesitated. He didn't know what to do. He wasn't a rookie, but he obviously hated the drill sergeant as much as everybody else. Yet it was his duty to report the incident. He didn't want to, though, so he decided to wait until the sergeant got back up on his own, but the sergeant didn't. He was completely out.

After five minutes, he said, "Sorry, I have to call the infirmary."

When two nurses came to take the drill sergeant away on a stretcher, another sergeant came and asked what had happened. People answered that he accidentally got hit in the head with the butt of a rifle. We left it at that, checked all the guns in ourselves, and went to bed. I was tired, but I couldn't sleep for the longest time. Assaulting a superior came with repercussions, and there was no love lost between me and the squealing pig. He'd definitely press charges. I had just sabotaged my military future.

Chapter 32

Rock Bottom

"Far better is it to dare mighty things, to win glorious triumphs, even though checkered by failure, than to take rank with those poor spires who neither enjoy much nor suffer much because they live in the gray twilight that knows not victory or defeat."

— Theodore Roosevelt, *The Strenuous Life*, 1905

The next day, two guys escorted me, with all my belongings, to the hole (military prison). After spending the night at the hospital, the drill sergeant told his superior that I'd knocked him out. He'd written a formal complaint. In the meantime, I was held in the camp's jail, waiting to find out what would happen to me.

I didn't feel bad about what I had done. It was self-defense, and I had more than eighty guys willing to testify for me. But would that fly with the officers? I spent the entire day in the jail, wondering if I had already doomed all my chances to enter the commandos. I had worked so hard. I'd suffered so much to make it. I didn't even know if I had qualified in the final competition. It no longer mattered. There was no doubt in my mind: I would be court-martialed.

I wondered what my sentence would be. It had only taken me a fraction of a second to jeopardize my future. I didn't feel any wrongdoing, but I regretted it. I had not been in a fight since I was fifteen years old. I didn't think I was a bad guy. I didn't want to elbow him. It happened so quickly. I saw the punch coming, and I saw the opening. I had no time to think about it. The sergeant was down, and my life was wrecked. Game over!

The cell wasn't much: a simple room with a bed, metal closet, desk, and chair and a locked opaque window. It wasn't meant to keep any criminals. It wasn't a real prison, just a basic confinement place to punish disobedient soldiers. If court-martialed, soldiers would become real prisoners and be transferred to a proper military jail.

I spent most of the day on my cell bed, thinking about my life. All that I had fucked up by not finishing school and by believing that I could spend my time in the army climbing mountains. And here I was, in the hole. I couldn't even see the mountains surrounding me.

I didn't know how long I would have to stay in jail after being court-martialed, but it didn't matter anymore because my remaining seventeen months would be spent guarding a gate or obeying orders from someone like the squealing pig. I would be in hell for seventeen months and not learn anything. It was an entire waste of my life. I could already imagine my family mocking me for failing what I had been so confident I could accomplish — the only thing I thought I could accomplish.

I wondered what I could do after the army. No degrees, no work experience, no money. I was nothing. The only option left meant following my father's suggestion and taking a *formation* to become a plumber or something else I had no interest in. I would live my life fixing other people's homes instead of traveling the world.

Maybe I could beg my dad to take me on as an apprentice at his optician shop. After all, that was his first goal for me when I was still in junior high. But without studies, I could only become his slave, paid at half the minimum wage for two years while taking night and distance courses for a CAP diploma, the lowest level of professional *formation* in France — the equivalent of freshman studies.

I could continue another two to three years to take a professional BEP, but that was actually an inferior education level to that of my high school, provided I hadn't dropped out. It would take me five years to reach that level while being paid near to nothing. And then, maybe, I would be able to continue my studies to take the Optical BTS, the equivalent of the university degree my dad held, something I could have reached in three years if I had stayed in school, but it would take me eight to ten via apprenticeship.

Eight to ten years of living off a meager salary. Then, in twenty or more years, when my dad finally retired, I could possibly purchase one of his stores. Maybe that was my best prospect. I could be my dad's slave for more than twenty years to one day inherit one of his optician stores. Twenty years of being the subject of his condescending remarks. Twenty years of being mocked by my family.

No, I could never do that. Maybe I'd just be a bum. My life was fucked up, all that for a fucking moron of a drill sergeant.

By the end of the afternoon, as I stood near the bars of my cell, stressed, upset with myself and deeply depressed, a lieutenant entered the hallway. The private opening the door saluted him. The lieutenant ignored the guard, calling for the sergeant in charge.

"Sergeant!"

"Yes, mon lieutenant," he replied with a rigid and perfect salute that showed both tremendous respect and fear.

"Get me First Class Soulé out of your joint. He's one of my guys, and nobody but me decides what happens to my guys."

"Yes, mon lieutenant." The sergeant, very intimidated, opened my cell door and let me out.

"First Class Soulé, I'm the commanding officer of the SR. Get your bag and follow me. Your drill classes are over. Now you're going to train and fight with real soldiers."

I had placed eighth overall in the competition. And this was how I entered the best elite team of the Mountain Special Forces. I had done less than three weeks of stupid Basic Training instead of the regular two months.

With immense happiness, I reflected on everything that had happened. How my life had led me all the way here. All the hurdles I had to cross. All the moments of doubt and sacrifice. All the radical changes in my life.

What if I had never fought back when I was bullied as a small kid? I certainly wouldn't have made it to the SR.

What if I hadn't won the cross-country run? Would I be a criminal, or in jail?

What if I had finished my studies? Would I have gone to university to learn a regular job?

What if I had done a Sport-Étude? Would I have become a pro athlete, an Olympian, or only a physical education teacher?

What if I had not been selected for the commando team? I would waste eighteen months of my life in a fighting company after rotting in a cell for who knew how many days or weeks.

I realized that despite society's molds, we had choices. We, and only we, could decide the course of our lives. There would always be obstacles. Like a river meeting a boulder, we could go over it or around it — that decision was ours to make. Or we could take an entirely new course. Nothing was impossible.

Yet everyone I knew had believed that my goal was unachievable, that I was not up to the task. Since my Pyrenees mountain experience, I hadn't stopped believing in myself. I listened to no one and followed my dream. I had to have even more faith in myself to make up for all those who thought I'd never succeed. I wanted it so much that I never imagined failing. I had doubts and fears at times, but deep within, I knew I could do it. I wanted it so bad. Luckily, even the squealing pig had not been able to stop me.

I did it. I had made it to the SR of the 27th BCA.

I had opened a huge door, turning my imaginary world into reality. This success revived my childhood dreams beyond just mountain climbing. It was a first step. Maybe I could become an adventurer after all.

Chapter 33

Hell Day

"Each man must look to himself to teach him the meaning of life. It is not something discovered: it is something molded."

— Antoine de Saint-Exupéry, *Terre des Hommes*, 1939

Arriving at the location for the commando team was very intimidating as the twenty-four people who made up the Special Forces unit gathered: eighteen commandos, the *adjudant-chef* (chief warrant officer), the lieutenant, two truck drivers, and two chefs. Chief warrant officer is the highest senior noncommissioned officer rank, and ours was the real commando team leader, a true badass, leading the best of the elite commandos in the field.

Our lieutenant was in his early thirties and our commanding officer. He was the liaison with the higher command, and he didn't always lead in the field—most often he led from his office. Many officers were not physically able to keep up with the chief warrant officer and the full team selected among the best athletes of the French Army.

Apart from the lieutenant, the chief warrant officer, the staff sergeant, another sergeant, and the four commandos who were career soldiers enlisted for fifteen years, all others were on a mandatory service. Every year, some of them would return to civilian life and needed to be replaced.

The eighteen operational commandos were divided into three teams of six, each led by a sergeant or staff sergeant. These teams were then split into two groups of three, or a subunit. One subunit was led by a sergeant, the other one by a corporal or corporal-chief. There were twelve new recruits, and only nine of us would remain.

The lieutenant introduced himself, the philosophy of the team, and the nine experienced commandos with whom we'd be training.

He then introduced us as the rookies. The speech was clear: we had passed the selection tests and made the team, but we were not yet officially part of the team. We had to survive the first month of commando training, and many of us would either fail or quit. We had to pay our dues to be allowed to bear the blue star on our shoulders that would distinguish us as the best of the French Army.

We were all athletes who had dreamed of being part of that Special Forces unit, but badasses we were not.

As new recruits, we didn't know one another. We'd come from various mountain battalions from across the country. We only knew we were among the very top athletes, but before us were nine well-trained elite commandos, the absolute cream of the crop of the French Special Forces. They stood straight and proud, completely unimpressed with our selection. They didn't care what our special skills were. They'd been there before, they knew our training had not yet begun, and that we were weak. Some of us wouldn't make it, and those of us who did had to earn their respect.

We newbies were very intimidated and clueless as to what would happen next. We studied them as they studied us, wondering who would crack first. I caught the eye of the most muscular of the lot, a corporal. He was one meter eighty tall and eighty-five kilos[1] of lean muscle. He stared me down like I was his enemy, and it gave me the chills.

As we moved on to our first task, under the eyes of our seniors, we quickly understood that the physical tests wouldn't be our only challenge. Some of these guys mocked us, and it was clear that they were going to make us pay our dues.

1. five-foot-ten and one hundred and eighty-seven pounds

It didn't take long for our feelings to be proven true. The tough-looking corporal stopped by our dorm room flanked by two senior privates. He messed up our beds and smacked one of the newbies on the back of the head. And then, as he flipped my bed upside down, he looked me in the eye, judging my reaction.

It was clear they'd heard about my fight with the drill sergeant. The entire battalion had. I was the wild beast they wanted to tame. I was the example they wanted to set, showing me who was in charge outside of the chain of command. They had to break me in front of the other rookies.

I boiled with rage and stared right back, but I didn't make a move. I hadn't come this far to be kicked off the team due to the provocation of a stupid bully.

We later learned that the corporal was the toughest in hand-to-hand fighting in the whole commando unit. He was a champion amateur boxer aiming to turn pro. He'd lost his first fight when he was sixteen to a poor judging decision and had vowed never to rely on the score again. At age twenty-one, he had won all his subsequent boxing contests by knockout, to be undefeated ever since. He wasn't the best runner, climber, skier, or even athlete, but he was the most powerful. He had the quickest hands, and he was talented in many fighting disciplines. All our seniors were strong, fast, and lean killing machines, but he was the strongest and meanest of them all.

In the middle of the night, they came back and kicked us out of our beds. I thought they only wanted to inspire fear in us, but I was wrong. They'd prepared a hazing ritual. The three of them grabbed a newbie, stripped his clothes off, and pushed him naked under a freezing cold shower.

Another newbie tried to ask them to leave the other guy alone and got punched in the stomach by a private. He dropped to his knees, unable to breathe, while the corporal flipped my bed upside down again and stood there challenging me, his face so close to mine, I could smell his putrid breath. I didn't know what to do. He wanted me to fight, but he wouldn't throw the first punch. He was provoking me. He wanted to be on the defensive and make me responsible for the altercation.

I really didn't want to fight him, but I couldn't let him bully me. I stood facing him, our noses almost touching. My eyes stared into the whites of his, proving that I wasn't afraid. I had to stand my ground. I knew that I was his target. I knew they'd only harassed the other guys to scare me.

They left, and we looked at one another, speechless. We helped our friend out of the shower and got the other guy on his feet, asking him if he was all right. We didn't know what to think. Was that part of our training? Was this sanctioned or even ordered by the high command? Or were they the bullies of the unit trying to humiliate us? But if it was sanctioned, where were the other seniors? Why weren't they coming to humiliate us too? Would there be another team of bullies ready to drop us out of our beds as soon as we went back to sleep?

We straightened up everything and tried to rest, but I'm sure my new friends didn't sleep much more than I did. That first night was long, and I was exhausted when the bell rang. It was 5:00 a.m. We had five minutes to jump into our running shorts and shoes and go downstairs to line up in the courtyard for our first day of commando training.

No breakfast, no showers. Our first day of training started with an eight-kilometer[2] run over rolling hills. A twenty-five-year-old enlisted staff sergeant led us. We could finally judge one another on the first exercise. The rhythm was too fast to uphold a conversation. We were amazing athletes, but we had to prove it, not to the staff sergeant but to ourselves. We had to show we had a place on the team. We weren't going to be the quitter among the newbies. So, we ran our hearts out.

The skinny guy took the draft of the staff sergeant. I ran into fifth position. After six kilometers, the staff sergeant picked up the pace on a gradual slope. The skinny guy dashed to the front and dropped the staff sergeant. I raced after him, leaving the others behind, but I couldn't catch him. He even put a gap on me. I was being dropped, running uphill in what I thought was my strongest physical abilities. It's true that at eighty

2. a five-mile

kilos, I was thirteen kilos[3] heavier than the man in the lead, a huge penalty to carry on a hill. We arrived fairly evenly packed, the staff sergeant trailing me just less than a hundred meters in third position.

We were spent and thought we'd go to breakfast. Instead, we moved to the courtyard, and the staff sergeant called it.

"Drop on your hands, fifty push-ups on my count. One!"

The count was slow, and the staff sergeant would scream, "The chest stops one centimeter from the ground without touching. Keep your feet together. Don't move up until I tell you."

"Up… Two, chest down, stay there… Up. Three… Up…"

I had done a minimum of a hundred daily push-ups for the past six years at school; I was ready for this, or so I thought. But the slow count made it harder. After thirty-five push-ups, one guy collapsed on his belly. My chest and triceps were burning, and my body twitched.

Fuck, count faster, I thought.

By the count of forty, two other guys kissed the dust. The count seemed to get slower every time, even though it wasn't. The last ten push-ups were excruciating. At the count of fifty, we all collapsed.

Without a pause, the sergeant yelled, "On your backs. One hundred sit-ups, on my count, one, two, three…"

The count was faster, but I could do as many as they'd want. I had played rugby for years, doing not only push-ups but lots of ab work. Later on, I continued to work my abs to take punches when I was brawling. My abs were rock solid, and a hundred sit-ups was a breeze. But this hundred set came after eight kilometers of intense running and fifty slow push-ups. My belly started to burn even before finishing the set.

As soon as we accomplished that, the sergeant gave the next order. "On your hands, a hundred push-ups."

My neighbor and I looked at each other in disbelief. Did we hear a hundred? That couldn't be possible, not with the slow count.

The first round had been excruciating. The count was a tad faster this time, which helped, but it wasn't fast enough. I collapsed at number thirty

3. twenty-nine pounds

along with one other guy. We were the last two who had not yet done so.

The staff sergeant said, "Boy, you're so weak. How the hell did you make the selection to come here? We didn't recruit warriors, we recruited little girls. Do you guys really want to be commandos? Anybody wants to quit? On your back, a hundred sit-ups, quick, I want to see some pep."

None of us could pass fifty. One guy puked next to me, even on an empty stomach.

"On your feet," the staff sergeant screamed before calmly saying, "Okay, boys, here is the deal. Every morning, we'll run eight kilometers, and you'll do five hundred push-ups and a thousand sit-ups, and we'll increase the number of daily pull-ups to reach a hundred by next week. If you can't do these within four weeks, you'll be off the team. Now, you have fifteen minutes to shower, change into your military uniform, and come back down to breakfast. Fifteen minutes to eat breakfast, and you line up here in front of me in exactly thirty minutes, ready for your training day to start. Go!"

No words were spoken other than, "Yes, Staff Sergeant."

We all ran up the two-story level stairway to our room, showered, and dressed quickly to have as much time as possible to grab breakfast.

We were too busy eating to have a long conversation, but words still slipped out. "Did he say we start our training day? What did we just do?"

We stuffed ourselves as quickly as possible. We needed almost two minutes to run from the eating hall to our courtyard, so time was very tight.

We lined up seconds before the thirty minutes had passed. Based on our few weeks of Basic Training, we knew that arriving even two seconds too late could yield the stupidest punishments. But that was not the case here. Our staff sergeant seemed much more lenient about the time. He didn't even care that two guys had arrived ten seconds late.

It was clear that the stupid drills we had done were something of the past. The job of this staff sergeant was to transform us into real commandos. All he cared about was our physical and technical training. He didn't play the dumb drill sergeant games we'd experienced before.

It was still early morning when we reached the shooting range. Finally, a chance for me to excel, and I did. We shot with the FAMAS automatic rifle without a scope at targets set one hundred meters away. One other guy had also done the sniper training. To the admiration of our friends, we put every bullet into golf-ball-sized holes in the middle of the target. We spent the entire morning shooting from both standing and prone positions to fixed targets at varying distances. Shooting gave us a welcome respite from the physical strain that the early morning exercises had inflicted on our bodies.

Before breaking for lunch, the staff sergeant said, "Back here at fourteen hundred for the obstacle course. Don't eat too much or you'll throw it up on the course."

Lunch offered us the first opportunity to really talk to one another. The morning training had been so excruciating, we had all forgotten about the experience of last night. We only talked about how impossible it would be to do five hundred slow-count push-ups, a thousand sit-ups, and a hundred pull-ups after running eight kilometers full speed. We couldn't even handle a quarter of that, and we still had to do an obstacle course in record time that afternoon.

We were highly trained athletes in our respective sports. The group was made up of elite rock climbers, mountaineers, cross-country skiers, and extreme skiers. I was the only guy with little experience in any of the mountain sports. Running was my strength, and even though I could do it well on mountain climbs, my mountain experience was very limited. But none of us were prepared for that physical abuse. The climbers could do pull-ups and abs, but the push-ups were too much for all of us. We thought our abs were made of iron, but all of us had sore tummies, which proved to be a problem in the afternoon for the obstacle course.

By fourteen hundred, we headed toward the obstacle range. We had done it daily during Basic Training. We knew how to go over every obstacle. There were twenty obstacles stretched over a length of only five hundred meters.[4] It seemed easy. Going through each individual one wasn't

4. just over a quarter-mile

too difficult for a trained athlete. It was impossible for many people without any practice.

It started with a speed climb on a five-meter-high[5] rope ladder, followed by a couple obstacles that required small but fast jumps. The fourth obstacle was a twenty-meter crawl under barbed wire set at a height of fifty centimeters[6]. There were two crawling techniques: one involved crawling on the stomach, the other one crawling sideways. The sideways technique was usually faster. It might have seemed simple, but it was the one that took the longest, so technique and speed were essential to avoid losing time. It required all the muscles of the body, and doing it at speed taxed the cardio system.

After the increased heart rate from a fast crawl came different obstacles that required coordination, balance, and various jumps. None of them were too technical, but all kept the heart rate high.

The next major obstacle was *La Planche* or *Table irlandaise* (Irish Table), halfway through the course. It was one of the most physical exercises. It was a flat, thick, and wide horizontal wooden board set two meters thirty[7] above the ground, and we had to go over it. The technique consisted of jumping up to grab it with both hands. Then we did a pull-up while lifting one leg to hook the board with the foot. Using both arms, the leg and abdominal muscles pulled the rest of the body over it, rolling to the other side and jumping back down to land facing in the running direction. It required most muscles in the body.

This exercise alone was difficult enough that during Basic Training more than half of the trainees couldn't make it over the first few tries. Scaling the Irish Table after nine other obstacles, and with our cardio already in the red, made it extremely challenging. Often the amount of energy we spent on it determined how fast or slow we finished the second half of the course.

5. sixteen feet
6. twenty inches
7. seven and half feet

The course was done at the limit of the anaerobic level; and by that time, most people were in hypoxia, forced to slow down to finish the course. The fastest people were those with the best technique who pushed the first half of the course at the extreme limit of their aerobic threshold and finished after the Irish Table in total anaerobic state. It was excruciating.

Another six obstacles led to the seventeenth on the course, which was often considered the toughest. *La Fausse*, or the deep pit, required a jump of two meters into a pit, and then we jumped out of it over a two-meter-twenty-tall wall. The jump down usually killed all momentum, and the four-meter-thirty length of the pit wasn't long enough to regain momentum. Similar to the Irish Table, jumping out of the pit engaged all the muscles in the body. During Basic Training, more than half of the people stayed stuck inside the pit, unable to lift themselves out.

Trained athletes went over it quickly, unless they had already exhausted themselves, which was often the case when we reached the deep pit. The best technique consisted of landing from the jump slightly forward and immediately putting pressure on the legs, running to regain as much speed as possible to jump over the wall. The less hesitation on the jump reception, the faster the momentum, and the easier it was to jump over the wall.

The next obstacle was the *Girafe*, giant climbing steps that took us four meters[8] high, from which we jumped down. The fastest people, who still had some energy left after the deep pit, ran and jumped to climb the steps without any pause.

After a technically easy but momentum-breaking high-cardio-taxing nineteenth obstacle, the last one was a succession of three trenches. Slower people jumped down and back up into each of them. The fastest people tried jumping over the trenches from one to the next. These were not straight but swaged walls, and with the cardio and muscular fatigue, missing one of the jumps and landing on the sharp cement edges could be very painful and inflict injuries.

8. thirteen feet

During Basic Training, we were the very best at this course. We had to do it in record time to qualify to compete in the final SR mountain test. So, we approached the exercise with great peace of mind.

The staff sergeant called our names, and we went two by two, racing each other on the course. We ended up being slower than we were in Basic Training, and much slower than our times on the selection tests. Our shoulders, triceps, pecs, and abs were so sore that we could barely lift our bodies over the obstacles, and our legs felt heavy from the fast morning run. The board crossing that we easily managed before proved to be extremely demanding with our burning, hard, and heavy muscles. Even getting out of the pit, which for all of us had been a breeze during Basic Training, was a challenge.

Once we had gone through, the staff sergeant gathered us for a briefing. We knew he wasn't anything like the stupid drill sergeants who had trained us when we started in the army. The staff sergeant commanding us now was an elite commando, a phenomenal athlete, a killing machine, and yet he seemed like a genuinely nice and smart guy. We all respected him from day one.

After we'd been through the course once, he gathered us around, ordered us to relax (an army command allowing us to move), and gently said, "Okay, guys, we have a problem here. The best time on the course was 3'15". The slowest time was 4'. You all did this course in less than 3'10" to be selected. Guess what? 3'10" is not going to cut it. I don't know how your drill sergeants taught you to pass these obstacles, but you're going to have to relearn it all because you need to run the entire course in less than 2'55". And most of the guys in the unit do it in less than 2'50"."

We were bewildered. "Less than three minutes? That's impossible!"

And for the first time, our staff sergeant said, "Okay, demonstration."

To our great amazement, he ran the course in 2'53". I had kicked his butt in the morning run, and he'd finished this course more than fifteen seconds faster than me. That was almost 12% faster than my time, which only trailed the best of the group by one second. That was a crazy gap to bridge. I'd finished exhausted. He was breathing hard, but he seemed much fresher than me. I think he even kept some in the tank. He was smooth on the obstacles, but he hadn't even run that fast between them.

We spent the afternoon learning how to properly go over each obstacle in the fastest and most efficient manner. We learned how to crawl, how to jump in and out of the deep pit, and how to go over the various gates. We wanted to stay on the team so badly, we did our best to improve on every obstacle.

But the board! The board was just impossible. We couldn't climb efficiently over that damn board. Our arms, shoulders, triceps, pecs, and arms were burning too much from the morning training. We were in pain, and the more we practiced, the slower we got. Even the pro climbers among us were too sore from the push-ups to be able to climb it well. After a few tries, we all collapsed.

At the end of the afternoon, to our great surprise, our staff sergeant congratulated us.

"You guys did good today. You have much progress to make. But for a first day, that wasn't bad at all. I'll let you go rest early, but remember one thing: you were far off from the required time. Tomorrow, I'll expect more out of you, and in a week, you need to be at full speed. Now go shower and rest."

We all said, "Yes, Staff Sergeant," and walked back to our dormitory with our bodies aching.

When we arrived at our rooms, all our beds had been flipped upside down and our closets emptied onto the floor. We were tired and pissed off. During the day, we had entirely forgotten about this. We showered and discussed our situation.

"Do you think this hazing is really part of the training? I mean, our staff sergeant seems like a cool guy," I said.

The skinny guy's eyes narrowed. "Are we just the victims of the corporal and his two buddies, or are we going to be visited by other seniors tonight?"

The rest of our group gathered round as Skinny and I discussed the problem.

"Who's going to be the next target?" Skinny asked. "Should we all get together to try to fight back, or just be patient and not risk being kicked off the team?"

We didn't know what would come next.

After dinner, we got to know one another a little more, where we came from, our experiences, our passions, and why we wanted to be part of the elite Mountain Commando team. It was a pleasant dinner, but we worried the hazing would continue in the evening.

Chapter 34

Sudden Impact

"Our greatest glory is not in never falling, but in rising every time we fall."
— Confucius

In the middle of the night, while we were sleeping, we got kicked out of our beds. The corporal was back with the two privates. This time, they grabbed me before I could completely wake up and pulled me toward the hard cement walls of the shower.

And then I heard the corporal say, "Pass me the waxed stick. I'm going to shove it up his ass."

And I saw the stick they had dug into the shoe wax. This was not going to happen.

I was already trapped inside the shower compartment as one guy held me against the shower wall with an elbow to my throat. The other one tried to rip my underwear down, and the corporal stood a couple meters back, holding a half broomstick with shoe wax on the end of it.

With one arm, I grabbed the guy who was going after my underwear and pulled him violently toward me and against the wall. I heard a huge bang as his skull made contact. The guy fell down, unconscious at my feet. Surprised, the other private let go, and I head-butted him in the nose, pushing him back to get out of the shower. I was full of rage, and no one was going to stick a broom up my ass.

Everybody stood speechless, looking at the guy I had knocked out and the other one bleeding from his nose. There was a short, very uncomfortable silence, and the corporal smiled, stood in front of me, and said, almost laughing, "Come on, bastard. I'm going to fuck you up."

I knew the fight was unavoidable. I had knocked out his buddy. He'd been looking to fight me from the beginning. And now I'd gone from the victim to the assailant. He was in a position of self-defense and could beat the crap out of me without any risk of being blamed.

I was so mad, I forgot who my opponent was, and I confronted him straight away. I instantly took a jab in the face that opened my lips. I could already taste my own blood. I didn't see anything coming. The bully was dancing like Muhammad Ali. His punch was painful. He moved quickly and smiled the whole time. He was so full of confidence, I suddenly lost all of mine.

I faced off with a trained and highly skilled killing machine and boxing champion. I stood before one of the toughest hand-to-hand fighting commandos of the French Army, and from the start, he had wanted to take me down. He was more powerful, faster, and much better trained.

I had a flashback to when I was nine years old, confronting the biggest bully of the school who had beaten me and terrified me for so long. And yet I had won.

I had no choice but to fight him because he wouldn't stop until I was down, broken, and beaten.

I thought to myself, He might knock me down, but he's not going to humiliate me. I'm going to fight this bastard until I can no longer.

So, I moved forward, trying to punch him, and bang, I took another jab in the face.

Undeterred, I moved forward and tried to throw another punch. He shifted to the side and jabbed me again on the nose. My sight instantly became blurry with tears. I couldn't hold them back. It took a couple of seconds for my vision to clear. The asshole still smiled, and I realized I couldn't possibly touch him. I didn't know what to do.

I had been in many fights, but I had never faced a trained fighter. I had brawled with bigger opponents, but I had always been fearless and quicker than them. This guy was faster than me. I couldn't see any openings. I was afraid, but I pressed forward again.

He dodged, and I took another left jab in the face. The pain registered all the way to the top of my skull. I saw his right fist at the ready. That one hook or uppercut would be enough for him to put me down. I realized he could have already thrown it and finished me. He hadn't. He was playing with me. He wanted me to try to hit him. He wanted to show all the guys he was superior.

He took pleasure in my helplessness and enjoyed every moment of it before knocking me down. Once he finished me, it would be with a devastating blow. No matter what I did, I couldn't defeat him.

I scanned my surroundings for clues and assistance. I was scared, and he knew it. He stood in front of the window, and it gave me a reckless idea. I jumped on him, taking another jab, but grabbed him and threw him out the window. He clung to me, pulling me with him. I ducked my head down, head-butting him at the same time. I then tucked my head on his chest while closing my eyes as the window shattered into pieces.

We free-fell from the second story. I kept him tight in front of me, looking at him straight in the eye, thinking, *You wanted it. Now we're both going to die.*

I pushed him down under my body to ensure I'd remain on top. People say that when we're about to die, we see our life flashing before our eyes. I didn't. There wasn't any time for it.

The impact from window to ground was violent. The corporal landed on his back with me on top. A thin mattress of grass was not enough to pad our landing. I had the wind knocked out of me and felt a bit dazed. I didn't notice any pain, but I couldn't move. I remained paralyzed, wondering if I'd broken my spine. After a minute that felt like an eternity, I started to breathe and rolled to my side. Then I saw the corporal. He didn't move. He was dead; I was sure.

He'd fallen on his back, with all my weight on top of him from a height of eight meters.[1] I still couldn't move and stayed down, checking the asshole for any signs of life. There were none. I had a killed a man, and my life was over. I was going to jail.

Dozens of flashlights appeared. My friends, with two nurse-soldiers and a doctor, ran toward us. I had not shed a single tear in a long time, but I suddenly let out years of pain as I wept silently and profusely. One of the nurses tried to roll me onto the stretcher, but I refused. I wanted to get up, but I couldn't.

"Is he dead?" I screamed.

The doctor said, "He's knocked out but breathing."

They called an ambulance and transported him to Emergency. They laid me down on the stretcher and loaded me into a jeep to take me to the hospital. By the time we arrived, my entire body felt like it had been run over by a tank. Although I hadn't suffered anything other than minor bruises and cuts from the broken window, I was in shock.

"How is he?" I kept asking. "Is he going to die?"

And all I heard was, "We don't know." But I kept asking the same questions over and over.

An hour later, the doctor returned. He had news from the trauma center. The corporal was out of danger, but most of his ribs were broken, and he had some contusions. Fortunately, he regained consciousness.

"Luckily, he had a very muscular back that saved his spine," said the doctor before leaving.

Relieved, I started crying again. "He forced me," I said to the nurse, who really didn't care about the fight. "I had no choice." I kept saying the same thing, but nobody listened to me. I was in the hospital, not yet being judged by my superiors.

I didn't know if I cried because I thought I had killed a man or because he might still die. Or maybe I cried because of the pain, or the realization

1. twenty-six feet

that my dream had just vanished. Perhaps I cried all the tears I'd never shed, releasing years of pent-up emotional pain and anguish, crying because I'd lowered my tough-guy shell, portraying the vulnerable me that I had always been. I guess I cried for all of it.

A few hours later, I regained my composure, but they kept me overnight for observation. They worried I might have lost consciousness because it took over ten minutes for my friends to get the medical team and arrive on the scene. Time during which I had no memories.

In the morning, the hospital released me and sent me back to my unit. A sergeant waited for me as I arrived, asking me to follow him to the lieutenant's office.

I am doomed, I thought. I'm going to go to jail and be kicked off the team.

I entered the office and saluted the lieutenant.

He looked at me and said, "You assaulted a superior and should be court-martialed." The lieutenant took a long pause, and I felt a chill run down my neck. "Your roommates told us the corporal started the fight, is that right?"

"Yes, mon lieutenant," I answered.

"I can't have any loose cannons in my unit," he said.

"Yes, mon lieutenant," I replied.

"Go back to your unit. I'll decide what to do with you later."

"Yes, mon lieutenant," I answered, saluted him, and turned around and left.

I had no idea what would happen. The guys in my unit had already returned from the run and were doing push-ups when I joined them. The sergeant instructed the newbies to be at ease and all applauded me. I was embarrassed.

The staff sergeant then said, "You're a crazy lucky motherfucker!" He tapped me softly on the shoulder as he continued. "Go have your breakfast and take a rest. You'll join us for the afternoon shooting exercise."

Before lunch, our lieutenant gathered the full unit together and called in the two privates who had joined the corporal in the hazing ritual party.

With a very cold look at the two guys, he said, "We don't do this type of thing to our own. Rookies need to be pushed to their physical and mental limits in the field. Not with dumb humiliations. You tried to stick a broom up his ass!"

"We weren't going to. We just wanted to scare him," replied one.

"Attention, Private! Nobody asked you." He continued, "Did he seem scared when he was kicking your asses? Three highly trained members of one of the best commando units taken down by an untrained rooky. You're a double disgrace to this unit. How could someone try to save your lives one day if you humiliate them? And obviously, you're not the fighters you were trained to be."

He moved toward them and tore the blue stars from their shoulders while saying, "You're immediately moving to another battalion. You'll finish your military duties with other morons like you in a basic infantry. Dismissed."

With tears in their eyes, the two soldiers saluted the lieutenant and went to their barracks to gather their stuff. A truck was already waiting to take them away to another region of France.

The other rookies were pleased with the fate of the two privates. It wasn't a feeling I shared. I still feared that I'd be the next soldier sent away for having been part of the fight. My fate had not been decided yet.

My friends comforted me, saying, "If they wanted to kick you off the team, they'd have done it today. I think you'll stay with us."

At least we could sleep soundly without worrying about being bullied. It was our best night. Our bodies badly needed a few good hours of sleep to recover from the intense training. My friends were asleep as soon as they hit the sack. I was uneasy and couldn't find sleep for the longest time.

I had signed up for eighteen months to make it to this unit. I was so confident I could make it. And now, because of stupid guys, I might be sent to guard a gate for my remaining seventeen months. I'd be wasting an entire year and a half of my life. Worse yet, I wouldn't achieve my dream of climbing mountains and eventually become a mountain guide. I couldn't do anything about it anymore, but despite my extreme physical and mental fatigue, I didn't sleep. My fate might be decided the next day.

In the morning, I resumed the full training as if nothing had happened.

By the end of the first week, most of us could do only slightly more than half of the punishing push-ups and sit-ups, and when we started the pull-ups, thirty was all I could achieve.

We learned to appreciate our staff sergeant. He was only our elder by a few years. He had enlisted for fifteen years and had been selected into the elite commando unit three years ahead of us. Like most people in the unit, he had joined because he loved the mountains.

The other sergeants, along with the senior privates and first class, sometimes joined us in training. They'd demonstrate the obstacle crossing and kick our butts every time, but they were nice.

It was an era before all the modern commando training movies and books were published. It was before Richard Marcinko published *Rogue Warrior*, but I had heard about the Navy Seal BUDs training and Hell Week. I had heard of the Green Beret and British SAS. And I had firsthand accounts from a commando paratrooper who briefed us on his training and missions when he tried to recruit us during my Military Preparation.

I knew what commando training could be like. I imagined the worst-case scenarios. Extreme endurance tests, sleepless nights, extreme cold exposure, physical and mental exhaustion. I was physically and psychologically ready for it. I had trained and thought about it for two full years. I knew it'd be tough, and I'd embrace that challenge and be the best. I was ready for all the physical and mental abuse they could throw at us — or so I thought.

But I never expected this level of suffering. Our superiors didn't play the mean, tough motherfuckers you see in movies today. They didn't scream their lungs out while projecting saliva in your face like my first drill sergeant. They didn't need to. They were the real thing.

They led by example and inspired us, but at times we felt discouraged when we thought we could never match their strength and skill.

But they never screamed.

The physical and technical level we had to achieve within specific timeframes was the only pressure we faced, but considering what they asked of us, the pressure was tremendous and the tasks seemingly impossible.

Some days, all of us rookies wanted to cry. We never broke down in front of the others. We were too proud, but we all felt like it, time after time. Not usually during exercises, but when we were alone.

Although I would have never admitted it then, more than once during the first month of commando training, when I was alone at night in my bed, I cried. I didn't cry because of any physical or psychological pain. I didn't cry because I was afraid of not making it physically. I was one of the strongest rookies, so I had confidence. I didn't cry because I thought I would get kicked out for throwing the corporal through the window, although I was genuinely worried about it. I cried because it just happened, and it felt good.

I hadn't shed a tear in all my boarding school years. I can't say why, but it almost felt like a relief for me to silently weep in my bed. It felt like a healing. So more than once, in my own moments of privacy, I let go. I let my eyes fill up and the warm tears glide on my cheeks to wet my pillow. Crying felt good.

Quitting was never an option for any of us. The only way we'd be out was if we got injured, or if we couldn't reach each level of fitness required by each deadline. But even though I had doubts at times, I'd never let it happen.

As young trained athletes, it was amazing how quickly our bodies became used to the morning training. After two weeks, most of us could do the full sets of push-ups and abs. The pull-ups took a little longer.

Two weeks had passed since the incident, and I thought and hoped the high commands had forgotten about me, but then I got called to the lieutenant's office.

I was worried. Maybe my file had gone up and down the ladder. Maybe I'd be kicked off the team. What would I do? Where would I go for seventeen months? I suddenly realized that without this, I had nothing, and I was nothing.

In the lieutenant's office, the officer said, "First Class Soulé, the corporal is going to need a few more weeks to heal from his broken ribs. He's not going to make it back to the team. You're causing me a huge problem."

I listened silently, waiting to know what my sentence would be.

"You've knocked out three people in less than a week, two of them were your superiors. Are you a troublemaker?"

"No, mon lieutenant, it was self-defense," I quickly replied, remaining at attention and saluting.

"Your physical results are good, and I don't see you to be a quitter. You're obviously not scared to stand your ground, and we need good mountaineers and skiers."

I thought to myself, That sounds good, but how am I going to get out of the good skier part? We'll see later. At least it sounds like I might be able to stay in the unit.

"As of today, you're a corporal, and you'll command two privates. You still need to finish your last two weeks of training, but you'll do so as a corporal."

Trying to hold back the tears, I replied, "Yes, mon lieutenant. Thank you, mon lieutenant."

He removed my first class rank insignia velcroed to my chest and replaced it with two yellow diagonal stripes showing my new corporal rank.

Then he looked me straight in the eyes and said, "Now, you're not going to throw another guy through a window. Are you?"

"No, mon lieutenant," I replied.

"Okay, return to your unit."

I saluted him again for the x number of times, turned around, walked out the door, and closed it behind me with a grin. I couldn't believe it. I had thrown a superior from a window, almost killing him, and I'd received a promotion to take his place. I was staying in the SR unit as a CORPORAL! The guy I nearly killed ended up being transferred to another fighting battalion, and I never saw him again.

When I returned to my unit, the staff sergeant had all the rookies called up. He asked them to salute their new corporal. With a huge smile on my face, I saluted them back, and the staff sergeant followed by saluting me with a warm smile. He had already been briefed. He knew.

"Corporal Soulé, you lead the men to the obstacle course," he said.

I gave my first order as a corporal, telling the men to jog to the start of the obstacle course, the staff sergeant following right behind me to give me pointers. For the next two weeks, he taught me how to lead men. At that time, it was one of the best days of my life. I felt immensely proud, and all the other rookies respected me. I appreciated the staff sergeant. I even suspected he might have put in a good word for me with the chief warrant officer and the lieutenant to keep me in the unit.

I was happy, and I felt good. I was more motivated than ever.

Before the end of our first training month, one rookie gave up and quit, and one suffered a knee injury. Even though only nine of us were supposed to remain, the ten of us who finished the training received the blue star on our left shoulders.

That blue star was not considered a medal or a rank promotion. It wasn't even a commendation, but we were more proud of it than any other accolade we received. It distinguished us from all others as the elite commandos of the French Army. We were now Special Forces, and we were going to start training in the mountains with the seniors. We had made it. I had made it. I couldn't have been prouder of that tiny piece of fabric.

I couldn't help but review the past few years of my life: All the years when I was a drunk, smoking two packs a day and brawling.

All the years my parents denied me the opportunity to live my dream of sports.

All the years during which I had lost all my dreams.

All the years when everybody told me that I'd never make it.

I may not have had the chance to go to the Olympics. I didn't get the opportunity to do a Sport- Étude. I was a high-school dropout in a country where diplomas were the only thing that mattered. I had no possible future, and yet here I stood.

I had made it into one of the world's best elite commando units. For the full duration of my service, I would train at the highest level and climb more mountains than I had ever dreamed of.

At age eighteen, I was the youngest member of my unit, and in less than two months, I had already moved up from first class to corporal. It was the greatest amount of pride and joy I had ever felt. However, there were more difficulties to come as I continued with my training.

I had placed eighth out of the ten newbies in the selection race, and we were now training with the full team. Most climbed mountains faster than I.

Winter would come and although my file stated I was a ski instructor, nothing could have been further from the truth. I dreaded the time I'd be tested on skis. I had a few months before we moved to our winter quarters, and I had to prove my worth. I had to excel at everything. No, that wouldn't be enough. I had to become the best, the alpha member of the team.

Chapter 35

The First Four Months

"The proper function of man is to live, not to exist. I shall not waste my days in trying to prolong them. I shall use my time."
—Jack London, 1916

We spent the entire fall season climbing mountains. We did a lot of hand-to-hand combat training and obstacle courses, but the bulk of our training was in mountaineering.

Some days we focused on endurance, when we'd climb three mountains in a row at high speed. Other days, after practicing rope drills for weeks, we'd climb more technical mountains. Sometimes we'd set up monkey bridges with ropes and a Tyrolean traverse to go over cliffs. We also learned and practiced mountain rescue techniques.

Our job had many facets. Besides our main duty of recon and commando operation, we were the mountain guide team for the entire battalion. It was our responsibility to set up all the safety ropes and to guide and assist all the fighting companies into crossing the most technical mountain terrains. We were their hands and their safety net for crossing technical or dangerous mountains.

When a fighting company trained in the high mountains, we ensured their safety when crossing the most technical pitches. Our unit supervised their progress. Their officers were no longer in charge. We were. They knew that their lives, and that of their company, were in our hands. Our specialty allowed us to give orders to the entire battalion, including its officers.

They knew that in a conflict situation, we were the eyes who assisted them in efficiently fighting the enemy.

They also knew that if they were ever stranded on a mountain in the worst possible weather, or stuck in a crevasse, we were the ones who would come to save their lives. If we were in the SR, we were not simple soldiers. We were not just another commando unit. We were the guardian angels of the entire battalion.

The BCA officers had the utmost respect for the SR, even if the SR member in front of them was a private, the lowest rank in the army. The function as a whole overruled the rank.

The physical training they asked of us was considered inhuman for most, but I loved it. I loved all the mountains we climbed.

The number of things they required us to learn was overwhelming. All the rope techniques. All the combat techniques. Mountain orienteering in fog with zero visibility. The radio communication skills to avoid detection. The use of explosives and all demolition techniques. The use of anti-tank weapons. The art of hiding and disappearing.

The biggest chunk of learning came in the form of memorization, specifically recognizing vehicles and weapons of both Soviet Union and allied countries.

We studied all the helicopters, tanks, airplanes, armored vehicles, troop transport vehicles, and all other war vehicles and equipment used by most troops around the world.

We had endless slideshows and tests. We had to know all our allied equipment, but the focus of our studies was on all the gear of the Soviet Union. We saw classified photos, sketches, and data featuring the most secret Soviet tanks and helicopters. These were not even supposed to exist. The Soviets had never released that information. It was highly classified. Nobody else in the French Army had access to these because our government didn't want the Soviets to know that we knew all about their latest weapons.

That was exciting, but I often felt overloaded trying to memorize all the Soviet weapons. It was essential for our recon job, though. In a conflict situation, our first task was to observe and inform our high command of everything we saw. The French Army needed to know if we saw troops and heavy weapon movements. They had to be aware of what the enemy planned so they could move all the regiments and protect and counterattack.

I didn't care much for the pure military tasks. Learning about all the Soviet Union tanks, helicopters, and warplanes didn't sit too high on my list. But I understood that in case of a conflict, we were the very first recon teams to be deployed in black operations, and we had to memorize it all.

It was a minor pain, for all the fantastic physical training and mountain climbing we were doing. And we all appreciated the fact that — apart from our sometimes military-zealous lieutenant when generals visited — we had virtually no discipline. We never did any of the stupid chores that were the norm in a fighting company. We never had to guard a gate. The only thing the army asked of us was to be the very best commando unit.

Over the months, our bodies had transformed into lean, efficient muscle. None of us looked like the bulky bodybuilder commandos that you see in the movies. It was impossible to keep that much inefficient muscle mass with the amount of endurance training we did. We were fast, powerful, light, and swift. We reached a physical fitness we'd never imagined.

We enjoyed all the training and thrived in pushing our bodies to our utmost physical limits. We were a group of alpha males who loved competing against one another. But we shared a great camaraderie and a common passion for climbing mountains.

Our chief warrant officer was thirty-eight years old, only two years younger than my dad. He couldn't have been taller than one meter seventy and heavier than seventy kilos.[1] He was humble and wore a permanent smile on his face. I learned early on to never judge a person's physical abilities based on their appearance. Apart from his self-assurance and great enthusiasm, if you saw him dressed in civilian clothes and standing next to

1. five-foot-seven and heavier than one hundred and fifty-four pounds

a tall muscular guy, you might not have even thought of him as an athlete, let alone one of the best commandos of the French Army. He was a real badass, and not in the negative sense of the term. You couldn't find a nicer more human guy, but he could be as deadly in hand-to-hand or knife combat as he was with guns and rifles. A mountain lover before anything, he was a five-time military national champion in orienteering, an excellent rock climber and skier, and a remarkable mountaineer; he excelled at every sport. He was one of the best athletes I would ever meet in my entire life — probably stronger mentally and more fit than many Olympic and world champions.

He pushed us to our physical limits far beyond any imaginable boundaries, yet he always looked after us to ensure our safety. He always had a smile to encourage us.

He was not only our superior in rank; he was a father and a big brother to us. While our lieutenant was a distant liaison between the team and the higher chain of command, our chief warrant officer was the heart of our unit and our inspiration, pulling us through all the physical hardship. More than any other of my army leaders, he made us appreciate the mountains and life. He would remain my role model not only during my time in the Special Forces but also for the rest of my life.

After a couple of months, I wasn't satisfied to have made the team. I couldn't contend myself with just being a Mountain Commando. I wanted to be the best.

I'm not sure why. Maybe it was my competitiveness, my well-hidden lack of self-confidence, or the years of humiliation I'd carried like a burden. Or maybe it was my strong need for recognition, but I had a burning desire to be the alpha of the pack and never stopped competing for it.

During those few months, I proved myself worthy of the commando unit and of my corporal rank.

I would never be able to match the best in rock climbing, it wasn't my forte, and I didn't feel I had to. I wasn't the most technical rock climber, but I strove to be better than all others in every other field. I achieved it in orienteering, combat, and many other activities. I dominated the obstacle course. I loved the thrill of rappelling from a helicopter next to a mountain cliff. I loved descending on the ropes headfirst, and enjoyed the mountain orienteering and all the rope techniques.

Orienteering was a new sport to me. Being a combination of reading maps, navigation, and running, it came easy to me. I had studied maps even before I could properly read, and since Frédéric had taught me navigation in the Pyrenees, I had read books and practiced it ever since I began running, so I naturally dove into orienteering to almost instantly lead the pack.

One had to have an excellent eye to find the marker once we were on the designated spot. It sometimes took some imagination as to where the course designer could have hidden the marker. The only person I couldn't match was our chief warrant officer, who, when he competed along with us, seemed to be attracted to markers like a magnet. He always knew their location instantly. He was unbeatable.

Yet all of this still wasn't enough. For me, the ultimate goal was to be the fastest endurance mountain climber. When we climbed challenging mountains, I wanted nothing more than to be the first one at the top. That was the holy grail.

In three months, I had almost reached that aspiration. In most sports, my only real competition came from Skinny; the third guy was usually far behind us. Skinny had grown up in Algeria with his French parents, visiting France regularly during his childhood to ski and climb. He had run marathons faster than I ever dreamed of approaching, easily beating my best teenage time by twenty minutes. I could never keep up with him when running.

I didn't mind that so much, but in the mountains we competed fiercely. Neither of us ever wanted to lose to the other. He had become a corporal just a couple of weeks after me.

Four years my elder, blond with blue eyes, he was good-looking, university-educated, and fluent in French, English, and Arabic. He was a natural leader, a good man, and just a cool guy. The type of guy everybody likes. I could not dislike him, for he was genuine. Yet, I could not like him, for he was too perfect, a perfection I couldn't match. I think I struggled with him because I wanted to be just as perfect and cool, but I didn't feel I could. I was the youngest. He was the oldest of the drafted members. His maturity made me feel like a kid.

So, I had to be better than him in what I was good at, particularly in the mountains. Although always in a nice way, he was as competitive as me. We respected each other, but friends we were not. We couldn't help but see each other as a threat, and we both fought to be the only alpha of the platoon.

I hated how he frequently kicked my butt in the mountains, not by a big margin, and not always, but often enough that the competition between us never ended. He was the skinny guy who had crushed me on both the run and the mountain race he had won during the selection tests.

Admittedly, I had the biggest ego on Earth. I had cultivated it my entire childhood to build the armor I needed to fend off my grief and lack of self-confidence. My ego was the fruit of my dire need for my mother and particularly for my father, my first childhood hero, to recognize me. I nurtured it to perfection, driving me to be the best to the detriment of all those around me. I had to be the best. And I had to claim it high and loud for the world to hear and recognize me. Since joining the Special Forces, I started to become aware of it, to understand it. I knew it wasn't a good thing, but I couldn't help it. I still had to be the best.

Feeling the need to be perfect is a curse. It didn't make me perfect, it only prevented me from enjoying the moment because I couldn't be satisfied with just being the best I could be.

The rivalry between Skinny and me had become so fierce that none of the sergeants, nor even our chief warrant officer, tried to compete with us. We were like crazy wolves going at it day after day without rest in every physical exercise until we'd both collapse from exhaustion. Yielding to the other was never an option.

The only two fields we didn't compete in were rock climbing and hand-to-hand combat. He was the better climber and I was the superior fighter. We had nothing to prove there. On mountaintops, we'd talk, waiting for the others to arrive. We recognized and respected each other as fierce rivals. But the war was never-ending.

Eventually, we each accepted that one could dominate the other in some disciplines to be crushed in the next. It took over three months for us to transform our rivalry into the easy companionship we had long experienced with all the others, but we eventually did. We continued to compete against each other in a more friendly manner, finally appreciating and inspiring each other.

I also loved being a leader, even though I only led two privates: a first class and a second class making up my subunit. Unlike a standard army platoon, our trio was entirely independent and sent on our own missions.

The way it worked was: whether it was training for a mountain search-and-rescue or a recon or a demolition operation, each of the three teams, or units of six operation commandos, were given a separate target or objective. Often, each team of six would split into two subunits of three, each targeting the same goal from a different angle. In commando missions, one subunit would sometimes succeed where the others couldn't. In mountain rescue missions, splitting into two subunits of three allowed us to cover more ground. We could be more than a kilometer from each other and stay in constant radio contact so that one subunit could come assist the other. I loved the independence we had, and I loved leading a subunit.

I noticed something important in the SR, beyond the competition, beyond the sports and the training, and beyond climbing mountains. For the first time in my life, I didn't feel lonely. I felt this constant drive to be the best, but I also had the companionship of other young people and our formidable chief warrant officer. Even though we all came from entirely different backgrounds, we understood each other. Despite the hardships, I lived life fully and enjoyed it thoroughly.

Yet as winter approached, I started to worry. The time for reckoning grew near.

Chapter 36

Just Like Bambi

"Even the fear of death is nothing compared to the fear of not having lived authentically and fully."

— Frances Moore Lappé, *O Magazine*, May 2004

By December, a thick coat of snow had covered the mountains, and by year end, we moved to our winter quarters. After a freezing transfer in the open back of our two trucks, we arrived in the small ski town of Le Grand Bornand. I was looking for barracks but couldn't see any. The trucks stopped next to a four-story chalet house with a huge parking lot. In front stood an empty flagpole.

We unloaded our gear and headed to the chalet. Rooms were flanked with two pairs of bunk beds. We were four per room, and each enjoyed a window with mountain views. It was fantastic. They were not barracks. It was not the battalion. There were no other officers present than our lieutenant. We were only a small unit of twenty-four, including two ace truck drivers and two real chefs — they weren't commandos but all four were masters in their own specialties. The chefs weren't random soldiers drafted into the kitchen because they couldn't do anything else, they weren't battalion cooks with no prior cooking experience: we had two professional chefs who had worked in restaurants.

They were so pleased to be in our unit rather than in a battalion cantina cooking for thousands of people, preparing disgusting food for the full regiment. They had a budget and did their own shopping for natural and local items, creating new daily menus made with fresh products.

On day one, our chefs welcomed us with a delicious first dinner that set the tone for meals to come. It was at least as good as a local restaurant. Wine flowed freely, and the mood was at its best. Even our lieutenant, generally cold and uptight when surrounded by higher commanding officers, seemed to loosen up in the mountain chalet. It was amazing. I couldn't believe we were in the army, yet I began to feel uneasy, for I knew my biggest test was yet to come.

The next day, after a morning run in the snow, the chores were all about logistics. Our chief warrant officer plotted our first mountaineering skiing day. We secured the guns and ammunitions, cleared the snow around the chalet, and finally received our skis, to which we adjusted the bindings.

Mountaineering skis are a little like Telemark skis. They use skins under the skis for a free open binding that allowed us to climb efficiently. To descend, we would peel away the skin that prevented us from sliding backward. We would lock the bindings and shoes, and the descent technique was exactly like downhill skiing, except in the wilderness without any groomed trails and carrying a fifteen-kilo backpack.

My skiing experience was far from what was expected, and my level of skill didn't compare to that of all my friends who had grown up on skis or at least done extensive backcountry skiing. I had never done any mountaineering skiing.

I had been on skis at the age of two, three, and four, which was a great start. Mom then decided she hated the cold and the snow. She refused to go on any other ski holidays. Dad continued his annual ski trips, but he couldn't be bothered with small kids. I didn't go skiing again until I turned twelve.

My friend Jean skied every winter. His parents had a small camping car, and they'd move the family to a winter camp at a Pyrenees ski area. They offered their two kids lessons every year.

When I was twelve, Jean's parents invited me. I slept with his family in the trailer, took skiing classes with Jean in the morning, and we'd race each other in the afternoon. That was my first and only week of formal instruction. It was great fun, but I didn't feel confident in deep moguls, even though I loved the speed. I was reckless enough to try to keep up with Jean, who had honed much better skills than I did.

From thirteen to fourteen years old, I went skiing with my brother and father a couple of times but quickly switched to monoskiing. The monoski, a single wide board on which the two feet were attached together, was the new sport in vogue. Although it was a winter sport practiced on the same slopes, the technique was different. I loved it and the speed, but it didn't help my traditional skiing at all — the last time I had gone was with my father when I turned fifteen.

My current level allowed me to go down any groomed ski trail. I was able to descend in the moguls. I was absolutely unable to ski in deep powder with traditional skis. That was where I had used the monoski. On traditional skis, descending in powder snow, I was unable to turn twice consecutively. I crossed or split my skis and always found new ways to fall. I looked like Bambi discovering the ice. That was far from the minimum level required to descend any mountains in any snow conditions.

For weeks, I'd felt the pressure building up, and for the past few days, I couldn't think about anything but how I would manage that first time on skis in deep powder snow. I knew I'd be in serious trouble.

The next morning, we woke up at 4 a.m., had a quick breakfast, jumped into the trucks for a fifteen-minute drive, and jumped out. We set the skins under our skis and clipped in the ski bindings. We tightened our backpacks on our shoulders and climbed toward the mountains. That was the easy part: going up. The climbing technique was like Telemark (which I had never done). The skins under the ski glide forward, but not backward, unless it's very icy. We'd do long transversal climbs, turn in the opposite direction, and climb again on another long transversal.

Even with little experience, I picked up the climb-turning technique. And with my stamina, I managed to be among the first on top of the mountain. It was even addictive. So far, so good.

The views of all the snow-covered mountain chains were fabulous. But for me, the moment of truth had come: I had to descend that mountain on two skis in deep powdered snow, something I had never done and for which I didn't have the skills.

The lieutenant took off first, and all the other commandos followed with superb style, carving beautiful turns in the fresh snow. Hesitant, I was the last to start, and I fell on my first turn attempt. I immediately stood back up, glided down a bit, and fell again.

The lieutenant had stopped a few hundred meters down to watch his flock descend. The others had already reached him, apart from the chief warrant officer, who was waiting behind me. All eyes stared at me, and I felt the stress rising. I tried to make a turn but couldn't. The snow was too heavy. I either split my legs or crossed my skis, but it always ended with me falling on every turn. They all waited for me. To say that I felt ashamed was a huge understatement.

I was too slow for the team. The lieutenant asked a sergeant to stay with me and continued with the rest of the unit. I crawled down that mountain the best I could. The sergeant only told me a few encouraging words. Even though he had become my friend, I didn't have the courage to look him in the eyes.

I arrived at the trucks fifteen minutes after the team, exhausted, having fallen over thirty times and my body under pressure from the incredible amount of stress.

I was so ashamed I couldn't bear to meet the eyes of my other friends either. I knew this moment would come, but I had never imagined I'd be this bad and feel this level of shame. I had deceived everybody. I couldn't belong to a Mountain Commando unit. I was the only one who couldn't backcountry ski. Nobody said a single word. I think they felt bad for me.

The fifteen-minute truck transfer lasted an eternity. Coming out of the shower, my roommates tapped me on the shoulders to comfort me but without any words, for nobody knew what to say. They all understood that it was my last day with the team. I was a fake, a fraud, a con artist tricked by his own game.

Two hours later, the lieutenant summoned me to his room. I entered with a salute and stood at attention, rigid like the Eifel Tower, as he sat without looking at me. His head down and eyes riveted to my file, he started to read.

"Ski instructor." As he raised his head to stare at me, he repeated with a question, "Ski instructor?"

I replied, "Mon lieutenant, may I speak?"

"Yes, I'd like to know about your ski instructor experience," he replied.

Then I answered, "I had no choice but to lie. It's been my dream to enter this unit since I was sixteen years old, but I didn't have any of the mountain experience required. The only requirement I couldn't be tested for in the summer was skiing. I thought I could prove myself before the season and then learn how to ski. I'm sorry that I lied about this, but it was my only chance to even enter the competition to make the selection. I'm a fast learner, mon lieutenant, I can do it!"

And he replied, "Corporal Soulé, you're unable to keep up with the speed of the slowest guy on the team. Imagine the shame you would have brought to our unit if a civilian or officer from any other unit saw you ski with us today." He paused for a few seconds and continued, "We're the elite Mountain Commando of the French Army. This is not a paratrooper unit, we're the MOUNTAIN Special Forces."

I stood still, speechless, like a scolded dog as he paused for a few seconds. Cold sweat ran down my body, bringing with it the chills. I was deeply ashamed. I did all I could to prevent tears from forming in my eyes. My dream was over.

After being a high-school dropout, I was being kicked out of the Special Forces. I would finish my time guarding a stupid gate. I had failed. I could imagine my parents telling me, "You see, we said you couldn't do it."

The lieutenant resumed talking, ready to deliver my sentence.

"For three months, you've proven to be one of the best assets of this unit. You've worked your way to be the fastest on the obstacle course. You've been an exemplary corporal. All the rookies looked up to you. You had gained their respect as well as that of your seniors, although today you may have lost it all."

He paused for a few seconds.

"You say you're a fast learner. I give you three days to keep up with the team. Three days, not one more. Pick one of the best skiers on the team to teach you. In three days, you'll join us for another mountain climb. If you don't reach the bottom of the mountain within the first two-thirds of the group, it will be your last day in the Special Forces."

Before I could even answer, he added, "And a few words of warning: don't even try to fool me by asking your friends to ski slowly. We'll do a steep technical run, and the last three to reach the bottom will have a full week of duty. Dismissed."

Standing still and nonstop saluting, I replied, "Yes, mon lieutenant. Thank you, mon lieutenant."

I returned to my room and told my friends, "I have three days to match your speed."

"Holy shit, it's impossible, man," many of them replied.

All offered to teach me, but I went to ask Cyril, an elder. The best extreme skier in the unit. He had been featured in all the mountaineering magazines for descending insane gullies. I didn't need a ski instructor. I needed a god, for I had a miracle to realize. He agreed to teach me.

The next morning, the platoon went to climb another mountain, and Cyril and I stayed at the chalet with the two chefs. We took our skis down to the parking lot. I started walking to the ski area, where we had free passes.

He stopped me and said, "No, this morning you're going to practice right here."

"Where?"

"Right here in the parking lot."

I looked at him, perplexed, and then he said, "Listen, nobody can learn how to ski deep snow in three days. It's impossible. If you try to turn in heavy snow using the technique they all use, you'll never make it. It would be incredible if you master this by the end of the season. I'm going to teach you the only technique that can get you down any mountain. It's the extreme skiing jump turn. Not all the guys even know how to do it, but it's the easiest. If you master it, you'll be able to descend the steepest slopes. Of course, when it's not steep, you'll look stupid using this technique to turn, but it will work. That's the only thing you could possibly learn in three days, and even that won't be easy."

"Why do you say many of the guys can't do it if it's the easiest?" I asked.

"Because it isn't a technique that any skiing instructor will teach you in a ski area. It's not pretty. It's only used when the slopes are over forty degrees, and particularly on narrow couloirs and canyons. Most guys never ski these slopes because missing a turn there often means that you'll die. Once you venture onto these slopes, you can't miss your turn. Mistakes aren't allowed. But the steeper it is, the easier it is to do this turn. That's why you're going to first practice it here on this flat parking lot. When you master it here on the flat, it will be a piece of cake on the slopes."

He showed me how I had to jump high in the air and then rotate an exact 180 degrees before landing with my two feet simultaneously, my weight perfectly balanced. I had to land with two skis precisely parallel. The rotation started with the shoulder, by pitching the down pole toward the back tip of the down ski. And then I'd jump, the hips following the movement of the shoulders and head, and the legs turning all by themselves. He showed me a few times. It looked easy.

I tried it, but I didn't lift both my skis at the same time, losing my balance and only achieving a 160-degree turn.

"You're dead," he said.

"If you were on a steep slope, you'd have died. You can't have your skis land until you've done a complete 180 degrees, and you have to land perfectly balanced on both skis. Your problem is that you didn't turn your shoulder enough before jumping off your legs. Do it again."

It took me dozens of times to manage something even close to a 180-degree turn without losing my balance.

Then Cyril left, saying, "Okay, practice, practice, practice. It needs to be smooth and automatic. This afternoon, when you have it well honed, we'll go to the ski area to practice it on the slope."

And so, I spent three hours doing the exact same motion over and over again. That's hundreds of jumps. On every jump, I tried to visualize myself on the slopes, steeper and steeper, and thought to myself, I can do it. I can do it.

In the afternoon, we walked with our skis to the ski slope. We took a lift and chose one of the steepest but shorter snow walls with nobody around. There, he showed me the jump in action on a thirty-five-degree slope. His jump was smooth and perfect. A little intimidated by the slope, I didn't push on my legs quite as hard as I had all morning, and I landed at 160 degrees with skis crossed. It was a left turn, and my left ski touched the snow first; as it was on the higher side, my right ski continued the motion and landed on top of my left ski. I fell immediately and slid down on my butt for thirty meters.

Cyril yelled, "Remove your skis, walk back up, and do it again here where it's the steepest."

I did. My second jump turn was better. I landed after a perfect 180-degree turn and was well balanced on my skis. But I had gathered some speed, and when I tried the next jump turn, I fell heavily, sliding down another thirty meters.

My friend left me there on that short steep wall to practice while he went to do a few runs. I jump-turned again and again, falling dozens of times, and after each fall, I walked back up that small slope and did another turn. After a couple of hours, Cyril returned. He'd had a blast skiing on his own and returned to check on me. For the last hour, I had been doing jump turns without falling, accomplishing four or five consecutive jump turns in a row with speed. Turning left felt easier than turning right, but I was getting the hang of it.

Cyril said, "You're ready. Let's take the highest lift, and we'll go on the steepest run of the ski area. You'll descend the entire slope nonstop, only using this jump-turn technique."

And so I did, again, and again, and again. After spending the entire afternoon on the slope, we decided it was enough for day one and returned to the chalet. The team was back. They asked me how it went, and Cyril said, "He's doing great." I was not in any position to comment on myself.

On day two, we put the skins on the skis and climbed into the deep snow over the hill. I tested out the technique. It was much harder as the slope was not very steep, but it worked. I was able to descend and turn where I wanted to in deep snow.

Then Cyril said, "Do you see that canyon up there? Since we arrived four days ago, I've had my eyes on it. I wanted to make a first track there. Let's climb on that ridge. If you can descend that, you'll be able to do anything."

I was game. I had no choice. We climbed up the first ridge that took us to the bottom of the canyon. There, the slope was much too sheer to climb with the skis on. We carved steps in the snow and used our ice axes to climb the wall with skis on our backs. It was steep. It was very steep.

But how am I going to descend this thing? I'm going to die.

Three-quarters of the way up, Cyril anchored a rope across the canyon. When we reached the top, he said, "Okay, the steepest part is the first hundred meters. This is why I set up that rope when we were climbing. If you fall in the first part here, you have to catch that rope a hundred meters below. If not, it's going to be a very long fall. But don't worry, this one is not exposed. There is no cliff for you to fall off. If you miss the rope, at most you'll break a leg."

I looked down and realized it was steeper than anything I could have ever imagined. I was terrified.

He said, "The first hundred meters are about fifty-five degrees, perfect for you to practice. I'll do the first turn to show you, and then I'll wait for you there on the side. You'll go first on the rest of the run." He paused for a second. "For the first few turns, come to a full stop after each jump. Don't try to make the next turn with any speed. Make sure you're well-balanced. You've already mastered the technique."

I got myself into position and twisted my hips and shoulders entirely. I pitched my left pole completely behind me, just under the tip at the back of my left ski. My body was so twisted and stretched that it hurt. I flexed my legs, ready to jump. And I looked down. I looked down and couldn't jump. My stomach cramped up. It was too steep and the slope too long. From where I stood, I couldn't even see the safety rope. If I fell, it might be for three or four hundred meters. I hesitated for too long. My body ached from the tension of my twisted hips and shoulders. My knees hurt too much. I was so stressed, my entire body threatened to cramp. I straightened up and aborted the exercise.

"I can't do it," I said, frozen in fear.

And Cyril replied, "Okay, look, you did it on the flat all day yesterday. It's much easier here. You don't even need half the propulsion you used on all those turns you've done. It will flow naturally. It's very easy. I'll show you again, look!" He went for a perfectly controlled turn. He didn't even gain any speed, coming to a stop after sliding less than two meters down. He did make it look easy.

I've done it hundreds of times already. It's the same thing. I have to fight my fear of this sheer, long slope. I can do it, I can do it.

And hop, I did my first jump, a perfect 180-degree rotation, well-landed. I slid down a few meters and came to a stop. It had worked. I'd done it.

Now I had to turn on my right side. I found it a little harder in training. I positioned myself, twisted my body to a full stretch, and jumped. My body followed my shoulders and turned by itself. I landed smoothly, sliding forward and coming to a stop.

Wow, I did it! I thought, ecstatic.

As my friend encouraged me, I continued. I jump-turned and came to a stop, jump-turned and came to a stop. I passed over the rope, marking the end of the steepest section.

Cyril said, "Continue, I'll take the rope."

The slope moved to thirty-five degrees and my fear was gone. I decide to no longer mark my stops and tried to make a few turns at speed. It worked. As I descended and gained more confidence, my speed also increased. Pretty soon, I was having a lot of fun. All fear gone, I enjoyed myself so much that as I neared the bottom, I just let it go entirely and made a mistake that took me down. I stood right back up and finished half the slope, waiting for Cyril to follow after packing the rope.

"Enough for today," he said.

"Oh no, I'm going to redo it."

So, we climbed another time. No more safety rope. And that time around, after the first six jumps in which I marked the stops, I let go of all my fear and jump-turned my way down the entire slope. Not elegant, but it worked, and I loved it.

After the team returned that same evening, I knocked on the lieutenant's door. When he answered, I said, "Mon lieutenant, I'm ready. I don't need a third day."

He smiled and said, "Are you sure? You have one more day, you'd better use it."

"I'm sure, mon lieutenant. Tomorrow, I'll keep up with the team."

I didn't want to spend another day wondering if I'd stay on the team. All I needed to do was what I'd done today. The faster, the better.

The next day, we all climbed a mountain, and after the full team reached the top, I volunteered to go first and took on the steepest slope. The full team did not follow me. They stood on top with the lieutenant and the chief warrant officer and observed. I didn't want to descend there, on that steep slope where everybody stood, dreaming of the perfect turns they would carve in a style I could never match. Instead, I walked up two hundred meters on the ridge over a rocky cliff.

Cyril immediately understood my goal. The steeper it was, the easier to turn. I had learned my lesson. The steeper the slope, the better it would showcase my new technique, and the more I could impress the lieutenant. I had to stay in the unit. The rest of the team watched us walk up that ridge. I chose to descend into a narrow gully with a fifty-degree slope surrounded by rocks. It was exposed. Falling wasn't an option. I chose this spot because I knew half the guys wouldn't dare descend it. I had done it the day before on a less exposed but steeper slope. It wasn't without any apprehension, but I knew I could do it.

And Cyril stood by me, saying, "You can do it. It's not harder than what you did yesterday. I'm right behind you."

Everybody stared at me in silence, making me feel some palpable tension. Many still wondered if I was really going to descend that canyon. Others worried they might find me broken and have to retrieve me from the mountain on a stretcher. I couldn't let the lieutenant kick me out. My style wasn't pretty. Either I would impress him with this impossible descent, or maybe I'd die if I fell, but I was determined to stay in the SR.

And with great pride, and even more fear, I did my first jump turn, slowing my speed to a stop as I skidded down the slope. I pushed a mini-avalanche under my skis. I took a deep breath and did another turn, slowing my speed almost to a stop. I did another four controlled jump turns at slow speed and let myself go faster and faster, taking one turn after another. I stopped two hundred meters below where the canyon linked back with the slope that the team would descend. The entire unit and the lieutenant were applauding. I had redeemed myself.

They all descended the slope. I felt less comfortable on the milder slopes and traversing through the forest. There, my jump turns were not as smooth as the perfect deep-snow turning techniques used by everyone else. But I took more risks and went straight down more often than most, to compensate for the time I lost on the few falls I had. I reached the bottom short of being last. I had done it.

Back down at the truck, the lieutenant called everybody together and said, "It looks like Corporal Soulé is going to stay with us after all." I could not describe the satisfaction and elation I felt. Cyril tapped me on the shoulder, and I thanked him.

Skinny sat next to me in the truck heading back to our winter base and said, "You did great. I'm happy you're staying." At last, we had become friends.

I loved the winter in the Special Forces. We did less running, and a couple times a week we did push-ups, pull-ups, and abs to maintain those muscles. We spent most of our time climbing and descending mountains on skis. Occasionally, we'd stop and do some rifle shooting exercises in the snow.

We also did winter survival training. We learned the quickest way to dig a snow shelter. We built igloos. We learned all the techniques to survive snowstorms in the mountains. We rappelled down icy rocks with crampons. We ice-climbed crevasses and frozen waterfalls. And we learned how to find and rescue people caught in avalanches.

Most of our time, though, was spent climbing and skiing superb mountains. We always raced each other, both climbing and descending. And we did so much daily elevation gain, we were completely spent at the end of each day. But we loved it. The camaraderie was great, the mountains magnificent, and we pushed our bodies to the limit day after day. The feeling of our muscles and lungs burning was both painful and deeply satisfying. We were addicted to pain and to the endorphins our bodies produced as a result.

The best part of it all was that our lieutenant, although a good athlete, was by far the weakest physically. He didn't train much with us. He'd very often go back to report to the colonels and generals of the battalion, leaving the chief warrant officer in charge.

And we adored our chief warrant officer. He loved mountains, and he loved people. Born into a poor family, he had joined the army with the only goal of being a mountain guide. Although he was a very good fighter and excellent with all firearms, he despised them. He hated firearms so much that whenever the lieutenant returned to headquarters, we'd check in all the guns with the local mountain gendarmerie. They were his climbing friends, so the guns would be safe and guarded. We would remove all our military clothing and go climb mountains and ski in colorful civilian clothes.

Under the leadership of the chief warrant officer, the military camp almost transformed into a holiday mountain camp. But the physical training always increased exponentially. We would train much harder than when the lieutenant was present, but we never had to salute the chief warrant officer or anyone else. And we never received a harsh order. He pushed us to our extreme physical limits but then talked to us as if we were his climbing buddies. Life was good.

Prior to the lieutenant's return after a week at headquarters, we would dress in our military gear and get the guns out from the gendarmerie. We knew that, we'd have a couple of easy days in the mountains because the courses would be chosen based on our lieutenant's abilities. He was a terrific athlete, maybe even one of the best officers, but that was simply not enough to keep up with the chief warrant officer or with any of us. It was like inviting the star of a local cycling club to ride with professional cyclists of the Tour de France. When the lieutenant was there, we had more shooting practice.

I thought that nothing could be greater than climbing mountains, but I discovered that winter climbing with mountaineering skis was even better. My last worry had gone. I was now a real Mountain Commando.

Chapter 37

Badass

"In the long run, men hit only what they aim at. Therefore, though they should fail immediately, they had better aim at something high."
— Henry David Thoreau, *Walden*, 1854

Most of our training was either done in Annecy, within the 27th BCA regiment, or all over the Alpine mountains. But twice a year, the SR was sent to do a special commando training camp in France's best commando training center, Fort des Rousses.

Located at 1,150 meters above sea level in the heart of the Haut-Jura Regional Natural Park, Fort des Rousses is the second largest fortress in France. From the end of World War II until 1997, under the command of the 23rd infantry regiment, it became a commando training center for the best elite troops from around the world, including the British SAS, US Navy Seals, Green Berets, and Rangers. It has also trained all the French Special Forces: the Foreign Legion, Paratroopers, Marine Commandos, and all the SR platoons.

During our week there, we practiced many things: the classic commando marches and all the rope techniques already used by the SR units, such as single rope crawling, double parallel rope knee crossing, and monkey bridge (triple rope crossing) to various rope-climbing techniques and

Tyrolean traverse exercises. All this was nothing new for the SR units, who practiced these on a regular basis.

The three main areas in which we came to improve our technique were urban close-combat fighting, hand-to-hand and knife fighting combat techniques, and the very challenging exposed obstacles.

For urban combat, we learned to take position inside a town. We secured room after room of a building, working as a team with a combination of rifles, grenades, and explosives. We learned to speed-climb walls up to a three-story level by holding a long wooden stick with three guys pushing on the thicker end. While holding it with two hands toward the thinner extremity, we'd run full speed toward the wall, and as we reached it, we'd continue to run vertically up against the wall. We did so by pushing all our weight against the building with our legs, while opposing all the force with our arms and body onto the stick. Our three friends continued pushing the stick as they ran toward the wall.

The first few tries were difficult as we'd run up and sideways until we'd fall. But we got the hang of it, learning to run straight up the walls to the third-story level. There, we'd lock the stick under our armpit, and while holding it with one arm, we'd break the window, throw a grenade, wait on the side for it to explode, and then jump through the window while firing our FAMAS automatic weapons. This was a technique the Nazis commandos used in World War II.

We also learned to place explosives under a rolling tank. We stood in front of it as it came moving toward us. We placed our hands atop the tank and let ourselves roll backward, lying flat on our backs underneath. We let the tank drive over us as we placed the charges under it, standing back up after the vehicle had gone. It was easy but looked very impressive.

In hand-to-hand combat, we always learned new techniques. None of them were about knocking out an opponent. Each technique was designed to kill or completely neutralize. Some of them involved sneaking behind sentinels and neutralizing them silently to access a target they protected. We used ropes to strangle them, knives to kill them, or our bare hands to either choke them or break their necks. Other techniques had us facing first one and then many opponents, either with bare hands or a knife.

Each strike had to yield a kill with a single blow. In case of fighting multiple enemies at once, there was no second chance. One strike, one kill. Not killing on the first strike meant we were dead. Commandos had to be ready for that type of situation, particularly when it was time to exfiltrate or if our positions had been compromised.

Our hand-to-hand combat instructor was a small, skinny warrant officer in his forties. He had served in almost all the French military corps as a combat instructor, and for many years at Fort des Rousses. The first time I did a commando training there with my unit, I thought we were good. But we could never touch the small warrant officer. He was fast and always had a powerful and efficient counterattack move. It didn't matter how much we learned from him or how much we practiced, we could never match him. We griped that we weren't given enough time to practice before he took us one-on-one. He said we shouldn't hold back because he wasn't. Every day, he inflicted a lot of pain upon us.

Laughing, he would share how he could beat the crap out of every commando from any country. And we believed him, since they all came to train with him for a reason.

Often during practice he would tell us that the Seals and the Rangers were much more muscular and powerful but slow. "If you make them run first, you'd have the advantage," he would say. "During a fresh confrontation, it would be speed over power. You're quicker, but they're a little more technical. It would be a tough call."

Another time he would say, "I'm not even sure you could hold your own against the best commando units of the Foreign Legion. You're on par with the French Paratroopers, but you'd get whooped by the SAS. They're also quick and have more experience and technique than you guys."

Hearing these words, I thought, *Great, Warrant Officer, you're really boosting our confidence. We came here thinking we were good, and you kick the crap out of us. We love hearing how strong you are. And we love hearing how every other commando unit would kick our butts in hand-to-hand combat. That's very positive.*

I kept my mouth shut, though. I didn't need to be picked to volunteer for another painful demonstration.

He said he couldn't be easy on us because maybe one day we'd have to face a Soviet commando in hand-to-hand combat — a situation I could not possibly imagine. For me, everything was a sport challenge.

After making us feel miserable for days, he finally told us something nice: "I heard you guys are killing it on the Risk Track."

That was the main reason we kept coming back to Fort des Rousses. Here, the obstacle course wasn't called the obstacle course. It was called *Piste du Risque* (Risk Track). And indeed, it was different. Each battalion had an obstacle course, and each commando training camp in France had a Risk Track. But the one at Fort des Rousses was famous for good reasons.

Some obstacles were complex and exposed. They required harnesses and straps to avoid death in case of a fall. I've already mentioned all the rope technics, and these we mastered. But we also learned how to speed-climb holding a small pipeline while climbing with our feet on a smooth, slippery wall. That was both technical and very physical. How to crawl horizontally inside a narrow pipeline. How to climb inside a completely smooth and vertical pipeline. How to walk and then run on top of a narrow iron beam spread between two of the fortress walls over a big drop. How to crawl under barbed wire that was too low to avoid touching.

But my two favorites quickly became *l'asperge* and *le saut-de-puce*. Funny names for the toughest and scariest obstacles, even though they were technically not difficult. It was the exposure and the risk of injury that gave everybody a mental block on these tracks.

L'asperge (the Asparagus) is a giant vertical metallic pole rising ten meters[1] above ground, with its top portion one meter and a half from a platform. Think of a firefighter's pole but wider, much taller, and not within arm's reach. The technique couldn't have been easier. We only had to jump a meter and a half to grab the pole and slide down, a distance anybody

1. thirty-three feet

can jump. The jump at ground level could be done by an eight-year-old. But everything changes when you do that same jump ten meters off the ground. Other than that pole, there was nothing but emptiness.

We all wore harnesses with straps and carabiners tied to a safety cable, so we couldn't die even if we missed it. It was impossible to miss that pole, but it was also nerve-racking on the first try, letting go of that fear to jump. It took me almost a minute of hesitation on my first try, and that was the average time it took everyone else. I was so afraid and jumped so far that I hit the pole hard and slammed my balls, legs, and arms on it. That was painful. Sliding down was the fun part.

The second jump was much easier, and then after three jumps, it was just a stroll in the park. The instructing sergeant told us that we were quite good. He had seen many commandos who took more than ten minutes, stuck on that top platform before they dared try. He even told us that it was frequent for some to cry, painting a picture of a big bodybuilding commando unable to jump, weeping in front of the obstacle. We laughed and moved on to *le saut-de-puce* (the Flea Jump). We didn't laugh for very long.

We climbed on another vertiginous platform. It took many ladders to reach the top. This time there was no pole. But there was another, much smaller platform under us. Upon reaching the top of the platform, we understood what the Flea Jump meant. The next platform down looked tiny from the top. We had to jump down on it. It was so small that I wondered if I would miss it. Even if I landed on it, would I roll, or do a step, or bounce back and take a deadly fall?

No, I thought, it can't be. The Asparagus was okay, but this was crazy.

The platform we had to jump on was only one meter by one meter.[2] That seems like a lot, but when the next platform was one meter fifty away, and two meters lower, that was a big jump. It didn't require leaping far. Only a tiny horizontal one, but it was a big fall to land on what seemed to be a minuscule spot, particularly when viewed from the top. It may only have been an optical illusion, but it appeared easy to miss. The main platform was sixteen meters[3] above the ground, and it would take eight jumps

2. three feet by three feet

each from a height of two meters to the small, one-square-meter platforms in order to reach the ground.

The platforms were all fixed to and around the main pole, so we rotated a quarter of a turn each time we jumped onto the next platform. This meant that when we looked at the next platform under us, we didn't see any others around, only the drop all the way to the ground. The technique is to almost not jump as we dropped two meters. We definitely wanted to start low by flexing our legs. It took no propulsion to cover the one-and-a-half-meter distance. The landing needed to be very soft, with both feet touching the metal platform at the same time, and our legs had to flex entirely to absorb the shock. There was no sidestepping or rolling possible. That would lead to a deadly drop.

There was a safety cable that ran from one platform to the next. We used a double-strap system tied to our harness and two carabiners to clip to the safety cable. Once we landed on a platform, we needed to clip one of our straps with the carabiner to the lower cable before we unclipped the other straps from the upper cable — a safety maneuver we repeated on each platform. Once we overcame the fear, the jumps took no time. However, the clipping and unclipping of the carabiners on the safety cable, even done efficiently, were very time-consuming.

The scariest part was the realization that without the safety cable, we could easily fall and die if we missed. Although the safety cable would save our lives, it also meant we would slide under that cable all the way to the next platform on which we were going to slam ourselves. It was like descending on a Tyrolean traverse, except the landing would be right on the side structure of the next platform. It would preserve our lives, but I thought it would break our bones or leave us with some type of injury. In other words, we had to avoid falling at all costs.

We hesitated for a moment before we made the first jump and the following two jumps. After leaping eight times from one platform to another, we were ready to do it again. By the time we reached the ground, we thought it was easy. Yet, once we made it to the top again, we still hes-

3. fifty-two feet

itated a bit before tackling the first jump. After three runs, this became one of my favorite obstacles. It was all in the head. We had to ignore the emptiness under us. We had to forget that we could fall because that would be painful even with the safety cable. We had to jump without pause from one platform to the next and not think about it.

For days, we practiced each obstacle many times until we all felt confident. We finally put them all together into a single timed event. It was amazing how this timed factor changed everything entirely. It was one thing to tackle an obstacle without pressure, but it was a different matter to tackle it with a pounding heart rate, gasping for air, with burning legs and arms. I did okay on my first run, but I was much slower than I thought I'd be.

We practiced several times, even at night. We would redo all the obstacles in pitch-blackness, which was actually fun and exciting.

After five days of training, I had one of the fastest times of the unit. I was pleased, but when the training sergeant told me the speed record on the course, it astounded me. The time was almost 30% faster than mine. I wondered what kind of machine could fly that fast through this course. On day six, I significantly improved my time, but it was clear that I would never set the course record.

When the training sergeant told us that, as a platoon, we were probably the best he'd seen, we asked him about the course record for the group. That's the average time each person takes in the entire platoon. That time had been set a few years back by another SR commando team. I told the guys that we could beat that record. So, we tried, and we came very close. We only had one day left to get under that time.

The next morning, I told my friends, "I know how we can be sure to beat it. Do you know where we waste the most time?"

And one replied, "Changing the carabiners when we reach a platform on the *saut-de-puce*."

"Exactly," I said. "And so, I'm going to do both the *saut-de-puce* and the *asperge* without tying myself to the safety cable."

There were a few long seconds of silence and then people started to argue. Some thought I was crazy; others thought it was a brilliant idea. In the end, most agreed that doing the *saut-de-puce* without safety cables was too dangerous. But all conceded that it was impossible to miss the *asperge* and nobody needed that safety cable. It could give us the ten seconds required to set the record. I argued that skipping the Asparagus safety cable didn't save that much time.

In the end, I, along with three other guys, skipped both safety cables, and most of the others skipped the Asparagus cables. We set a new course record. Doing so, I reduced my individual time, and I came closer, but I still wasn't able to set the individual course record.

All our trainers joined us for our last dinner. They started with a speech to congratulate us on setting a new course record. They told us that out of all the commando teams who had come from around the world since World War II, almost every time a record was set, it was done by an SR team. We all screamed, "Hooah!" We were proud. The fort had seen over forty years of commando unit trainings, and we had set the record.

One of the guys asked the trainers, "So who set that individual course record? Was he French? Was he from an SR unit? "

And the training officer replied, "It was someone in this room."

We all stared at the six commando trainers standing in front of us, wondering which one could be such a beast. I was faster than the guy teaching us, so it wasn't him.

And then the officer pointed his finger toward us and said, "Your chief warrant officer."

We were in awe! We applauded him until our hands hurt. He had crushed my time, skipping none of the safety cables. It was very humbling to learn that the individual course time record was done by our very own chief warrant officer, who had never bragged about it. His record still stood year after year.

We celebrated with our trainers, enjoying a party that eventually led to our very own training officer removing one of his boots, pouring white wine into it, drinking from it, and then passing it around to the rest of us. And we all drank from it. Disgusting, I know, but we were too drunk to care, and it was an amazing fraternity bond.

Following the commando training camp, I was promoted to corporal-chief, which I felt extremely pleased about. But, in the end, I think I gained much more from that camp than a new rank.

I realized that no matter what I did, I wanted to be the best. That was all that mattered to me. I had to beat everybody else. I couldn't beat Skinny on the run and the mountain climbs, and I couldn't beat our chief warrant officer on the Risk Track, on something I had thought I was the best at.

I also realized that no matter who, what, or when, there would always be someone stronger. And it was okay to not be first. First place on the podium wasn't what mattered most. I just needed to be the best I could be. Not against other people, but for myself. That was a major life lesson I learned. It didn't fix my huge ego problem, but it made me more aware of it.

The other thing that impressed me was that our chief warrant officer had never even told us, not even when we tried to set the course record, that he was the individual course record holder. Something he had set ten years ago, and none of the hundreds of commandos after him had been able to match. That was an incredible achievement, and he would have kept that hidden if we hadn't asked about it.

He never said things like "I was a five-time national champion in orienteering," or "I set the record for the commando Risk Track," or "I was the first one to ever climb this mountain this way," or "I set the speed record on this mountain," or "I was a fucking badass fighter."

He was all of the above, but he never said it. He would always say things like "Come, kids, you're going to love this mountain," or "It's a beautiful climb, the view from the top is amazing," or "There is a small technical part before the final ridge that you're going to love." We all knew what that meant: a technical section in which some of us would be dead scared.

It was never about him or his skill and accolades. It was about us and how much we were going to love everything he taught us. For him, his sole focus was on us and the experiences we had training with him. He talked like someone who lived for the mountains and only cared about sharing his passion. He never led with harsh orders, he led by example. He was a pacifist, anti-militarist, leading to perfection one of the best elite Special Forces. He was someone you could only like and respect, a fabulous man and a true inspiration to me and many others.

I couldn't match him, not in sports, and not in modesty. I understood that, and yet I continued to crave recognition. Maybe, despite all I had already accomplished, I was still feeling a lack of self-confidence. I pondered this, realizing it would be extremely difficult for me to fix this aspect of my character. It might take years, or a lifetime, but at least I had become self-aware.

Chapter 38

No Time for Recovery

"You are so brave and quiet I forget you are suffering."
— Ernest Hemingway, A Farewell to Arms, 1929

Pushing our bodies to the extreme was part of our daily life. We never walked down a mountain. We skied down in the winter, and we ran down the rest of the year. Following trails was often too slow. We would usually take a shortcut and run straight down on the steepest slope. As long as we kept good speed, we didn't slide. We just had to focus on each step to be precise, making contact with ground that didn't have either holes or stones.

Sometimes we reached places where running wasn't possible. We arrived at speed and either stopped suddenly to then scramble down or risked it all and jumped from a height of one meter to over two meters with our heavy bags. We learned how to do this in commando training camps and obstacle courses, but that scenario was different. In the mountains, we weren't in a confined situation with leveled, flat ground. We descended the mountains at full speed, sometimes exhausted, never knowing where or how the next obstacle would come up. We didn't know how the terrain would be for the landing. We had to be quick, demonstrate great coordination, and anticipate.

Injuries were inevitable. Knee injuries happened, but the most frequent were sprained ankles. The way we descended these mountains, it was almost obligatory to one day miss a landing and twist an ankle because of a hidden hole or loose rocks or stones.

The biggest problem with these injuries wasn't the pain; it was the SR rules for injuries. Career commandos had their own guidelines, but for drafted guys like me, the rule was simple: regardless of the injury, we had fourteen days to recover and be fully operational. On day fifteen, we had to be at full speed with the rest of the unit. It meant that a knee injury would be the end of our adventure in the SR. And even for young men, fifteen days was never enough to fully recover from a badly sprained ankle, which happened time after time to us all. We learned from the nurse how to create bulletproof strappings with medical tape. We made them so thick we could barely fit our feet into our shoes. It offered our recovering ankle minimal up–down movement but completely prevented any lateral movements. It was rock solid, and on day fifteen, we'd always be running down mountains and jumping again.

We were young, invincible, and a little stupid. But dropping off from the SR to end our service in a fighting company was inconceivable. We were the elite of the French Army, with all the benefits, pride, and respect that came with it. It wasn't something we could ever give up.

Everything we experienced in our training, even the injuries, prepared us to be of service to our country and those who needed us most. Lives depended on the excellence of our physical and mental training. Unfortunately, there were civilians who needed us all too often.

Chapter 39

Life & Death

"For us the mountains had been a natural field of activity where, playing on the frontiers of life and death, we had found the freedom for which we were blindly groping and which was as necessary to us as bread."

— Maurice Herzog, Annapurna, 1951

The only time we weren't sure we'd all come back alive was during mountain search-and-rescue missions.

When temperatures dropped far below freezing, when storms with high winds prevented people from standing straight, when total whiteout would envelop the mountains with fog so thick we couldn't see our own feet, when helicopters couldn't fly, when rescue dogs could no longer operate, and when it was deemed impossible for human beings to survive, that was when they called us.

The toughest of all training ended up being some of the winter mountain rescue missions. It was never as technical as our usual training, but each minute was of crucial importance for those we were rescuing: truly life or death. No mountain or commando training could ever push our physical limits as much as a real mountain search-and-rescue mission.

We were always called as a last resort. The GHM (*gendarmerie de haute montagne*), another amazing corps of the Gendarmerie, was one of the best mountain rescue forces in the world. They had the world's most talented helicopter pilots and were excellent climbers. They mastered rope techniques and perilous evacuations like nobody else. In some regions, they were also backed up by their fantastic counterparts in Civil Protection. But sometimes both were overwhelmed, most often in the winter, and that was when they called us.

It was no longer a drill. I had never been in the line of fire, but for us, this was a war. A war against the elements, a war against cold, a war against time, a war against our very own selves.

For my first mountain search-and-rescue mission, I was a young corporal, and my team was first to find a thirty-year-old woman. When the fog came in, she had lost her directions from the top of a lift and ventured outside the ski area. We split our six subunits and spread them to cover as much ground as possible.

After a full night of searching, we found and followed her ski tracks, locating her skis. Then we followed her footprints in the half-calf-deep snow. They kept coming back and crisscrossing each other with no logical patterns. We found her bag, and then we spotted her. We saw her lying down on her stomach, face in the snow. It was 4 a.m. We ran with our flashlights, and the sergeant turned her over. Her body was partly stiff, her frozen arms were rigid and didn't flex at the elbow. Her eyes were open. Her face was blue and frozen.

The sergeant gravely radioed the other teams. The rookies and I were in shock. She had died less than three hundred meters from the top of the ski slope. I was eighteen years old. It was during the first weeks of my first winter. I thought I was a tough guy, but I wasn't ready for this. It marked me profoundly. For weeks I couldn't stop thinking about her blue face and vacant eyes every time I laid down to sleep. I couldn't stop dwelling on the fact that she had only been three hundred meters from the top of the lift. I imagined it could have been my mother or one of my sisters.

It didn't take long for us to understand that a mountain rescue mission wasn't an exercise. Each and every time we were called, we went to war. We were in the line of fire, where our enemies were the elements and time.

On a mountain rescue mission, we never stopped to sleep. We'd walk in the mountains for up to three full days and nights without ever sleeping. It's impossible to describe the levels of physical pain and exertion we put ourselves through to conduct these missions. We'd only take three- to five-minute breaks max every four hours to grab food from our bags, rest our backs, stretch, relieve ourselves, and race again against time and death. We knew that we were the only chance these people had of survival, but to succeed we had to find them rapidly. The clock was always ticking.

Unless they were experienced mountaineers who knew how to dig a snow cave, there was an 80% chance that people who were lost wouldn't survive a full first night in the mountains.

I learned more about life in the few days of these search-and-rescue missions than in any other situation. It wasn't the mountain that taught me; it was the people we rescued. When we found them, we carried them out in a *cacolet*, a small harness to transport a victim on our back the same way we would carry a backpack.

They were saved. All they had to do was survive the eight- to sixteen-hour journey as we carried them on our backs out of the mountains.

Our only goal was to keep them awake. Sleeping meant dying. We tried to warm them up, sometimes giving them our own clothes. We placed our small combustible hand-warmers between their shoulders and on their chests. One guy would run ahead, light a stove, and boil water. Then we'd regularly give victims a hot drink. We kept talking to them, asking them questions about their lives, their jobs, their wives, their kids. We did anything to force them to talk and stay awake.

Sometimes we would find someone with a minor injury or mild hypothermia. There was no reason for us to doubt they'd survive, but no matter what we did to warm them up and keep them awake, some didn't have the will to fight and died on us. They would fall asleep and die on our backs. We felt helpless.

It was the toughest psychological experience a nineteen-year-old could live through; at least it was for me. Still today, writing this on my computer keyboard thirty-five years later, I cry just thinking about it.

During search-and-rescue missions, many of us would also suffer from hypothermia. Sometimes we also had frozen fingers or we would freeze other body parts that were accidentally unprotected. Physically exhausted beyond any imaginary state, the only thing that kept us going was our mental strength.

When you've been walking for three days and three nights in the worst winter storms without any sleep, your only chance of survival is hope. When someone you're trying to save dies on you, you lose all hope. You lose all your will to fight. When you stop believing in what you're doing, your body collapses.

Walking out of the mountains after losing a person we had rescued became an extreme survival challenge. But we still had to save ourselves. The mental blow of losing someone put us all at risk, and it became a mission for the strongest of us to help the others survive and make it out. And every single one of us had a weak moment when all we wanted to do was sleep, which would have caused our deaths.

On other missions, sometimes we'd find people in a deep state of hypothermia with frozen feet, hands, ears, and nose. They would have died within the hour if we hadn't arrived. Despite everything we could do, we knew it would be almost impossible for these people, in their state of hypothermia, to survive a ten-hour or longer foot evacuation. We never thought people in that state could survive, and yet they did. They fought so hard. They found an incredible power of will. The will to stay alive.

We did everything necessary to warm people up and keep them awake. But we could never decide who would live or die. Only they could.

I'll always remember one man I carried on my back. He was in the worst state we'd ever seen when we found him. And yet each time I asked him a question, he fought sleep so hard to answer. He fought death. It was amazing how answering the simplest of questions — how old are you? — required so much energy when dying of hypothermia. But this man stayed awake for the twelve-hour evacuation. We took turns carrying him, talking to him, warming him up, but he was the one who kept us going. He saved our lives as much as we saved his. That day, he taught me the biggest life lesson. Everything that seems impossible is possible. We're all able to go twenty times beyond any boundaries we ever imagined. There are no limits to what we can achieve. We only need to believe and fight. Dying or staying alive, it is all in the head.

The physical and mental challenge these mountain search-and-rescue missions required was beyond anything we could ever train for. It was a double benefit for the army. It was a way for them to save lives nobody else could. And it was also a way for them to train their elite Mountain Commandos to operate in the absolute worst conditions, where most human beings can't survive. These were always high-risk missions. But if we died, it didn't count in the military quota because these were not military training exercises, but real search-and-rescue missions.

Throughout my childhood, I had experienced my mother facing death so many times that it seemed to numb me to it. No matter how close she came, in the end she never died. And although I always felt the guilt of her misery, more than I ever should have, I still became indifferent to death. As if it didn't exist.

It wasn't until I really faced death in those mountains that I came to realize how tangible it was. How the sudden existence of a human being could simply stop. Death was no longer defined by my mom's suicide attempts. Death was not the end goal of people who didn't want to live. Death was the end of those who loved life.

Between my eighteenth and twentieth birthday, I learned a lot about death, but more importantly I learned what it meant to be alive. It is in our toughest moments that we really discover who we are.

After these experiences, I understood that life was extremely precious, and I had this epiphany. My childhood fantasies were not fantasies at all. I could be Tarzan and Jacques Cousteau if I wanted to. I could be whoever I wanted to be. I could achieve whatever I wanted because I was young, strong, and healthy. And most importantly because I understood the beauty of being alive. Life was too short not to live it to the fullest.

A few times during my first years in the Special Forces, I had several people tell me that they loved my smile and that I smiled all the time. I'd never thought of it before then, and I didn't remember smiling much as a teenager. But I realized that it was true. I spent most of my days smiling. Climbing mountains, doing sports, sharing that experience with great people. I was happy for the first time in many years.

Life was beautiful and I planned to live it fully. I didn't know how at that time, but I promised myself I would never become the person people wanted me to be. I'd always be me.

Chapter 40

We're the Terrorists

"I learned that courage was not the absence of fear, but the triumph over it. The brave man is not he who does not feel afraid, but he who conquers that fear."

— Nelson Mandela, *Long Walk to Freedom*, 1995

A little after my first year, the lieutenant promoted both Skinny and me to the rank of sergeant. We each led one of three commando units, and I extended my service from eighteen months to twenty-four. It was the longest we could do the mandatory service. After that, we either returned to civilian life or enlisted for a minimum of fifteen years.

I wasn't sure which one I wanted to do yet, but I thrived on the training. I loved climbing mountains, and I enjoyed leading a small unit of six commandos. Extending my service offered me more time to think about my future while gaining more experience as a sergeant and climbing more mountains. My time spent in the Special Forces became an amazing school of life.

Shortly after that, our lieutenant was promoted and replaced by a twenty-six-year-old, the star of the St-Cyr Officer School. Our new lieutenant could keep up with half the guys. He was nice, athletic, and zealous but still a military-first man. He changed the dynamic of the team as he climbed many more mountains with us than the previous lieutenant.

This meant that we had to carry our guns more frequently and didn't climb mountains in bright colors as often. That alone wasn't a big deal. On the one hand, I enjoyed kicking his butt in the mountains. On the other hand, we had enjoyed the companionship of our chief warrant officer on mountain climbs, and we wished we could continue climbing with him alone. It wasn't the same when the lieutenant joined us. Luckily, he would also be called away to perform liaison work with the generals of various battalions.

Besides all our mountain, fighting, rescue, and commando training, each year two competitions among the SRs of the six mountain battalions were held as specific skills exercises. The SRs competed against one another in mountain climbing, mountaineering skiing, igloo making, shooting, recon, and fighting exercises — all timed and graded.

Because we were from the 27th BCA, we were expected to always win, and we did. We were told that if we didn't win, we'd lose many of our privileges. One of our greatest privileges was that we lived our military lives without any strict discipline. We enjoyed a great amount of freedom with minimal chores, as long as we pushed ourselves and delivered the results expected.

One of our most interesting training exercises was entirely different. It was a biennial joint-force training with the National Gendarmerie, a French National Police Force that is a branch of the military. Due to its military status, the Gendarmerie also fulfills a range of military and defense missions. They have many divisions, including the GIGN (*groupe d'intervention de la Gendarmerie nationale*), which is the world's most famous counter- and anti-terrorist group. Many other divisions also work to fight terrorism.

Apart from the GIGN being frequently called into action — both in France and around the world for most hostage situations — there is a need for the other divisions of the Gendarmerie to do real-life situation training. Something that isn't easy to organize without a terrorist group at hand.

This was where the joint-task force came in. The SR teams made perfect terrorist groups for the gendarmes to practice on: catching and neutralizing "bad guys."

For us commandos, it was a real-life experience to practice infiltration, recon, demolition, and exfiltration.

One would say that the exercise was unfair. There were three specific targets that were defined and located in three different valleys. Each target was protected by a platoon of thirty armed gendarmes. The gendarmes also used mobile divisions. They used a motorcycle division, a dog search division, and a communication and spying division, with all the high-tech equipment to catch and locate all radio transmissions. They had helicopters and many other vehicles. Overall, four hundred gendarmes took part in this operation to protect the three known targets from a terrorist attack. A terrorist attack that we, the SR team, were in charge of doing for this exercise.

Our lieutenant and chief warrant officer stayed back as observers to be on the intel-receiving end and evaluate our recon work. The drivers and chefs also hung back as observers. We had eighteen operational commandos for the mission. We had to infiltrate, do recon, blow up the three targets protected by four hundred gendarmes, and exfiltrate, with only a week to do it. We'd only be safe once we reached the base camp on the other side of the lake after accomplishing our mission.

The higher command of the army and the Gendarmerie must have thought that the exercise would be too easy for us, as they decided to give us even more of a challenge. They added an escape situation. The eighteen of us would be prisoners being transferred by boat on the Annecy Lake. In our full military uniform, we'd have to jump from the Gendarmerie boats at full speed in the middle of the lake.

We would have a two-hour lead to swim to shore, grab our bags waiting for us on the beach, and run away before the four hundred gendarmes were sent in to catch us. It removed all elements of surprise, instead of starting with a secret infiltration and blowing up targets they didn't expect. The gendarmes knew where we would jump into the lake, where we had to pick up our bags, what our three targets were, and how much time we had to accomplish our mission. It was impossible from the start.

If they caught us, they'd win. If we didn't blow up the three targets within the week timeframe, they'd win. Yes, it didn't seem fair.

The rules of engagement were simple. For the gendarmes, we were a terrorist group and we should be treated as such.

For us, we had to blow up the three targets protected by enemies. We needed to infiltrate their lines, neutralize the guards, blow up the targets, and exfiltrate. They were not gendarmes; they were enemies.

The gendarmes had handguns and rifles loaded with blanks. We had sniper rifles, automatic FAMAS rifles, and handguns loaded with blanks. This meant that all firearms were useless on both sides. The gendarmes didn't care, but for us it was a big drag because FAMAS were bulky and heavy, and we had to carry them everywhere. We couldn't hide and leave automatic weapons in the open, for they could be found by people who could sell them to real bandits or terrorists.

The gendarmes had fighting sticks. They could and were ordered to use them. They also had handcuffs.

We had long bayonet knives. Our orders stated we could use them only to neutralize gendarmes, but we weren't allowed to stab or cut. The knives had to stay in their sheaths. To be clear, that meant that we had big knives that we were allowed to use, except we weren't allowed to use them as weapons. At least they'd serve as can openers when we needed to eat. We had explosives that we were only allowed to use to blow up the three designated targets.

The gendarmes had dogs. They briefed the dogs, telling them that we were nice guys and that it was only a game. These German shepherds were trained to find and catch terrorists, and we were the terrorists. We knew we'd better not let them close to us or we risked ending up in the hospital with multiple stitches.

The summary was simple. There were four hundred gendarmes with sticks and biting dogs. They were supported by helicopters, many types of vehicles, and all the modern anti-terrorist equipment, and we had…

What did we have? Our hands and legs!

We'd be soaking wet after a forced one-mile swim in the lake wearing our military uniform and boots. We were eighteen guys on foot, and we only had our bare hands to fight the gendarmes.

It really didn't seem fair!

Before we started, our chief warrant officer briefed us. "Okay, kids, come on, gather up. Listen, the cops aren't joking. If they catch one of you, they'll beat you until they break a few bones. They have sticks, and they have the order to use them. They know you're highly trained commandos, and they are afraid of you. That makes them dangerous. This means that if they get a chance, they'll be extremely violent."

He continued, "Our government thinks this is a good exercise for the gendarmes and for us commandos. On paper, it is. In reality, it sucks. Don't get this wrong. It's not a game. You are now in a war situation. The war is real. Take care of the dogs immediately like we taught you, and don't get caught. Good luck."

We divided into three six-man units. As sergeants, Skinny and I each led a unit, with the staff sergeant in charge of the third. All of us were highly trained. We were the best, but after listening to the pep talk from our chief warrant officer, I couldn't help but get the chills and growing knots in my gut. He encouraged us but urged us to be careful. That was quite unusual coming from him.

He'd always led us on all the exercises with a huge smile, telling us things like "This is a piece of cake. You're going to love it!"

Apparently, this wasn't going to be a piece of cake, and I was in charge of my men, of the success of our mission, and of our safety.

We boarded the gendarmes' speedboat. The loud twin engines going at full throttle prevented any conversations. The boat violently jumped up and down with the speed, even with no waves. A huge wake sprayed water behind the boat. We needed to jump out of it at full speed. We were anxious. We'd never trained for this before.

When we reached the middle of the Annecy Lake, they gave us the signal and started the clock. In two hours, they'd all be chasing us. We had seven days to blow up the three targets and return to the designated base camp located on the other side of this lake.

The clock was already ticking. Without any hesitation, we all jumped out of the boat, protecting our heads with our arms as we knew the impact would be hard at the speed the boat was going.

The water was chilly, and our military boots filled quickly, making our legs heavy to swim. Our movements were hindered by our soaked military pants and jackets sticking to our bodies, yet we had to swim as fast as we could.

We swam the mile separating us from shore, retrieved our bags, and removed our wet and heavy jackets, hanging them to dry on the backpack. Dressed only in wet T-shirts and soaked boots and pants, we ran to regroup in the forest.

The very first thing we had to do was neutralize the dogs. Those damn dogs would find us quickly. We couldn't outrun them, and we learned commando techniques on dummies to break a dog's neck with our bare hands, but they'd be coming as a pack, so it would be impossible for us to fight them. Even if we hit them with the cross of our rifles, we stood no chance.

I loved dogs. As a kid, I grew up with a German shepherd and two Briar shepherds. I would normally never hurt a dog, but the gendarmerie dogs weren't pets. They were trained fighting dogs. They were dangerous beasts. If one or two caught any of us, we risked severe injuries at best. If they attacked as a pack, a few jumping together on one of us, they could kill us.

We had prepared our bags. They were heavy, mostly with food. Water was a challenge. We couldn't possibly carry enough. We only carried one bottle and had large, empty foldable jugs and purifying pills to fill up later. We had old jackets we'd been wearing for days while training to infuse them with our smell. Each unit brought three kilos of black pepper mixed with a tenth of very thin, dried cayenne chili powder.

When the dogs were nearby, we would set traps with the old sweaty jackets filled with the black pepper and chili mix. Upon smelling the jackets, the dogs would inevitably breathe the powder, burning their snouts and destroying their olfactory system for many days. It may have been cruel, but this was war. If we didn't neutralize the dogs, they'd get us. So, we used all the old commando tricks without any bad feelings.

Before we split, the staff sergeant said to the full platoon, "Remember, like we've trained before, maximum eight-second radio communication. Ten seconds and they'll localize you. We stay in minimum radio contact. We change channels every four hours. Good luck."

We set our radio, and we split into three teams of six. We each had our own target. We knew that thirty gendarmes guarded each target, and there were three hundred other mobile gendarmes actively looking for us. I took my team to target two.

We ran fast but not straight toward our targets, as this would be too obvious. We knew from the beginning they'd send all their forces after us. We decided to head straight to the mountains. That way they wouldn't be able to use their vehicles. If they were on foot like us, they'd never catch us, and they would use the dogs right away. That was what we wanted. We needed to get all the dogs out of the picture from day one because those canines would keep finding us no matter how much we ran, and we didn't want any of them near the targets.

After four hours of running and climbing through the forest, we heard the barking. We stopped and looked around for the best place to set our traps. There was a trail heading straight up, with a narrower section of the path surrounded by rocks a hundred meters from our position. It was perfect. To chase us, the dogs would have to go exactly through this narrow section of the trail. We dumped two jackets ten meters apart. With the traps set, we kept running. We heard the dogs getting excited. There must have been four to six of them.

Then we heard them coming. We could tell by the way they were yapping. We ran as fast as we could with our loaded bags and dropped a third jacket-trap in our wake. A minute later, we heard the dogs crying. It worked. We still had half of the powder mix and we could use some T-shirts we were wearing now if we had to do this again.

After losing the dogs, we changed direction. We ran nonstop for four hours. Not too fast. We knew nobody could outrun us in the mountains and didn't need to exhaust ourselves.

We heard helicopters flying over us frequently. Each time, we stopped moving and took cover until they were gone. Luckily for us, in those days, helicopters weren't equipped with heat detection. They only had light-intensification for night vision, the same technology used in our scopes and binoculars, but that didn't help them find us during daylight hours.

They believed they had the best chance of catching us when they still knew approximately where we were. We found a cave with a small entrance and decided to take a rest, hiding the opening with branches. They couldn't possibly find us there, and they'd take at least twice as long to hike up as we did. We could rest a few hours to continue moving under the cover of night. We took turns napping and maintained radio silence while one guy monitored the radio and the mountain for movement. It wasn't necessary to communicate with the two other teams. We were self-sufficient with our own targets and would only break radio silence if one of the teams needed assistance or we had to share recon info.

The gendarmes would look for us the entire night. But apart from the night vision on their helicopter, they were on foot in the mountains and couldn't do anything. In the darkness, we moved at least three times faster than they could. And if they were lucky enough to find us, we could head to technical mountain grounds where they wouldn't dare follow us, particularly when it was pitch-black.

We stopped before daylight in a wooded part of the mountain, took our shovels out, and started digging a large pit to hide in. For four hours, we took turns digging. We excavated everything through a small hole and dumped it under a bush, where it couldn't be seen. We made a wood frame around the hole and a cover that we hid first with earth and then with leaves. We got inside and buried ourselves, making small holes on the slope of the hill to breathe and see outside. Then we moved that camouflaged cover over the tops of our heads to conceal the hole. It would be impossible for them to find us. This was a technique used by all SR teams when doing recon work.

Now we could sleep the entire day before heading toward our target that night. We still had six days, and we were doing great.

We knew they'd be looking for us everywhere for the first forty-eight hours. Even if they didn't catch us immediately, they assumed their actions still stressed us, putting the pressure on, thinking we would be exhausting ourselves. They believed that by harassing us, we wouldn't be able to accomplish our mission. That we'd get sloppy and make mistakes. We knew better. We let them look for us all day while we slept and waited.

The first two nights they most likely wouldn't sleep, expecting us to attack. Which meant we had to wait for them to get exhausted.

At sunset, we came out of our hole. It was too small, and we were cramped, but we all managed to sleep at least six hours. That was excellent. It was a relief to be outside. Pissing wasn't the problem, but for the rest, it was so much more comfortable to relieve yourself away from friends while breathing some fresh air.

We didn't hear a sound. We assumed that by now, they'd moved most of their mobile brigades closer to the three targets, and that was exactly where we headed. Finally, we started the real infiltration work. Up until that moment, it hadn't been infiltration; it was almost like an exfiltration. They knew where we were but also where we had to be. That was why we took a different route.

After descending the mountain, we had to cross a road. We waited thirty meters from it and observed for a while. Two patrol cars crossed. We waited a couple more minutes. When we didn't hear anything and didn't see any lights, we raced across and disappeared into the forest on the other side.

We walked half the night and reached the vicinity of our target. I gave the orders to the guys. We split into two subunits of three. The corporal led the other subunit. The other subunit took a different position around the target. Our target was an old water tank reserve with an ancient yet still standing building next to its base. It was located near a hilltop in a semi-forested area.

We found a steep slope from where we could perfectly see the water tank, the building, and everything surrounding it. We were less than one hundred and fifty meters[1] from it and fifty meters inside the woods. It had a few horizontal rabbit holes through the tree roots. It was perfect. We started digging from the top at a distance so we could make a vertical wall that used the rabbit holes going through the roots. These holes provided our natural openings for air and vision. We couldn't have hoped for a better environment.

This time, we knew we had to stay in that hole for a few days. We would only get out at night if necessary, but we had to stay in our pit as much as possible. Even though there were only three of us, we had to make this hole long and large enough so we could all lie down. And we needed an extra space to use as a toilet area.

We dug the toilet area much deeper so that we could cover part of it each time we used it. We excavated all the earth through a small hole to keep an opening where we could fit through with arms extended. This time, we dumped all the earth a few meters from us on a slope with roots. Spread evenly, it didn't show at all. The two guys inside the hole dug hard. The guy outside dumping the excavated earth had to do it quietly. We dug most of the night.

This was similar to the tunnels used by the Vietcong. My shoulders could barely fit, with my arms extended over my head. A bodybuilder could never have gone in or out of this hole. The wood structure helped ensure the earth didn't drop constantly at the opening. We found a large flat stone that covered it perfectly. We just added a small bush in front of it to blend in. Even if the gendarmes came right on top of us, they wouldn't find us.

We had a hidey-hole and good visibility. Because of the natural rabbit holes, we were able to dig fairly far from the outside slope. That meant the earth walls were thick, allowing us to talk without anybody outside being able to hear.

1. five hundred feet

We hurried in and covered the hole before daybreak. We would only shit in the hole if we really had to. If clear, whoever needed to would go out and take the water jug to fill it up at the nearby river at the same time. We were all settled, waiting for the agreed time to break radio silence and communicate with our other subunit. Just before daybreak, we stuck the antenna through the top hole to do a short radio call, finding out that they were buried at two o'clock from us. They also had a global view of everything and were 100% sure that they couldn't be found. Everything was perfect.

We relaxed, waited, and started our recon work. During the day, we counted the gendarmes over and over. It wasn't always easy because they moved. There were supposed to be thirty, but we were sure that there were thirty-four. Thirty-four guys with sticks. Six of us with our bare hands.

At nightfall, we saw ten gendarmes guarding the target. Others were eating and chatting. In the middle of the night, we checked the situation. There were no longer ten, but only six guys guarding the target. The others were all sleeping. Still too many. We couldn't surprise all six at the same time. It would be easy with rifles, but not with our bare hands.

We went back to sleep.

Eventually, we sensed that the gendarmes were getting tired. They were a lot less on edge. The mobile teams looked for us everywhere, and the cops had probably started to think that we'd never be able to approach their targets. If only they knew we were already here. We waited the entire day and tried to sleep as much as possible. At night, we observed. After midnight, there were only four guys guarding the target. One of them was falling asleep. The three others seemed alert, but one's head lolled back and forth. It was a good sign.

They'd been in operation for three days, and it was their third night. They were already getting tired, but they weren't tired enough yet. We waited again in our hole. It had been agreed that we'd try to blow up all three targets at the exact same time, around 2 a.m. on the fifth night.

We knew that the gendarmes would be exhausted by then. They'd think we couldn't come close to them because their defenses and mobile brigades had prevented us from approaching. We also knew that by targeting them all at the same time, they'd take much longer to get organized and chase after us. We didn't want to wait any longer than day five, keeping some margin of operation.

We did a quick radio check with our subunit to confirm they were all good to go. The reason we were in two different places was that if one of the subunits couldn't accomplish the mission, the other team, being in a different position and having a different view, could get the job done. It gave us two chances to succeed instead of one.

We slept all of day five, and from 10 p.m. we observed. At 1 a.m., there were only three guards. Everyone else slept. We got out of our holes and took position. Two of the guards weren't far from us. One was on the other side of the building. We didn't see him, but our friends did. They'd take care of him.

A real war situation would have been much easier. We could have used silencer guns and knives to easily eliminate all the guards. Even without weapons, the easiest technique to neutralize a sentinel was to come behind him and simultaneously place one hand on the chin and the other on the top of the head. In a quick snapping motion, pull both hands externally in opposite directions. The neck snapped instantly, killing the victim immediately. No sound, no blood, almost no traces. Of course, we weren't allowed to kill the gendarmes. We had to use a different technique. We had to choke them until they passed out.

One of our two guards fought to stay awake. That was fantastic. We crawled behind them, and at the exact same time, we locked them into a rear naked choke hold, then formed a triangle hold with our elbow, blocking carotid arteries and jugular veins. It took five seconds to put someone to sleep. It was impossible for them to scream, move, or even breath.

The guards were unconscious in seconds. We dragged them away quietly. We didn't know how long they'd be out. Maybe not long enough for us to place the charges. We needed to neutralize them more permanently. We dragged them through the forest behind the hill, where we tied them up, the SR commando way. One of us waited near the top of their heads with the rifle. If one of them woke up, *boom*, we'd knock him out with the butt of the rifle.

I tied my guy quickly with a small rope, first with the two thumbs, his hands behind his back, while he was flat on his stomach. From the thumbs, I moved to the wrists, looping the rope between the two hands until it was very tight. From the wrists, I looped the rope around his throat while extending his arms up behind his back a little toward his head. I folded his legs up toward his butt and swung the rope around his feet, bringing them back to his hands. We put a piece of his own cloth in his mouth.

He woke up, but it was done. He couldn't move or scream. We saw the terror in his eyes as he realized what had happened. But he had no idea how uncomfortable things would be for the next few hours. He was not going to have a good time. Another commando matched all my moves. The two cops were tied with one of the best — or worst, depending on which role you play— rope techniques to immobilize someone.

The rope going around the throat forced the cop to have his head bent backward. If he barely moved his feet from their current folded position, he choked himself. The same was true if he moved his hands or arms. He couldn't make the slightest move without choking himself. It wasn't too dangerous. As soon as he began to choke himself, he would instantly fold his legs or raise his arms back up to remove the tension on his throat. But there was no way out of this. Until someone found them, they'd have to stay in that painful position.

It took less than two minutes to tie them up. We radioed the other team. They had neutralized their sentinel as well. Everybody else slept. We were ten minutes ahead of schedule, but this was within the acceptable range. We didn't want to risk having one of the other thirty cops wake up. No matter how skilled we were in combat, we didn't stand a chance against so many men. We walked right next to a couple of sleeping cops and placed our charges. We set them with a ninety-second timer. We had to be close to ensure they blew without misfiring, and we wanted to make certain nobody woke up and stopped them while we headed back into the woods.

We retreated toward the top of the hill, deciding not to take a direct route back down and out. We waited twenty seconds and checked. The explosive charge blew. The explosion was small enough that it wouldn't do any damage to any structure or injure the cops. It simply proved that we had accomplished our mission. We ran into the night as all the cops began to scream.

None of these guys would ever be able to catch us at night in the woods. We had the terrain advantage and that was where we excelled. We knew they'd try to block every area of the woods around the lake to prevent us from returning to base. This was the exfiltration. But again, they had a major advantage. Not only did they know where we were as we blew the target, but they knew exactly where we were going. We had fifteen to twenty minutes before helicopters would be all over us. Nevertheless, we stopped and assembled the large folding antenna for the long-range communication. We needed to ensure all teams had blown up their targets; otherwise, we had to go and blow up the missing targets for them.

Two minutes later, we got the confirmation. We were all green. All targets destroyed. We had stung, now we had to disappear. For us, the toughest part of the exercise had just begun. We ran down the mountain, and as we approached a road, we saw a gendarme vehicle blocking it. Their blue flashing lights were visible from afar. Two cops were outside, standing on the road. Looking at one another, we didn't need to talk. We knew exactly what to do.

We crawled into the ditch to reach the car level. When we were less than two meters from the cops — we couldn't get closer as they were standing in the middle of the road — we rushed them, charging when they both faced the opposite direction. They never expected to be attacked. They believed that because we were on the run, we'd try to hide and sneak out. A big mistake, with all the gendarmes deployed, to have a single car with two cops by themselves.

Before they could reach their radio or their stick, we knocked them out and tied them naked around a tree with their own handcuffs. They were very lucky. At least when they woke up, they'd be comfortably hugging a tree. By now, their friends were most likely uncomfortable, trying not to choke themselves.

Two of us dressed in the cop uniforms. Not me. I had just turned twenty years old, and my baby face looked too young to pull off a cop uniform. The two oldest guys got dressed and sat up front. The rest of us stretched out between the backseats and in the trunk. The cop radio was on, and we could hear all the dispatches. We drove the cop car into the night and reached the safety zone without trouble. We were safe. We had won.

The chief warrant officer hugged us. He was so happy to see us his eyes got wet. The lieutenant arrived to shake our hands. We had the cop car, and we could follow all the dispatches. They didn't find the other teams.

One team arrived on foot an hour after us, and the third team made it to safety before daybreak, all dressed in civvies. Six days: "*Mission accomplie.*"

It wasn't fair from the beginning. It was a biennial exercise, and the SR from the 27th BCA had never failed on their mission. We were not going to be the first ones to fail. The gendarmes never stood a chance.

We told our lieutenant where we had left all the cops tied up so they could perform a rescue mission.

In the evening, there was a giant open buffet planned for the joint forces. It was a chance for us all to meet and exchange stories. As soon as they heard the mission was over, our two talented chefs prepared a Méchoui: two sheep cooked all day over a fire pit.

We were surprised and disappointed when only three gendarme officers came to have dinner with us. We were waiting for a few hundred.

They told us that they didn't understand how we were able to do it. They had prepared six months for this, and they thought that we didn't stand a chance.

What amazed us was that all the SR teams before us had also kicked their butts. How could they believe that we didn't stand a chance? It was good for us, though. The fact they had believed we couldn't do it made our job easier.

Lucky for us, in case of a hostage situation, French civilians can rely on the GIGN. If those guys had been drafted into this exercise, it would have been much more challenging for us. Then it would have become a fair fight.

We celebrated with twenty times more food than we could eat, and the same was true for the booze. We were all ecstatic and couldn't stop exchanging our experiences with the dogs, the recon pits we made, the positions we took, the way we neutralized the guards, and, for us, the way we stole a cop car.

After congratulating us, the gendarme officials said we were a fearless commando unit. Truthfully, it was one of the scariest things I'd ever done. When it was over, I could enjoy myself because we won and none of us got injured or beaten up. I never doubted that we could do it, but we weren't fearless at all.

We were scared when the dogs chased us. We were scared when we had to neutralize the guards. We were scared to walk across a field of thirty sleeping cops to place the charges. We were scared when they knew our position after the explosions, aware that we'd have the entire force going after us. We were scared to engage the two cops. We were scared to encounter roadblocks while driving the cop car. We were not fearless. We were scared the entire time.

A lack of fear would not be normal. It would be reckless. The danger was real. This type of fear forces us to properly assess a situation and make the right decisions. We had to control our emotions. We had to find the strength to move on and successfully complete our assignment.

That we conquered our fear and put all we had learned into swiftly accomplishing the mission was incredibly satisfying. Our skills were no longer skills. They had evolved into experience: something that was part of us and became who we were. We all felt intensely proud.

This exercise further reinforced my belief that it was a good thing to be scared but that being afraid should never stop me. Fear allows people to make the appropriate plans, and fighting fear allows us to accomplish what we set out to, even if most people consider it to be impossible. The same thing is true any time and for anything in life.

This exercise cemented what I had already learned from mountain rescue. Trust and perfect communication were the keys to a strong team. Failure wasn't an option. Perfection was essential. A united team would always be stronger than an individual, and victory as a team was more satisfying than an individual victory.

Although all these things were obvious, they didn't occur to me in an instant or immediately following the exercise. Even though it was something I already felt at that time, it always took me a few weeks to reflect and process information.

I understood that my experiences in the commandos had not only made me physically stronger, skilled, and more confident, but had also made me a better human being. It had made me a better me. Someone I could finally be proud of. Even though I still didn't understand who I really was, I understood who I wasn't and who I didn't want to be.

Chapter 41

Life Choice

"It is in the compelling zest of high adventure and of victory, and in creative action, that man finds his supreme joys."
— Antoine de Saint-Exupéry, *Wind, Sand and Stars*, 1939

During these two years in the SR, my training moved up into another dimension. All of us felt the same way. We were machines; we were invincible, almost immortal. We were ready to take on anybody or anything, and it was a great feeling.

Six months into my service with the commandos, I had been promoted from corporal to corporal-chief. A year later, before I turned twenty, I was promoted again to the rank of sergeant. I had received a sniper rating, multiple commando training certifications, and the mountain and skiing certifications. Before the end of my term, I was decorated with the National Defense Medal for excellence in the field.

As my fitness and technique improved, and as I moved up the ranks in the SR team, my vision of life also changed. There was nothing I thought I couldn't achieve.

When I had first joined the SR, my only dream was to make the team, pursue sports, and climb mountains. I had forfeited my deepest childhood dream of being a world adventurer because my parents and teachers had convinced me it wasn't a job. It was just a child's imaginary wish. It wasn't possible. But during my two years in the SR, I learned that nothing was impossible. With a renewed confidence that I could accomplish anything I wanted, I started dreaming again.

My lieutenant and chief warrant officer had both highly recommended me to the higher chain of command. Two months before the end of my two-year service, the army offered me the opportunity to attend an officer school so I could return and lead one of the SR teams. This came with a fifteen-year career contract. It was very comforting to receive this offer. During my two years, I had considered enlisting for a career in the army as it would guarantee me a secured job with good benefits and an excellent retirement plan.

My parents and grandparents all urged me to take it. I wanted to continue to climb mountains and push my physical limits. But I wanted to do so in complete freedom, without the constraints of a military uniform. I had revived my dreams of far-flung places and mountains on other continents. The adventurer in me was ready for a new experience.

When I turned down the officer school offer, I learned of another opportunity to work for the French government by joining the GIGN, the elite police tactical unit of the French National Gendarmerie and one of the world's best trained and most efficient counterterrorism teams. Their missions include hostage rescue, surveillance of national threats, protection of government officials, and targeting organized crime. They often train other SWAT teams in many allied countries.

The GIGN recruited the best Mountain Commando operatives at the end of their service. Because of my SR experience, sergeant rank, sniper training, and military commendation, I could transfer directly from the army to the GIGN training program, skipping the months of selection tests other candidates had to follow.

I had no interest in entering the regular police or gendarme forces. But not only was the GIGN prestigious, they also enjoyed lots of physical training and lived a great life of adventure, and all for the good of saving people. It would certainly be exciting. An adventure all paid for while I was being paid well. Benefits and retirement plans were exceptional. It was hard not to take it.

On the one hand, I could join this distinguished tactical force, guarantee my future, and live a good life. On the other hand, I could turn it down and face nothing but uncertainty. I was still a high-school dropout with no job opportunities. I didn't have any money to travel.

I tried to imagine what my life would be like if I joined the GIGN. In many ways, the training would be similar to what I had done for the past two years. The GIGN's numerous successful missions had set high expectations from the French government, and the team was sent all over the world to handle delicate situations. For example, their first major operation that made worldwide news was the 1976 Loyada hostage rescue mission. Due to the high risks and the difficult location on the hostile Somali border, the rescue was considered one of the greatest and most successful anti-terrorist and hostage-saving missions of all time.

It would be a real honor to join this unit. It was also my surest path to secure the recognition and admiration of my entire family, but I'd be living in a city far from the mountains. For many weeks I couldn't come to a decision.

If I chose not to join the GIGN, I couldn't really imagine what my life would be like. It was a big unknown. But I couldn't help but think that since I had succeeded in accomplishing my secondary dream of joining the Mountain Commandos, maybe my deepest childhood dreams were also possible, even if I didn't have the means yet to back them up. It probably wouldn't be easy to become a world adventurer, and I had no clue how I could do it without any diplomas, job, or money, but there was nothing I desired more. It was something that even the allure of being part of the GIGN couldn't steer me away from.

In the summer of 1987, at the end of my two-year term, I simply quit the Special Forces — and gave up all the present and future benefits — to return to civilian life. I wanted to take a shot at following my heart.

My two years in the Special Forces didn't set me up financially. It didn't even offer me any skills I thought I could use in a real job situation.

But it made me feel physically invincible, able to take on any challenge. It boosted my confidence in following my dreams and flying solo to go discover the world.

Education and work experience were still big hurdles for finding jobs and being able to live the life I wished, but I was determined to try. It was only years later that I comprehended the true experience I had gained during those two years in the SR. I didn't understand it all at the time, but it was one of the best schools of life.

It took a great leap of faith to follow my dream instead of staying anchored to what most people consider a comfort zone. The comfort of living in a region surrounded by friends and family. The comfort of a secure job. The comfort of knowing and believing we can control our own lives.

But this is a preconceived life that society molds for us. We are not in control. We are set to follow a path, one that society has designed for us, that tells us what is good and bad for us. A path that defines success and failure based on its own guidelines. Staying in that comfort zone was easy.

Most people I knew lived their entire lives within the same town or at least the same region where they were born. They always existed within this small world surrounded by the same people. Nobody ever made it out of their towns. I didn't want that.

My dad never dared to attempt living his dream adventures. I vowed that I wouldn't do the same. Life dreams aren't fantasies for the imagination; they are real goals to pursue. I believed that my dreams could come to life if only I dreamed strong enough and put that same energy into trying to accomplish them. I wanted to live my dreams (or die trying).

My life would have been drastically different if I had stayed with the army or joined the GIGN, but it was not to be my destiny. The stronger I became, the more combat skills I developed, the less I wanted to fight. I had gained the confidence I needed to never get into a physical confrontation again. I didn't have the soul of a soldier. I'd never wanted to kill anybody. I learned how to do it, but I didn't want to spend my life training with that goal in mind.

I wanted to climb mountains. I wanted to cross oceans. I wanted to discover jungles. I wanted to meet people from different cultures and explore the world without hiding behind a gun and a uniform. I wanted to be a nomadic and free adventurer. I wanted to be myself.

I was twenty years old. The world was mine to discover, and I intended to follow my dreams of adventure.

Chapter 42

The Bank Job

"The joy of life comes from our encounters with new experiences, and hence there is no greater joy than to have an endlessly changing horizon, for each day to have a new and different sun."

— Christopher McCandless, in Jon Krakauer's *Into the Wild*, 1996

I had just spent two years living life to the fullest with a team of smart and talented world-class athletes. I had gained a tremendous feeling of confidence in both my physical and intellectual abilities. I knew I could make tough decisions and lead a team. I was ready to face off with the entire world to follow my dreams.

But when I left the Special Forces, I had no savings — and reality hit. I was still a high-school dropout. I hadn't gained any useful diplomas. Besides becoming a mercenary, I was unemployable.

Confronted with that harsh truth, I started to understand why ex-commandos were easy prey for mercenary contractors. Those jobs for us were plentiful and paid beyond imagination. You would just have to fathom the idea that it was okay to sell your soul to the Devil, kill innocent people, and be able to live with it.

Even in a war situation, I never wanted to kill anybody. I loved the commando training, but I couldn't adhere to the "enemy" concept. And even though I have the highest regard for the work of the army, I couldn't stand the idea that one day I might be sent to war somewhere to kill without understanding the real cause or purpose of that war or, even worse, maybe with feelings that would be opposed to that war. I respect and admire soldiers who can serve their country in this capacity, but maybe I wasn't one of them.

If I was that sensitive about killing for the greater good of my country as a soldier, despite all my skills and training, I was definitely not a mercenary. I don't think I could have done it, and if I'd tried out of desperation for some quick money, I couldn't have possibly lived with myself. I never considered it. However, in these times of difficulty, readjusting to civilian life with absolutely no future to look toward, I understood how easy it would be for ex-commandos to embrace the dark side.

I didn't need much. I just wanted to save enough to purchase a plane ticket and launch my first great adventure. I figured that I wouldn't need a lot of money where I was going. I would just find a way to make it as I went.

My first adventure goal was to cross Asia on a bicycle. I had never cycled, and I was clueless about all the different bikes. I figured I could do that on any type of bike. I would purchase a used bike for nothing in India and just go. I had envisioned a crossing of the Himalayas. I would start from the Indian state of Sikkim, ride through Nepal, and then back to the Himalayan regions of Northern India all the way to Kashmir, cross into Pakistan, and finish either in Pakistan or Afghanistan.

My plan was to ride through the mountains and stop in places to climb some of the best summits that didn't require any expensive permits or gear. I knew I couldn't afford major mountain climbs, but I just wanted to experience the beauty and freedom of high-altitude, nontechnical mountaineering in the Himalayas. I would be trekking off the beaten path, to high mountains where trekkers didn't usually venture. But there would be no Himalaya crossing unless I could reach India. I needed any job that would help me buy my plane ticket.

Unfortunately, I couldn't land any minimum-wage jobs anywhere. After months of searching, I had only been offered a security guard position for minimum wage, but they required a two-year commitment that I was unwilling to give. Doubt started to creep in. Did I make the biggest mistake of my life by turning my back on both the military and the Gendarmerie?

The "Bank Job" sounds like the title of a thrilling movie, but for me it was a short experience in my life that wasn't worth mentioning, except that it reinforced my conviction that I wasn't meant to be stuck in a system doing a routine job.

I told my high-school friend Paul that I had tried every possible outlet to get a small job with no success, and I was left without any options.

He told me that he had talked to his mom, who was the director of the national bank in Bordeaux. They were looking to take apprentices under a *formation*, which is a short-time apprentice job sponsored by the government where the employer pays less than half of minimum wage to young trainees and the company receives substantial tax cuts from the government. The purpose was to train young, undereducated people for a practical job they could pursue for the rest of their lives.

Paul's mom came through, offering me the *formation* position in her bank. She made it clear that I couldn't tell anyone I knew her, the director, as I was going to enter the bank at the very lowest level. I would never interact with her at the bank. She agreed to take me on a *formation* basis only, knowing that I had no desire to work there full-time. Normally, these three-month *formations* were meant to recruit the best trainees into the bank. She was going against her own establishment's rules and against the system to help me. Regardless of the inadequate wages, I was grateful as it would help me move closer to buying my plane ticket out of France.

My first day working at the bank was a surprise. I met my team of a dozen people working in a small noisy room where machines constantly counted and sorted deposited bank checks. The job was ridiculously simple. We had to sort all the checks by bank brands and then by dates, and then we had to enter all the amounts onto printed spreadsheets. We handed that off to someone who checked our work, who handed that off to someone who entered all that information into a computer.

It was the most boring job ever: all day sorting through checks. But I didn't mind. I didn't even mind that I was only making less than half of minimum wage. This job, combined with my current meager savings, would allow me to get my plane ticket.

What shocked me, though, was the behavior and mentality of my co-workers, or should I say tutors, as I was the only trainee and everyone else had their bank jobs as a career. Their conversations varied between stupid jokes, complaints about the upper management, union talks, and very often criticizing one another.

Some even counted the number of minutes people took going to the toilet. All stopped for legally authorized smoke breaks. That's right. There was an official amount of time people could take a break to have a smoke. I couldn't believe it, and the full team would go out of the building and smoke. I don't remember the exact time allowance. It was something like twenty minutes per day that could be fractioned into minutes every few hours. It bewildered me. People would stop working to smoke.

Of course, not everybody was going on the smoke break at the same time, and often the group still working would complain about such-and-such person who was out smoking.

"That girl spends over an hour in the bathroom each day."

"That guy overextends his smoke break by five minutes four times per day. That's twenty minutes of his work we have to do."

It was all ridiculous talk.

Everything was so insignificant and so far from the active life and great team spirit I had experienced that I just didn't talk much to anybody. I felt that I was back in my first week of Basic Training. I had returned to "*La France Profonde*," where people had no desires and no goals whatsoever. They just lived their lives as sheep in a system they never tried to change yet kept complaining about.

It is this particular French mentality about unions, strikes, and complaints that so characterizes a significant percentage of the French population. France is a society with excellent social benefits over-abused by unscrupulous, lazy people who always want more while working less. At the time, I didn't have much work experience outside of the army, but I knew the meaning of work. I knew the sacrifice it took to reach a goal.

I was appalled by the lifestyle and mentality of these people. I didn't belong there, and this further reinforced my strong convictions that I absolutely had to leave France far behind me to seek the life of adventure I always dreamed about. I couldn't fathom being part of this French society, entering at the very bottom of the ladder with absolutely no future prospects. I'd be surrounded by this type of union worker my entire life. Who knew? Maybe even after decades of brainwashing, I'd become one of them.

I didn't belong in this society. Not in this bank. Not among these narrow-minded people. Not in France.

Each experience, good or bad, joyful or painful, is a piece of the puzzle that makes up our lives. It's up to us to choose how complex the puzzle will be.

The bank job was not my puzzle: it was only a tiny but importance piece, for it made me certain that I wanted my puzzle to be complex. I wanted my life to be filled with experiences.

I wasn't afraid to leave without any money or even without an education. I was willing to take the risk to live my dreams and escape from this sad reality that swallowed most people. I had nothing to lose.

I was still addicted to mountain trekking and climbing, and I couldn't stand staying in Bordeaux. Every weekend, I drove to the Pyrenees to climb mountains. I had registered for a civilian trekking guide test at the end of summer, for which I had to trek all the mountains and learn all about the fauna, flora, economy, and culture of my chosen valley. I chose one of my favorite Pyrenees valleys and went there every weekend to run every single trail and race up to the top of every mountain.

At the end of July, there was a two-week forced summer break in my bank *formation*. I decided to use that break to run up the entire mountain chain of the Pyrenees, from the Mediterranean Sea to the Atlantic — a dream I had a few years ago watching these mountains from my school.

Some people do that trek in a month, usually following the easy GR10 trail, the Pyrenees equivalent to the US Pacific Crest Trail.

I had imagined my own route, which would go through some of the highest mountains of the entire chain and rarely descend back into the valleys. It was a combination of the GR10 and the more technical HRP trail, and I included some bushwalking outside of any trails to climb up and descend mountains that were not on any marked paths.

I didn't bring a tent. I wanted to run the entire length, and I needed to be as light as possible. I also forewent the sleeping bag and only took a light bivvy-bag shell. My backpack didn't weigh more than four kilos,[1] including some warm clothing, a rain jacket, food, and water. I didn't carry much water. At that time, I was drinking from all the rivers without worrying the least about Giardia or any other possible diseases. I felt physically invincible, and I believed that my body could fight anything, including any disease. What wouldn't kill me would make me stronger.

I didn't need a warm sleeping bag. I wasn't planning on spending long nights, and I could handle the cold. I knew that in some high mountain locations I could occasionally find some *refuge*, small mountain dwellings built to host mountaineers and trekkers. Some of them had a keeper and were heated, others were open for all, and some even had blankets. I only purchased whole wheat bread, cheese, bananas, and dried fruits when I went through villages.

It was the first time I ran in the mountains entirely by myself without a military mission. I experienced a fantastic feeling of freedom. I enjoyed the ever-changing landscape of the Pyrenees and every moment of my small local mountain adventure. I met shepherds, who invited me to sleep in their little cabanas and shared their homemade cheese with me. They appreciated the company. I enjoyed a roof, wind protection, and free food. I didn't idealize the shepherd's life. I knew it was a tough and lonely existence, but I still thought they were much happier than the bank workers.

My Pyrenees crossing was such a fantastic experience, I knew I wanted to do the exact same thing in the Himalayas. I wanted to get off the beaten

1. nine pounds

path, discover the world's most majestic mountains, and meet people who enjoyed different lifestyles, living in harmony with their environment. I wanted to be far from the unions, the strikers, and all the people who kept complaining about their lives without ever trying to change anything.

Decades later, I would learn that in 2016, the world record would be established for a Pyrenees crossing on the GR10 in twelve days and fourteen hours. I had done my crossing twenty-eight years before, with road running shoes and rustic equipment, on a more challenging trek with greater elevation gain and difficult technical routes, in a little over thirteen days, which would have been a world record too. But without GPS and satellite tracking, it remained unrecorded.

I resumed my bank job and continued to drive every weekend to trek in the Ossau Valley. A week before my *formation* ended, during a quick training in the mountains, I met Laura, an American woman who was ill-prepared for the route and the mountains she wanted to climb. I suggested a less technical route and left to run up and back down my peaks. Five hours later, when I returned, she had set up camp by a lake less than three kilometers from where she'd started. She was carrying a dozen books up the peaks and had made virtually no progress, even though she looked very fit.

I only had five days of work left at the bank, so we decided to meet the following week when I could guide her on more technical and higher mountains since I had to be in that region to take my civilian mountaineering test two weeks later.

Laura had traveled a year and a half through Europe after graduating from Harvard. She had learned fluent German and French in a few months. Her savings were running low, and she was on her way home. She promised her family in Boston, Wisconsin, and Texas that she'd visit them before Christmas.

My passion for the mountains and adventure impressed her. She convinced me to first accompany her to the United States, where I could easily find small jobs under the table to save more money for my great adventure. In the time Laura and I spent together, we had developed strong feelings for each other, and she didn't need much time to convince me. Yes, I wanted to cross the Himalayas, but after all, visiting the States was still going to be an adventure. However, I needed more funds. Other than my plane ticket, I had to at least have some pocket money to land in the USA.

Chapter 43

It's Not the Destination, but the Journey

"No one can absolutely control the direction of his life; but each person can certainly influence it. The armchair explorers who complain that they never got their 'one lucky shot' were never really infected by the incurable drive to explore. Those who have the bug—go."

— Jacques Cousteau, *The Human, the Orchid, and the Octopus,* 1997

My new travel plans required a larger purse.

As I struggled to figure out how I could earn more money for my trip to the States, my childhood friend Jean came to the rescue. While I was in the Mountain Commandos, Jean had landed a full-time job working in a Ford factory as a mechanic. He didn't have a high salary, but he knew that I had nothing and really wanted to fly away.

In September, he'd purchased an old car needing a lot of work. He was very handy with all manual things and mechanics. I wasn't, and he really didn't need my help, but he told me that he did, and he paid me to assist him with the final mechanical work, full polishing, and repainting of his car. I spent a few days helping him, for which he offered me more than I'd received for a month's work at the bank *formation.* I didn't realize it at that time, but Jean had basically become my very first sponsor.

After I had entered the Special Forces, my relationship with my dad improved. We would see each other once every couple of months for a meal. Nevertheless, like my mom, he never believed in me. Along with my paternal grandfather, whom I really loved and respected, they never thought that I would become a Mountain Commando. When I did, my grandfather congratulated me, expressing how impressed he was by my accomplishment. But neither my father nor my mother seemed the least bit impressed. If they were, they certainly never expressed it. Once again, I was denied any recognition. Even worse, Mom mocked me, repeatedly mentioning how stupid the military parade marches were. I think my father was relieved, at least, to know that I had finally found my way and could have a job in the military for life.

When I left the SR unit, they absolutely didn't understand why I hadn't followed a full career in the army. I had found the one place where I was really successful. I had been offered an opportunity to go to an officer school. I would have had a guaranteed career and retirement with all benefits, and I was doing what I always said I loved doing: sports and mountaineering. What stupid idiot would turn his back on this opportunity?

They strongly disagreed with my decision to leave the army; and after I did, their feelings were further reinforced when I couldn't find a job. Dad suggested I follow a *formation* as a baker. *Seriously, a baker!* He knew that it was a hard, physical job, but the businessman in him also knew that there was a lot of work for bakers and possible opportunities for me to one day open my own small business.

A baker! He thought that I had left the Special Forces to become a baker. I was bewildered. Not that there was anything wrong with being a baker or having any other job, but obviously that wasn't for me. I couldn't believe that even after my time in the Special Forces, he still had no faith in me or in what I could achieve.

Our conversations led nowhere. For them, I was still an immature kid living in my own imaginary world of travel adventures. Maybe I had fashioned my body to look like Tarzan, but Tarzan wasn't real; and the Jacques Cousteau crew didn't hire mercenaries, they only selected the world's best marine biologists and scientists.

Since I never got any recognition from my parents, and was always too offended by how little they thought of me and all my ideas, I chose not to tell them about my goal to cross the Himalayas. I planned on letting them know just a few days before my departure so as not to be berated for days and weeks concerning how stupid and foolish I was, that I should reconsider all my dreams to fit into the mold, take a *formation*, and look for a real job.

My dream didn't change, but my immediate travel plans did. After purchasing my ticket, and two weeks before my departure, only Jean knew I was leaving for the USA. I didn't tell my family until I had my ticket in hand. I had sold most of my meager belongings. My small backpack was ready, and I had a total just short of $200 in savings.

When I announced my imminent departure, my grandfather summoned me for an emergency meeting. He couldn't let me go travel on another continent when I didn't speak a single word of English, had no degree, and no money. I would certainly become a bum. I needed to stay in France and get a job, then after years of hard work, I could take a holiday where I wished. Now wasn't the time for me to go on vacation.

My father gave me the same speech. The amazing thing is that he genuinely looked worried. He had no faith in me, but he actually seemed to care about me. I don't know what I felt more strongly at that time: the fact that he had absolutely no clue of who I was and what I was capable of, the fact that he believed I was a loser, or the fact that he might actually love me, something I hadn't felt since I was a little kid. It was a strange cocktail of emotions.

Mom was slightly more supportive, probably because she knew I wouldn't listen to anything they said anyway or maybe because she cared even less than my father did.

My parents didn't seem to understand or appreciate in the least what I'd accomplished. They had no interest in my experience and I never shared with them any of my training. When I quit, they only saw the army as a steady and secure job for their kid who was probably unable to do anything else. And even though they were clueless about my experience of the past two years, they at least knew I had succeeded in making a team they were certain I wouldn't.

On that note, I left my native country for an undetermined time. My parents were certain that I'd return right after Christmas, entirely broke. Their only comfort was that I had a six-month open return ticket, which was mandatory to enter the States.

For me, going to the States was the first step toward living my life in total freedom. I was ready to break all my chains and become the adventurer I had always longed to be. I didn't plan on going back to live in France. I was ready to embrace the unknown, certain that it was my destiny.

Chapter 44

Not a Word

"If you don't get out of the box you've been raised in, you won't understand how much bigger the world is."

— Angelina Jolie, 2011

On October 4, 1988, Laura and I boarded the plane for New York. She told me we had to go through US customs separately. There were different lanes for foreigners and US citizens, and foreign lanes took much longer. We would meet at the baggage claim.

I was nervous. I had never paid attention, let alone studied, in English class. I had hated all my English teachers and skipped most of these mandatory classes during my youth. Laura comforted me by having me memorize a sentence.

She said, "Don't worry, you won't get lost, but if you do, say this to any young woman you see. Don't ask guys. American ladies are much nicer to French people." I memorized the sentence I'd have to use for my survival in case I got lost.

I waded through the queue for the foreign lane for two hours. I was clueless when the custom officer asked me questions, so I spoke in French and he rolled his eyes. I had a return plane ticket. I had a credit card. Little did he know that it was a debit card with zero funds on the account, really zero. I only got it to be allowed entrance into the USA. And I only had almost two hundred bucks in cash. That was good enough for me to get a stamp. I was now officially in the United States.

I met Laura at the baggage claim. We boarded a train to Boston, where we visited Christine and Ric, her sister and brother-in-law. I had plunged into a foreign world where I could no longer comprehend anything. People talked around me, spoke to me, and I couldn't understand or say a single word. It was a strange feeling, like being a little kid discovering a new reality. I couldn't express myself, so I spent more time looking at people, following all their gestures and facial expressions. Despite not being able to communicate, I could sense that American people were much friendlier and more open than the French. It was very pleasing.

When Laura explained to Ric and Christine that I didn't speak a word of English, they nodded, but it didn't stop them from talking to me. And then Laura told them that she'd taught me one sentence. She asked me to deliver the survival sentence she'd taught me, and so I did.

Ric and Christine burst out laughing. They laughed so hard, they wept. Seriously, crying from laughter. I couldn't believe how rude they were, making fun of my French accent. I'd tried my best to deliver those words.

Finally, after at least five minutes of the three of them laughing and crying, they caught their breath. Ric tried to explain the meaning to me. That made Christine and Laura laugh even more because Ric didn't speak a word of French. He was a movie fan, and he loved *The Pink Panther*. He thought that if he spoke English with a caricature French accent, imitating Inspector Clouseau, that I'd understand everything he said. I didn't understand anything other than him talking funny in his own tongue. But I was even more clueless than Inspector Clouseau.

The longer I failed to follow the conversation, the more Ric genuinely tried to explain with his best caricature French accent. It sounded French to him, but the words remained purely English. He could have spoken Arabic or Chinese with a French accent, it would have been all the same to me.

We had to wait until the girls wiped their tears for Laura to translate the first English sentence I'd memorized.

"I'm French. I have no money. I'm lost. I'm good in bed. Take me home."

I was a little embarrassed, but I had to admit that it was hilarious, and it broke the ice. Ric and I became instant friends.

I had a long way to go before I could follow any English conversations. After spending two weeks in Massachusetts, we took a train to Madison and spent a few days at Laura's uncle's place, from which she bought his old Subaru station wagon. With it, we planned to go climb mountains in Colorado. We went to the first climbing shop, where Laura showed me a big sign on the wall and translated it.

Urgent

Climber Wanted

$50 per hour

It couldn't be real. $50 per hour. It was 1988, and my biggest salary to date had been working for ten days with Jean for $400. I had worked three full months in the most boring bank job for a monthly income of $400. And I had risked my life on a weekly basis, working my ass off in the Special Forces, for $300 per month. I couldn't believe there was a job where I could make that much money in a single day. I could make $500 in a day!

Laura called the number and found out the City of Madison was hiring. They wanted to meet us immediately. They gave us an appointment at the Madison baseball stadium.

The deal was simple. They'd had two teams of professional painters who quit on them because it was too windy. Nobody wanted to climb to the top of the baseball field's giant projector posts to scrape off the rust layers and paint on one layer of anti-rust and two layers of new paint. They couldn't find a single professional painter willing to climb. All those who came had turned back down halfway up. They only had one university student, a climber who would come after school to work two hours each day. But he was too slow and didn't work enough hours to make any progress.

It was urgent that the job get done because winter had come early, and the weather forecast called for the first snowstorm in less than five days.

The paint could no longer hold with freezing temperatures. They had to finish painting the projectors before that snowstorm settled in.

Laura translated, and I nodded and said, "No problem, we can do that. They need to provide us with two climbing harnesses, six webbings, six carabineers, and two climbing ropes." I asked for all the equipment we'd want to use later on in Colorado to do the job.

They agreed and then said they weren't actually paying per hour. This was an estimate based on the work the student had done. They were paying a $1,000 per projector post. That was for scraping rust and painting one layer of anti-rust and two layers of paint. It was a fast-drying paint, and we could do the next layer a few hours after the first one.

Laura explained that I was on a tourist visa. They replied that it wasn't a problem. They didn't have time to do any paperwork, but it was a job for the city. They gave us a contract and said that in case of an accident, they'd cover us and would then go through with all the paperwork. Otherwise, they were in a hurry and would pay us cash with no taxes to declare. They were that desperate.

The next day, Laura and I climbed on the posts, and we each attacked one of them. I showed her how to climb, how to secure herself and her gear, and she was game for the experience. Physically, the job wasn't that hard, but I had to admit that hanging under the top basket in the wind was quite the experience. I'd done some swinging on rappel ropes under helicopters, grabbing a mountain cliff and rescuing people in the middle of storms. I was unfazed by the experience, but it impressed me that Laura had the guts to match my moves on the adjacent post.

In the evening, the city representative came to watch our progress. He couldn't believe that we had scraped both poles and already painted two layers. We'd be done the next day for sure. The student had called in to say he couldn't come because of his studies. We finished his work and made $3,000 in three days. The city representative was ecstatic with a job well done, and we had made more money in three days than I'd made in my entire life. Even with Laura's help, I wasn't sure I could have lasted until Christmas. Now we had money to travel. We drove through the great flat plains of Nebraska; went rock climbing in Boulder, Colorado; and climbed Pikes Peak in deep snow.

After three months of extensive travel, visiting many of the famous national parks, we'd eaten through half of our savings. It was time for us to find a place to settle temporarily and look for a job. We'd heard that Seattle was stunning and surrounded by mountains. A place where the economy was booming, where the people were liberal, and where it might be easier for me to land a job as a mountain guide or mountain rescuer at Mount Rainier National Park. It was also a great place for Laura to put her genius to good use in the high-tech industry.

I still didn't speak any English. I had picked up a few sentences but traveling with a French speaker hurt my progress. I was willing to get any job I could. It was time for me to learn some basic English and save a little money. We had a plan. Laura was going to get a job that required no speaking, like a cleaning job. And I'd do that job while she found another one using her academic skills.

On our first day in Seattle, she got hired as a dishwasher in a sorority. It was located two blocks from where we rented a cheap room in an old house on the verge of collapsing. We shared it with drug addicts.

She told the sorority she was interested in the job as she was going to school for her Ph.D., but there were two meals a week that she wouldn't be able to work. She introduced me, saying that I could replace her on those two days.

The sorority offered free meals but not a very high salary, and they'd had a hard time filling the position, so they accepted us. All they cared about were the dishes getting washed well and on time. Laura came with me on the first day to work and then only showed up to eat her daily free lunch and dinner.

I jumped into the job and worked harder than anybody else. Jerry, the chef, was fond of me. He had gone to France to master his cooking and loved it there. He even spoke a few words of French — not enough for a conversation, but we managed. He had his own resort and a big restaurant in Minnesota, but a divorce had blocked all his bank accounts. It also forced him out of his restaurant until the court decided the division of the business and properties. This process should have taken a few months, but it had been dragging on for over two years. Jerry had no choice but to take a low-paying job in this sorority while he waited to get his business back.

We had a bond. Because I worked harder and faster than anybody else, I had some spare time. Jerry used up some of my time as his assistant cook. It was hilarious, as cooking was absolutely not my thing, but I was great with knives. I could cut all his vegetables and fruits in no time.

Jerry taught me English with a great sense of humor. "That's a saucepan. No, not that one, this one."

"Hey, open the corn cans, would you? No, not the corned beef, the corn." We spent a lot of time laughing.

Jerry was in his late sixties, and he didn't appreciate the girls we served. He tried to explain to me what I already knew: They were rich girls living a life of luxury in a sorority while studying at the University of Washington. They acted like princesses and wanted to be treated as such. They had never worked in their lives and had no respect for people who weren't as wealthy as their families — something they made us feel all the time with their condescending attitudes.

Two months after I'd been hired, the manager of the sorority had heard that many restaurants were being cited for illegal workers. They asked me to legalize my situation and sign the work contract. They didn't know that I was on a tourist visa. I quit the dishwashing job and started a newspaper delivery route the next day. Not the best job in the world either, but until I could converse in English, my opportunities were more than limited.

Chapter 45

The Corporation

"Now is no time to think of what you do not have. Think of what you can do with what there is."

— Ernest Hemingway, *The Old Man and the Sea*, 1951

It had been a couple of weeks since I'd left the sorority. After my newspaper route, I'd spend all my afternoons in Laura's office at Microsoft, sitting in front of her second computer. I was learning its basics, as I had never even turned one on before. Laura had told me about what her new job entailed. She'd said it was so easy a twelve-year-old could do it. There was no need to speak English or even know much about computers.

The formatter job was simple. The language proofreader wrote text corrections on a hard copy, then the editor wrote font and format corrections on that same printed copy to give to the formatter. The formatter had to enter those corrections into the text on the computer. The current project was a Dutch software manual, but no one was worried about the language. It was the responsibility of the Dutch proofreader to spell out the text corrections.

While I learned computer basics as well as the formatter's job, Laura's boss, Matt, stopped by her office three to four times a day to talk about various work topics I couldn't comprehend. Based on his appearance and constant smile, he seemed like a nice guy. A small man wearing glasses with semi-long dark hair, he looked like the musician he was. That weekend, he planned to play the drums with his band and invited us to come. We ended up going, and luckily for me the noise of the band was too loud to have any conversation.

A couple of days later, Matt stopped by Laura's office while I was on a bathroom break.

"What is your boyfriend doing in your office every day?" he asked.

"He's helping me on the project. You know we're short on time."

"Really? Is he good with computers? You know we need two part-timers to finish this project, and we don't have time to find and train any."

"Oh yes, he's really good. That's why he's helping me."

"Could you ask him if he's interested in the job? We only need him for two weeks, but if he wants the job, we'll hire him as of tomorrow."

"I can ask him," she replied.

And this was how I landed my first job at Microsoft without an interview. I couldn't have followed any English conversation unless it was about saucepans, peanut butter, plate servings, and dishwashing. Up until the week before, I'd never touched a computer, and I couldn't type on a keyboard.

An opportunity isn't a free pass to success. It requires courage to try and a will to succeed.

It was crazy, it was impossible, and it was an opportunity I seized because I loved the challenge and the chance to try.

There was nothing to the job that I hadn't already helped Laura do, and I could do it in my sleep. Laura and I were perfectionists, so 100% accuracy was all we'd settle for, when the average team worked at less than 80% accuracy.

During our daily morning meetings, Matt would assess the progress on the project, give a few directions to his team, and ask them about a potential project getting behind schedule. I had absolutely no idea what all the people were talking about. I'd just stare at the person talking and eventually give a few soft nods here and there. I smiled when everybody did and just never opened my mouth. In fact, I never said a single word to anybody on our team. They all thought I was an introvert. Me, the teenage boy who played the snake charmer and scorpion eater to the crowds of tourists I guided. Me, the commando unit leader. An introvert! It was so ironic.

I could have almost been deemed a mute because I never opened my mouth to say more than hi, yes, and no. There was more to my vocabulary than that, but saying anything else would have revealed that I didn't speak English and never understood the conversations.

The few times Matt asked me a question, I just discretely looked at Laura to know if I needed to answer with a simple yes or no. If the answer required more than a yes or no, I would just lower my head and not respond. I managed, and nobody bothered me as long as my work was perfect — and perfect it was.

After a week, Matt wanted us to use a new tool, and he had a senior formatter give a demonstration. She asked a coworker to come up and type a paragraph so we could see how the automation could auto-correct a few basic words. He did so at lightning speed. Then she called me up, asking me to try it. I was embarrassed, as I had never learned how to type. I just pretended to be extremely shy and stupid, not moving from my chair until she called someone else. My cheeks burned red with shame. They probably assumed I was too shy to be put on the spot. The truth was, I couldn't type, and I couldn't let them know it.

That same day, I asked Laura to teach me the correct typing technique. She showed me how to use all my fingers to strike the keys. It wasn't complicated, it just required practice.

"How much practice?" I asked.

"People who take three classes per week can usually learn how to type in three months," she replied.

I did a quick calculation of three hours times twelve, realizing I needed to put in thirty-six hours of practice time to learn how to type. If I worked hard at it, I could probably divide that time by half.

That night, I didn't go home. I started typing the sentence "The quick brown fox jumps over the lazy dog," which includes all the alphabetic letters. Thousands of sentences later, I was still typing when Laura returned to the office in the morning.

She pushed the door open and greeted me.

I replied with a smile, and she froze before saying, "I can't believe it ... you're typing." She sat next to me to see if all my fingers were hitting the correct keys. "Seriously, I can't believe it. You're typing that sentence five times in less than a minute. That's forty-five words per minute."

"Yes, thanks for teaching me," I replied.

"You don't understand," she said. "Nobody can learn how to type overnight."

I joked that it was much easier than being a Mountain Commando, surviving hypothermia or exhaustion. But I was pleased with my achievement. I wasn't fast yet, but good enough to avoid another shameful situation.

The project ended three weeks later, and Matt, in our last morning meeting, announced that another team wanted to hire me for a three-month project. I didn't understand the details, but I knew it was good news, so I smiled and the next day I moved to another team.

This meant that Laura and I would no longer share an office nor attend the same meetings. A few weeks later, she moved on to a highly technical position anyway.

I had a new boss and a new office I shared with the lady who was my editor. She was the person in charge of giving me the corrections to enter and checking the accuracy of my work as a formatter. It was either fate or that rumors had already spread that I was not a talkative person, but I found a silent companion in my new editor. Helen was, in fact, the true introvert of the team. She hardly ever talked to people. She felt uncomfortable in all conversations. We made the perfect introvert nonspeaking team.

Days passed and Helen became impressed with the consistent 100% accuracy of my work. Not only did that make her work much easier — as she never had to check my work anymore — but I also found many formatting mistakes she wrote on paper or missed altogether, and I just corrected whatever was needed. She realized her mistakes on multiple occasions, always thanking me while apologizing for her errors. Our conversations were limited to basic greetings and questions.

"Do you want a drink?"

"Can you correct this?"

"Here you are. I'm finished."

I could manage even more than that, but those types of interactions were all that was required to work with and share an office with Helen.

After a couple of weeks, she had a question. It was the first time she spoke a few consecutive sentences to me and I didn't understand a word of it. So, I decided to tell her the truth.

"I'm sorry. I don't speak English. Can you talk slowly with simple words?"

She froze, speechless. It was the first conversation we'd ever had. No, I never used my secret sentence that Laura had once taught me. This one was the first real sentence I had delivered after a month at Microsoft.

Then she smiled and said, "No problem."

She took the time to explain as I pulled out a dictionary and we both looked for the words. We managed to communicate, and she enjoyed it. She ended up talking more with me than any other team member. That helped boost my confidence and prompted me to try to speak, even though I made grammatical mistakes with every sentence and looked for my words all the time. I'd often insert a few French words when I didn't know the English ones to patch the holes, assuming she'd understand.

I didn't rely solely on our conversations to learn English, though. I spent every evening binge-watching movies in English, I studied new words from my dictionary, and at work I took the tutorials of every Microsoft software that I could.

Before the end of our project, I started to speak in meetings. To the great astonishment of all, I was not shy. The team finally realized I was quite an extrovert. I loved talking, I just made mistakes with every sentence. At that point, the entire team understood that I'd sat in on those early meetings without understanding or speaking any English, not a single word of anything they'd said to me. Yet the accuracy of my work had preceded me, and everybody wanted to work with me when Helen and I finished early.

I spent countless nights at Microsoft. Since I had spent weeks taking all the tutorials, I knew that Microsoft had many in-house tools that could automate a lot of our work, but we weren't using them. I started writing basic macros, small formulas to automatically correct some of the formatting. These also did complex Find and Replace tasks for frequent operations.

When I was ready to test all my macros, Helen gave me a pile of pages to correct. There were over three hundred pages, something that would have taken the average formatter a good week of work to enter, followed by three days for the editor to check and correct the work. Then it would take another day for the formatter to correct any last issues and another day for an editor to do a final check. That was ten days of work shared between two people.

The next morning when she entered the office, she found the three hundred newly printed pages neatly piled on her desk. I had done them all before 3 a.m. and went home to sleep. That morning, I arrived at work after her, and I couldn't believe her expression when I entered the office. She couldn't stop asking, "How did you do this? Seriously, how did you do it? You even corrected things I didn't mark down."

The answer was easy. We were working on the printed manuals of the next version of Word for DOS. We had access to all the Microsoft beta software, but all the formatting teams were still working under DOS. What good was it to work for one of the most advanced high-tech companies if you used the dinosaur version of their software when you had access to the newer ones in development? I just learned the ins and outs of the newer unreleased word-processing software, made the best use of all the tools and macros that were already functional, et voilà.

The word spread quickly, and two days later I was hired as a full-time employee. I was given three new guys to train and manage; lucky for me, two of them were programmers who had entered Microsoft through the small door, hoping to move on to the programming department as an inside lateral move like Laura had. I was the boss, and I knew how to operate a team.

As a Microsoft manager, I understood that I couldn't lead my team like the squealing pig had done in Basic Training. Barking out orders was not in order. The best way to lead a team was exactly the way I had done as a sergeant, guiding my Special Forces unit through tough commando training and dangerous mountain rescues. It was exactly the way I had been led by my chief warrant officer. Not by giving orders but leading by example, earning my team's respect, and inspiring them.

My work as a formatter was well over. I was now a Production Team Lead, and I intended to guide my small team of expert programmers, producing 100% accuracy but working ten times faster than any other team. We did it time after time, and together we continued to develop new tools to further speed up and improve the process of the other teams. If we hadn't been at Microsoft, we'd have put our coworkers out of a job. But Microsoft exploded with new projects all the time, and they needed to be released faster and simultaneously in multiple languages on the same release date as the English versions. As a Production Team Lead, I managed the French and German languages to be released on the same date as the English versions for WinWord, the codename of the first version of Word for Windows. It was a huge success.

I was then asked to hire on a massive scale. My team grew from three to twelve and then sixteen, twenty, and twenty-four. In less than a year and a half, I'd been promoted so many times that I was a management level above the first boss who'd hired me.

I put the same focus into my work as I had previously done in my outdoor pursuits, but I also had other motivations driving my actions. Laura came from a very successful family full of doctorates, while I had dropped out of high school. I suffered again the stigma of not being good enough. The entire family urged her to break up with the low-class loser. I felt pressured to be a success, working incredibly hard for her so her family wouldn't be ashamed of her boyfriend. Unfortunately, my focus on proving I was good enough probably killed my relationship with Laura.

I never even thought that I was making a terrible mistake.

While I spent my nights working, Laura ran off with a programmer. He was also a poet, pianist, and artist: everything I wasn't. I had lost it all.

Laura's mother was a respected professor in immunology and infectious disease and head of a prestigious hospital. Before Laura and I left her family home to drive to Seattle, her mother explained to me that her daughter was the smartest. She had received a Harvard scholarship and graduated with top honors two years early. She had won the national mathematics contest at age sixteen. She was a genius — one of the nation's prodigies that all the leading corporations would be fighting over.

Being a high-school dropout, I was nothing and would never be anything.

She further said that I had no morality. I should be ashamed to be a dead weight on her daughter's future. She offered to pay me thousands of dollars to break off the relationship and move back to France. It didn't end well.

The message was clear. I was not only a loser, I was a parasite.

It took me days while visiting the amazing national parks on our way to Seattle for this experience to stop haunting all my thoughts. I finally let the scenery seep in and lighten my mood as we trekked through the Grand Canyon, Bryce, Zion, Death Valley, Sequoia, Yosemite, and Crater Lake to finally arrive in Seattle, where I was in awe of Mount Rainier, the Cascades, and the Olympic Mountains.

But her mother's words stayed in the back of my mind. And working as a dishwasher for spoiled girls only reinforced their meaning.

When I finally had the opportunity to work at Microsoft, I had to embrace it with all my will and strength. I had to make the best of it and climb to the top. I had to show that I wasn't the loser I had once again been branded. And rising up the management ladder at Microsoft would be a statement nobody could dismiss.

For Laura's mother, however, I was still a bug she had to smash, a virus she had to eradicate. Unable to reach her daughter directly, she enlisted Laura's uncles and their spouses to work on her — anything to put an end to her relationship with the uneducated French loser. Laura never budged. At best, her mother only fortified her beliefs that I could do as much without any academic credentials as most people who were considered to be educated. (Despite the end of our relationship, I will always be grateful to Laura. She not only helped me see that I was as intelligent as I was athletic and that my failure within the school system was due only to poor guidance, but she truly believed in me and boosted my self-confidence in my intellectual abilities. She helped me recognize that cognitive challenges were the same as physical challenges: you learn, you train, and you set your own limits.)

Although the family tension weighed on us, in the end it was not her family who destroyed our relationship. No, the responsibility was entirely mine. I was the one who dove into my work like no human being ever should. I thought I'd done it for the good of our future. I was wrong.

I even abandoned most of my sports activities to focus on work. During my first two years at Microsoft, I spent at least two nights a week in my office. I took seminars every other weekend and worked almost all others. As managers, we could take as many training seminars as we wished, so I traveled at least twice a month to learn more about management, team building, presentations, and communication.

I wasn't dating Bill Gates, but from home it probably looked as if I were. I had the constant drive to improve the process and move projects forward. Days and nights, I was living and breathing Microsoft.

I didn't realize it at the time, but there was no space for any social life outside of Microsoft. There was no space left for anybody to share my life in any way. I had become a workaholic.

I couldn't blame anybody but myself, but breaking up with Laura devastated me. Luckily, my friends were there to support me during this emotionally draining period.

Microsoft offered an amazing environment of bright, highly educated, and open-minded people. Best of all, I worked in the International Department, sharing a building with a wonderful international community. We were a group made up of 30% American staff and a majority of translators, programmers, and testers from all over Europe and Latin America. When I first started, there were only eight buildings, but most hosted a restaurant, and each had its own specialty food from diverse countries. It was always a great gathering place where we enjoyed meeting. This was where I met two of my lifelong best friends.

Gilles was a Frenchman who had grown up on the island of Madagascar off the African Coast. Two years younger than me, he was a software developer working as a tester. We shared the same passion for mountain trekking and climbing. Our personalities were opposite in every possible way, yet we formed an instant bond. Gilles became my little brother, following me into the craziest of adventures without a worry.

If I was a dreamer as a child, Gilles lived in another dimension. He'd fall asleep on the back of my motorcycle going over two hundred kilometers[1] an hour when we'd go rock climbing in Eastern Washington. Most people would be terrified. No one but Gilles could fall asleep at a speed that made passing cars look like we were in a video game. He was fearless because he had already seen his death. He didn't know when and where, but he knew how. He would describe it to me in great detail. It constantly came to him in his dreams, and it wouldn't happen on my motorcycle or climbing with me.

Gilles didn't own a car. The few months he had, he'd been in a couple of accidents and received a few tickets for not stopping at traffic lights. He was always living in his own world, fearless and unaware of any possible danger.

He saw and felt things most human beings couldn't. No matter how often he described a person's aura and how, based on their colors, he knew if people were healthy or not, or stressed, or even lying, it didn't make much sense to me at first. I was the opposite, Cartesian and earth-rooted, yet

1. one hundred and twenty miles

together we seemed to be able to meet halfway and understand each other when it came to the most important things in our lives, even without speaking a word.

We each lived in an apartment and longed for a home with a garden and nonsmoking neighbors. We had already started looking. Then one day we went rock climbing at the Vertical Club next to Microsoft. There we met Jim, ten years my elder and a software architect in a high-tech medical company. He was looking for a way out of his apartment. Gilles and I had just found a huge three-story house for rent with six bedrooms, three bathrooms, two large kitchens, and a nice garden with a stream flowing through. It was in Kirkland, a short drive from Microsoft. It was perfect, and the three of us moved in as roommates, living there for years to follow.

Jim was like our American big brother. Highly educated and an avid reader, he shared a wealth of information we enjoyed learning from. We all loved the mountains and the outdoors. We trekked, skied, rock climbed, and scuba dove together. We often organized great dinners, inviting all our friends. Jim and Gilles loved to cook; not my thing, but I was great at opening oysters.

Little did I know that ten years later, Gilles's accidental death on a bicycle, exactly as he'd described it to me dozens of times, would be one of the most traumatic experiences of my life. It happened as he turned thirty, the day after I left his house in Palo Alto when we celebrated our getting together after a couple of years apart. Gilles had become more than my little brother. He had become my spiritual soul mate.

Shortly after meeting Gilles, I met Dominique, another French compatriot at Microsoft. He also shared the same passions and interests. He was very laid-back, not quite as much as Gilles but much more than me. He had perfectly mastered English and was in a great position at Microsoft.

Dominique had been one of the very first French translators at Microsoft and the first French-language manager. He moved on to become the first language terminologist, a position he created for himself. Later on, he moved to a Microsoft research position and transferred to the company's top-secret building. We're not even sure he had a real boss. Frankly, we had no idea what he did.

Anytime we would take a break to have a drink or grab a bite to eat, Dominique was there. He stood out in the crowd, dressed in his bright, colorful fluorescent clothes that used to be the fashion among French climbers ten years before. He always seemed to be at one of the company's restaurants or cafeterias, surrounded by a large crowd of women, single or married, all crazy about this wild French guy. He spoke French and English with the same eloquence and conveyed a kindness even men couldn't resist, unless their wives worked at Microsoft. He was married himself and his wife also worked on campus, and he never went further than flirting; he didn't even seem to be doing it on purpose. (As he told me when reviewing this book, he wasn't even aware of doing it — but how could you resist a French man offering you chocolate all the time?)

Dominique became my other big brother. We shared a passion for skiing, big motorcycles, and sailing. Dominique had a sailboat on which I occasionally joined him.

Gilles, Jim, and Dominique made up my family in the States. They never judged me on my differences. All three believed in my wildest dreams, and they always encouraged me to follow through. They believed in me. (Thirty years later, Jim and Dominique are still my brothers, and Gilles's photo sits above my computer, always reminding me of the amazing friendship we shared.)

When I started to find success at Microsoft, I thought a lot more about my siblings, how I had left them behind for boarding school, to join the Special Forces, then move to the USA. Olivier, Karine, and I had all been close when we were younger, but by the time I was ten I had essentially abandoned them. (When Aurelie came along, her father was still living with my mother, and she had the full attention of both parents and Karine.) We never talked about our parents or our situation: we all lived through it entirely differently and didn't know how to express any of it. I was starting to understand the guilt I had always felt but couldn't put into well-defined thoughts.

Now that Olivier, Karine, and I were older, I wanted to spend time together, and I hoped to show them a different world from that of our childhood. I wanted them to see with my eyes, and to embrace new opportunities and join me in the American Dream. I invited them both to visit, but only Karine made the trip over for a month in the summer before her last year of high school; Olivier was too busy with his optical studies and his sailing race addiction.

Karine and I had a wonderful time touring around Seattle, trekking on the Pacific Crest Trail, and visiting every national park in the region, including a big stretch of Vancouver Island. Of course, she also got to see the inner workings of the entire Microsoft campus, where we shared a few lunches. But we had to face the reality of the rift that existed between an eighteen-year-old girl who had never left her hometown before and a twenty-four-year-old ex-commando who led a team of engineers as an expatriate in a foreign country, culture, and language. Our perspectives on the most important matters of life were too different; she wasn't ready to understand, and frankly I wasn't either. I was unable to see the world through her eyes.

Upon her return to France, she started dating her long-time childhood friend. And big brother was clearly no match for the young man who would soon become her husband and the father of her children. I never got to tell her that I had hoped she'd come live with me in Seattle to study at the University of Washington. Instead, she stayed home, attending medical school to become a nurse. We each got busy moving forward with our opposite lifestyles. At the time, there was no email, no mobile phones, and long-distance calls were forbiddingly expensive. I felt an emptiness but didn't know how to reach out to her.

I continued to live with a deep guilt. The guilt of having abandoned my sister, my ray of sunshine at home. The guilt of being the cause of my mother's misery, an emotion deeply anchored in me that even logical thinking couldn't overcome. I also continued to feel the years of being unworthy in my father's eyes. No amount of success could erase these wounds.

Even after my two years in the Special Forces, even after landing a job at Microsoft, a part of me still felt that I would never be good enough.

My boss, friends, and coworkers often praised me for all that I had achieved in a few short years, yet I often felt torn. I thought I could do anything, even the most impossible things, but in the back of my mind I always harbored this fear of failure. A duality of overconfidence and total lack thereof made me feel that no matter what I achieved, I still wasn't good enough. It was probably one of the reasons I needed to vocally claim all my victories and accomplishments and could never be like the humble heroes I had most admired.

Yet, both my parents and grandparents were truly impressed when I finally found a stable job at Microsoft. I had succeeded far beyond what they would have ever imagined for me. My grandfather couldn't stop talking about it with great pride. Every time Microsoft was in the news in France, he would cut paper clippings and place them with my photos in the family album.

A few months after starting work, I took a one-year evening course in sport and massage therapy, graduating with a license from Washington State. It wasn't because I wanted to work in that field though; I simply had a thirst for learning. As an athlete, I was interested in better understanding the human body, particularly the muscle system, and in traditional healing techniques. That year-long training gave me that knowledge.

But once my year of school was over, I had to find new things to learn.

After a year and half, I'd taken almost every seminar that caught my interest, so I started to look outside of Microsoft to continue learning.

Chapter 46

Discovering the World of Jacques Cousteau

"I swam across the rocks and compared myself favorably with the sars (bream fish). To swim fishlike, horizontally, was the logical method in a medium eight hundred times denser than air. To halt and hang attached to nothing, no lines or air pipe to the surface, was a dream. At night I had often had visions of flying by extending my arms as wings. Now I flew without wings."

— Jacques Cousteau, *The Silent World*, 1953

While working at Microsoft, for the first time in my life I was making a steady income that allowed me to do things I could have never done until then. I filled my free time with small adventures. I didn't even wait to be hired full-time before pursuing my interests. In my first four months as a temp, the very first thing I did to follow in the steps of Jacques Cousteau was to take a PADI scuba diving class. I did consecutive classes to take my Open Water and Advanced certificates. I was planning my very first holiday, diving in one of the world's most fascinating natural aquariums: the Red Sea of Egypt. I had seen it in a Cousteau documentary.

The environment was different, though. In Seattle, after all the academic classes and the heated pool training, we learned to dive in Puget Sound. The water there was so cold that even with a thick wetsuit, we couldn't stay submerged very long. Hypothermia was a real danger. We also used thick neoprene hoods, gloves, and booties. All this neoprene was very buoyant, and to dive, we had to weight ourselves with lead-weight belts. That was a lot of heavy gear to carry on the beach until the water entry point.

Practicing in the pool was nice, but it was nothing compared to the feeling of slowly gliding deeper and deeper into the ocean. Even though the visibility was very poor, we saw fish, starfish, and often octopi. I enjoyed playing with octopi. Puget Sound is home to some of the world's largest species. Once, I played with a large octopus that wrapped itself around my mask. The instructor told us if that ever happened, we shouldn't try to remove it. I stayed calm, observing it up close as the suction cups of the tentacles covered parts of my field of vision. I waited a couple of minutes until the octopus got bored and swam away, nonchalant. It was an amazing interaction. I remembered all the Cousteau documentaries, and there I was, underwater, living similar experiences.

After graduating, I flew to Egypt for a two-week holiday. My first highlight there was climbing on top of the Great Pyramid of Giza to watch the sun set over the desert: a forbidden practice that was legalized with a five-dollar bill. I crossed the desert to visit the world's wonder of Abu-Simbel. But my greatest highlight was diving the Red Sea.

Cousteau mentioned it as one of the world's best diving sites, and it did not disappoint. I dove for three days in Dahab, before there were any dive centers there. There was only a Syrian dive master who took two divers at a time on a small fishing boat.

Diving in water with over thirty meters[1] of visibility, I discovered an incredible world where thousands of colored fish swarmed around us. Moray eels were everywhere. Even small sharks came to say hello. It was like being in a giant aquarium. I was finally discovering a world that had fascinated me since my youngest childhood years.

I continued my diving on the other side of the Egyptian peninsula from the town of Sharm El Sheikh. That was the most famous Red Sea dive site that Jacques Cousteau filmed. On board the ship, the dive master

1. one hundred feet

warned us that sometimes large Napoleon wrasse would follow divers because they were used to being fed. Our dive master took boiled eggs for that purpose. Halfway through my first dive, I didn't see any and completely forgot about them because there were so many other things to observe. When the dive master's tank was half-depleted, he turned around and signaled for me to do the same.

When I turned, I freaked out, almost screaming underwater. The giant head of a Napoleon wrasse was less than thirty centimeters[2] from mine. That green fish was very impressive. Three of them had followed us, hoping to be fed. They had a giant toothless jaw. They were very peaceful. The dive master handed me an egg, which I fed to the wrasse closest to me. It swallowed my entire hand and half of my arm almost without touching me. I removed my hand and tried to pet the fish, but it moved enough to be out of reach by less than five centimeters. It was a magical experience.

Another day, a film crew was on board to film a deep canyon. They invited me to follow them. Coral and giant gorgonian covered all the canyon walls as I slowly glided down, deeper and deeper, into a magical 3D ocean world beaming with so much colorful sea life it overwhelmed my senses. I plunged into the abyss in pursuit of the dive master, who was following the film crew. It was, and would be, the most spectacular dive I'd ever do in my entire life. I had the feeling we'd descended for a long time, yet the visibility was amazing.

As I followed the dive master, I didn't worry much about the depth. At one time, I looked at my gauge and thought something was wrong. It marked forty meters,[3] but I could see the film crew so far down below that they appeared quite tiny. I thought my gauge wasn't working properly, and I kept descending, but the gauge kept going down. When it marked fifty meters, I stopped and looked up. I couldn't see the surface, with the colorful golden, orange, and red coral wall and all the giant purple gorgonian dancing with the water flow. It was an impressive sight. But I was

2. twelve inches
3. one hundred and thirty feet

certain that I had gone down much deeper than the twenty meters I was qualified for with my advanced certification.

I stopped, and the dive master turned around and came up to my level. I showed him my depth gauge, and he showed me the sign OK. It wasn't okay. I gave him the Up sign. I had never dived at that depth and knew that I couldn't stay down there without risking the very serious effects of the bends. The dive master and I slowly came back up.

The film crew went down to eighty meters. They took forever to return to the boat as they had to stop at a ten-meter depth where they'd left extra tanks to safely resurface while avoiding all decompression sickness problems.

Diving, I floated amid an entirely new ecosystem filled with creatures and vegetation that seemed to beckon me in. The responsibilities and worries of my life couldn't penetrate the gleaming waters, offering me a weightlessness in both body and spirit. This was even more true in warm water, where we only needed thin neoprene shorties (no legs, no hoods, no gloves) and thus much lighter weight belts.

Diving the Red Sea was the realization of my very first childhood dream. I had gone a long way from trying to hold my breath in the bathtub after watching Cousteau's films when I was four years old to diving one of the world's best sites. The Cousteau team had beautifully captured it on film, but living it was an incredible adventure.

I was so excited about my Red Sea diving trip, I wanted to continue to learn. As soon as I returned to Seattle, I enlisted in a new class to take my Rescue Diver certification. But after the Red Sea, I found diving in Puget Sound to be not only freezing but also not as exciting. After a few months, I eventually stopped diving to focus my free time on learning other things, like communication and management with Microsoft seminars and massage therapy. I also realized yet another dream of mine I had once thought impossible to pursue.

Chapter 47

Flying Like Saint-Exupéry

"One of the miracles of the airplane is that it plunges a man directly into the heart of mystery."

— Antoine de Saint-Exupéry, *Wind, Sand and Stars*, 1939

In the spring of 1992, Gilles had started to take flying lessons. Being a pilot was one of my childhood dreams since reading Saint-Exupéry's *Wind, Sand and Stars*. But as a kid I'd always been told that I couldn't fly because of my lazy eye and strabismus. My mom had also said that I would need to be a genius in physics to be a pilot. Physics was one of the subjects I'd hated in school and never felt that I would ever need in my life.

Gilles convinced me that physics was the easy part, and that he could help me with it. He also told me that perfect vision was only required for a commercial license, but pilots could fly recreationally even if they wore glasses with a strong correction.

He said for him, the toughest part was the actual flying, but considering my addiction for speed and adrenaline, and the way I drove my car and my motorcycle, it'd be a piece of cake for me.

Speed was, for me, another escape, an outlet for my life. It gave me a sense of freedom. As soon as I had my driver's license, I raced my cheap car in the French mountains. I couldn't take a switchback without skidding most of the turns. There was only one way I could go between points A and B: full throttle. Speed was a vehicle to transport me into another dimension.

As soon as I started to work for Microsoft, I bought a used fast-racing motorcycle. I couldn't bear being stuck in traffic. Speed was an addiction. The rest of the world ceased to exist. It was only me and my motorcycle racing at over a hundred and twenty miles an hour: brief moments of intense living that could end in seconds. I never felt more alive and free than when I moved at full speed.

I didn't want to just fly airplanes, I wanted to throw them into spins. I wanted to dive down and full throttle back up seconds before crashing. I had dreamed of that for years. Yes, Gilles was right. I didn't think that the pilotage would be a problem.

Once he told me I could do it with my eye problem and that he would help me with the theory, I immediately booked an appointment at his school for a test flight.

On my first flight, I had the plane under control within minutes. After a couple of demonstrations, my instructor let me take off and land on the first lesson. I was hooked. I signed up and speed-raced my motorcycle from Microsoft to Boeing Field every evening. Against all odds, I beat the record for the fastest training ever done in Boeing Field.

On July 27, 1992, I became a licensed VFR pilot within three weeks, with the lowest number of flying hours that FlyTech had ever presented a student to their final exam. Gilles, who had gathered as much flying time over the past two months, had yet to fly solo. He was still having trouble keeping the aircraft perfectly leveled on a straight line. The theory, after all, wasn't that difficult. Bernoulli's principle and its effect on aircraft wings was logical, as was everything else. The most challenging thing was the radio communication, but that was fun too. After being a certified pilot, I continued my training with classes in acrobatics, and I loved it.

All my friends wanted to experience flying. Every week, three of my friends shared the expenses of the plane rental for a few hours. I'd fly us next to the majestic snow-covered Mount Rainier volcano. We then followed the North Cascades range while the sun set over the mountains in a burst of crimson and ombre flames. We looked at the Olympic Mountains standing high on the other side. At nightfall, we would fly to San Juan Island, where we would land to have dinner and gorge ourselves on decadent seafood. In the middle of the night, we would fly back over the water to enjoy the spectacular view of Seattle, with its grand towers and Space Needle illuminated, before landing on the Boeing Field. It was a blast.

I had finally accomplished another one of my childhood dreams: I was a pilot. I could never fly commercially, but I could fly recreationally, and I thoroughly enjoyed it. I especially loved flying in Washington State. Between snow-covered mountains, oceans, lakes, islands, and this superbly illuminated city, Seattle was one of the world's best places to fly a small plane. As I soared over islands and this spectacular coastline, the giant water mass below didn't look that cold from six thousand feet. It was calling me.

Chapter 48

The Spell of the Sea

"The sea, once it casts its spell, holds one in its net of wonder forever."
— Jacques Cousteau, *Life and Death in a Coral Sea*, 1971

After getting my pilot's license and running out of Microsoft learning seminars after more than three years, I was researching jungle and tropical destinations. The diving bug had returned. But I decided that if I resumed diving, I would do it fully by not only taking my dive master certificate but aiming directly for my instructor rating. It was the beginning of winter, and I looked at the PADI dive centers offering an instructor course I could attend not too far from me. Most of them had just finished, and the only one that worked in terms of distance and time was one in Vancouver, BC. It was scheduled for early January, and I decided to register.

There was only one problem. The cold winter temperatures made open-water diving more challenging, and I had not been diving in three years. To take it, I first needed to graduate as a dive master. Doing so was not just a matter of finishing a class. There was a lot of theory to learn, but it also required assisting an instructor in teaching classes, both in the pool and in open water. Because it was winter, some dive shops didn't have enough regular classes scheduled.

I called the largest dive centers around Seattle. They all had the same answer: it took six months to train as a dive master. "Sorry, we can't train you in less than three, that's impossible."

I went through the entire phonebook, calling every single dive shop in the entire region. And I'd always get similar answers. One person told me that it might be possible in four months during summer, but that wouldn't get me to Vancouver in time. Desperate, I called the very last number on my phone list. I knew what the reply was going to be, but I called anyway.

The owner of the dive shop, an older lady, didn't seem to know much about diving lessons. She took my number and said she'd have the dive instructor contact me. That was the end of it. I didn't even expect a call back.

Three hours later, I received a phone call from a man with a very enthusiastic voice. The instructor introduced himself as Percy. I explained that I had my rescue certification, and I wanted to take my dive master classes, but I needed to accomplish them in less than three months to take my instructor rating in Vancouver. He listened attentively and didn't answer right away. I knew it. I'd heard it more than two dozen times in the past two days. It was impossible.

Percy replied, "It's a tight schedule, and it will require a lot of work. When can you start?"

Still unsure that he had actually agreed, I replied, "Now." It was 10 p.m. on a weekday. Percy had just finished teaching a class.

He said, "Come on over. I'm at the dive shop."

I jumped on my motorcycle, and fifteen minutes later, I knocked on the closed dive shop. Percy opened the door, saw my motorcycle, and said, "Oh, you're a motorcyclist too. Hey, come in, nice to meet you."

The smile on his face said it all. Percy and I became instant and very close friends (a friendship that still lasts thirty years later). We talked through half the night. We laid out my training program. Between the private lessons I would do with him and his scheduled classes, I was going to assist him in the pool and in open water.

We also shared all our life experiences. I was a VFR pilot, and Percy was taking flying lessons. We had both been in the army. We loved riding our motorcycles at high speeds. We loved the outdoors. We had a lot in common.

Percy also had unique life experiences, from the Vietnam War, to working as a private eye, to diving commercially in Alaska. We had so many stories to share.

At the end of the night he said, "When I mentioned it was not impossible on the phone, I hesitated and almost told you no. The truth is that after we hung up, I thought I'd made a mistake because it's probably impossible to master the skills you need in that timeframe. And in addition, you haven't done any diving in three years. But after meeting you, I'm confident we'll succeed."

I was not only amazed at his belief in me, but that he took it as a personal challenge to ensure that I would succeed. It would be a success we shared. That boosted my confidence.

Percy ended up being the best instructor I'd ever had in any field. A genuine nice guy, all the students loved him. His explanations were always very clear. His navy background showed how well-organized and methodical he was, and we shared one more thing in common: the word *impossible* was not in our vocabulary.

I went to train and work with Percy every evening. Winter was so cold that one night, when I arrived home after being in the pool, my long, wet hair had frozen. It was solid and as horizontal as a flag. I only realized it after removing my helmet, feeling something heavy pulling my hair. I touched it and felt the ice. I went to the bathroom to melt it with a hot shower.

I graduated as a dive master in eight weeks, with plenty of time to attend the Instructor Training camp in Vancouver.

Shortly after the New Year, I drove to Vancouver for the training program. Percy had taught me well. I gave perfect demonstrations of all the techniques in the pool.

As part of the instructor exam, we had an eight-hundred-meter[1] timed swim we had to do with a mask, a snorkel, and fins. During the training, the dive director wanted to ensure that we'd all be able to do the timed swim. He placed us two by two, covering the eight-hundred-meter distance.

When I finished my swim more than two laps ahead of my fellow trainee, the director nicknamed me The Shark. Apparently, I had broken the Canadian national record of any Dive Instructor Development Course. The director went on to say that I left a huge and impressive wake behind me.

The day before the final exam, we had a last practice in the pool.

Since I'd moved to the States, I had grown my hair long. In four years, it almost reached my butt, stopping somewhere on my lower back. I had also grown a full beard, a sharp contrast to my commando look.

During the last pool practice, I started the demonstration of removing all the diving gear underwater and putting it back on. I hadn't tied my hair well, and when I removed my BCD (buoyancy control device) to teach the technique, my hair got tangled in it. Being stuck with my head pulled back, I turned my head to try to untangle myself. At that time, my mouthpiece came apart from the breathing apparatus. I was still holding the mouthpiece between my teeth, exhaling air while looking back at my hair. I didn't notice that I was blowing bubbles in the pool. The twelve other apprentice instructors around me were laughing silently underwater.

Luckily for me, one of them wasn't just laughing. He understood that I hadn't realized what had happened, and once I breathed in, I would swallow a lot of water and choke. And that's exactly what I did. But instead of having to dash up to the surface for air, which presented no danger in a pool but was the worst thing to do in a real diving situation, I only had to grab the secondary stage regulator that my friend held in front of my mouth. I only swallowed a small sip of bleached water, coughed it through the mouthpiece before clearing it, and then resumed breathing. After un-

1. half-a-mile

tangling my hair, I switched from my friend's regulator to my secondary regulator and restarted my full demonstration.

Back on the surface, and thanks to my savior, the dive director congratulated the both of us for an excellent demonstration on how to manage an unexpected situation. Everybody had a good laugh.

The next day, having tied my hair well, I became a PADI-certified scuba diving instructor.

I stayed at the dive center another week, taking advantage of a full class teaching us many dive specialties that we could in turn teach to students. This included cave and wreck diving, underwater navigation, underwater photography, boat diving, deep water diving, night diving, equipment specialist, and underwater naturalist.

Back to work at Microsoft in Seattle, I didn't want to stop with the specialties I had learned in Canada. I had acquired knowledge in many others, but one of the most intriguing types of diving I had never experienced was ice diving. It was nothing we could learn just anywhere, and that was one specialty I was keen to sink my teeth into.

Percy was not only one of the very few PADI instructors licensed to teach it, he was by far the very best. His commercial job in Alaska involved diving in frozen waters with outside temperatures that would sometimes go below -45 degrees Celsius.[2] He had to dive in visibility so poor that he could not even see his own hands. He wore a heavy-duty diving suit and sealed waterproof gloves that were so thick he couldn't possibly feel anything with his hands. Blind, he had to understand how the machine he had to retrieve was positioned at the bottom of the water. He had to find the places where he could safely tie cables to pull it out. Sometimes he would stay hours underwater in those conditions while machines constantly broke the ice at the surface so he could come back up. Percy was called all over Alaska to salvage million-dollar machines in the most unimaginably dangerous diving conditions.

2. -49 degrees Fahrenheit

Teaching ice diving from the safety of a frozen mountain lake was a walk in the park for him. But as always, his attention to every detail ensured everybody's safety. I was delighted to learn from the best.

As a dive instructor, I enjoyed introducing people to the experience of diving under the ice of mountain lakes and swimming with playful sea lions in Puget Sound. Teaching diving on evenings and weekends was like sharing my passion for sports, adventures, and the sea. It was about inspiring people as I had been inspired by Jacques Cousteau.

Cave, wreck, and ice diving, as well as playing with sea life, also reminded me of all the summers I had spent with Uncle Philippe — my mentor for all things nature, my guide to unique spelunking adventures. And I remembered that before becoming an alcoholic, Uncle Philippe was my Indiana Jones–like role model. He offered me precious months during which I could reignite all my passions about adventure and life. Teaching diving, I was also giving a little bit of this back, by introducing people to new adventures and helping them discover a fascinating underwater world.

While teaching more specialties every week, I reached the highest level of instructor, becoming a Master Scuba Diver Trainer, and continued to dive with Percy when time allowed.

In the USA I did well, managing to fit my dreams within the confines of a job that took more time than any job should take. But work drove my life. I had reduced my childhood dreams to mini-dreams, one by one, over weekends and holidays. I was happy but not whole. I had become a holiday adventurer, living the Tarzan and Cousteau experience as if they were weekend seminars. A few ephemeral moments of real life before returning to a normal working life, like a drug addict reaching for a high, rushing to escape reality before descending again. I wanted a different reality.

Imagination is the source of all adventures, be they real or fiction. It was time for my fictional world to become reality. A permanent reality.

I didn't want my life to be an occasional adventure. I wanted adventure to be my life.

Chapter 49

The American Dream

"Every man's life ends the same way. It is only the details of how he lived and how he died that distinguish one man from another."
— Ernest Hemingway

For my first few years at Microsoft, I worked in the International Department. At that time, only people working in the Domestic Department were eligible to receive stock options. Eventually Microsoft reunified and I suddenly became eligible. It changed everything.

Until then, I'd made a good living but always saw it as temporary. One day I would quit Microsoft to follow my dreams. I'd stay as long as the situation afforded me learning potential: first with all the Microsoft seminars, then with the recreational courses I took.

Life was good. Too good. I could do everything I wanted and only lacked time. At first, I worked an average of eighty hours a week and slept in my office at least two nights per week. I've always been extreme in everything I do, and I had become a workaholic.

Being a workaholic was, in some ways, a continuation of cultivating my ego. I had slowly learned that it wasn't always a good thing to try to be the best. A better approach to measuring my own success meant being the best I could be, regardless of how I compared my performance to others. I found it a much healthier way of life.

I had stopped competing in sports due to lack of time, and even though I wasn't competing with anybody at work, I was competing with myself in everything I pursued. And I still enjoyed the praise people gave me when I accomplished the unaccomplishable in record time. This constant drive to be the best I could be sometimes put pressure on people around me. *Zealous*, *driven*, *intense*, or, more often, *crazy* are just a few of the words my friends used to describe me over the years.

I understood, back in the Special Forces with Skinny, that I wouldn't kill my ego overnight simply because I realized I had a big one. I had made slow progress in not allowing it to run my life. Yet, I wondered how I could keep the drive I had in sports and life, and the will to achieve all my goals, without telling everyone about my accomplishments. I wasn't born with the humility of my chief warrant officer.

People always asked me how I managed to do or even attempt everything I did. My favorite answer was "It's all in the head." Yes, I truly believe that physical or technical abilities can be improved. Often, they aren't the limitations; the mind is. The only limits are the ones we set for ourselves.

As I mentioned, this mindset often earned me the label of *crazy*. Yet, *crazy* was the best compliment my friends could give me. It would take a lifetime of effort to soften my ego. What I considered an undeniable strength when it came to achieving goals also became my biggest weakness, a double-edged sword. I was a workaholic, a learning addict, and constantly driven to achieve success and recognition in everything I did.

My work ethic and accolades within Microsoft had propelled me up the management ladder, and my performance reviews were always excellent: two important factors in determining a candidate for stock options.

In the summer of 1991, I received my first set of Microsoft stock options. I'd heard a lot about them before becoming eligible to receive some, but I didn't quite understand how this was so magical. They gave you a certain amount of stock options worth *x* number of dollars, but you only received those stocks once they were vested (became exercisable). And when vesting them, you still had to pay for the value at which they were first offered to you. It took four and a half years to fully vest the stocks received, and it was done incrementally every six months. The first increment of 25% started after a year and a half of employment from the day you received them, followed by 12.5% increments every six months.

That meant if I quit Microsoft the day after I received the grant of stock options, I would quit with nothing. If I quit after a year and a half, I would only vest and thus receive 25% of the first set of stocks. I had to stay more than four years in the company from the day I received options to vest these stocks.

The amount I first received didn't seem like much. A potential bonus I couldn't touch as it remained virtual until vested. Six months later, I still had not vested any of them, but it was the bull market period and the stock value had significantly increased. At the same time, I received a second — even more important — lot of stock options that would take another four and a half years to fully vest from this new date. A year later, the value of the stocks had again increased by more than 50%, and I received a third and even larger value of stocks. I still had to wait six months to vest the first 25% of the first lot I received, which had already more than doubled in value.

I thought back to how my father used to talk about how much money he'd made or lost on any given day in the stock market. Living in the States and working at Microsoft, I came to the understanding that although my dad had been a successful businessman and had done very well in France, his wealth level couldn't be compared to those of many Americans. In France, my father had risen toward the top of the middle class, but he wasn't rich according to American standards.

I didn't have to be a calculus genius to understand that if I kept receiving a larger amount of stock options every few months, and that even if the Microsoft stock value only increased by half of what it had in the past year, I'd be a millionaire in less than twenty years. Wow! That was unreal.

Despite the tight deadlines and constant pressure, Bill Gates made it easy for us to have a good life within the company. All the benefits and the promises of a high return on vested stocks for those willing to spend years at Microsoft made it a painfully tough decision for many to even think about looking somewhere else. In essence, Microsoft owned us.

In the winter of 1993, two months before the first increment of 25% stocks would vest, I had a very important decision to make. It wasn't an astronomical amount of money yet, but with the tremendous value increase of the stocks, that first small share had already become a nice bonus. At the same time, my work review had been excellent, and I was bound to receive a fourth lot of stock options.

A quick count of all the stocks I had received to date, but not vested, at the current value of the stock already garnered me enough value to purchase a house. Of course, I'd have to wait another four and a half years to vest that money. And in those years, it was almost certain that I'd continue to receive stock options, and the stock value would continue increasing. Microsoft was quickly becoming the world's richest company.

That was when I fully understood the meaning of a phrase that folks at Microsoft always talked about: "the golden handcuffs." A few thousand developers and managers who preceded me by a handful of years had already become millionaires thanks to the Microsoft stock options.

Bill was a real genius. Even more than his programming skills, he was a corporate genius with a vision, and an amazing marketing and business leader. And the stock options allowed Microsoft to pay fairly low salaries while compensating the best employees with the potential of high returns on stock options at nearly no cost to the company. This further fueled the demand on Microsoft stocks and helped rocket its price up. Microsoft made even more money from its stocks than it did from its products. Innovation not only happened on the software side, it happened in and all around the Microsoft campus, turning the grounds of Redmond into what we later called Microsoft Town, an almost utopian community where all the daily things you could dream of doing were at your disposal for free or at a very discounted price. For workaholics, life at Microsoft was easy.

Over the past year, I had reduced my working schedule to a more reasonable sixty hours per week and only slept in my office once a week. I usually took my full weekends off campus and had the time to enjoy life with my friends.

With the money I would vest in two months, I could quit Microsoft and travel for a year. But I was currently living the American Dream. I could always travel in another few years. Now was not the time. I could just go with the flow, work a few more years at Microsoft, and have all the money I needed to do whatever I wanted later. Quitting was inconceivable; I had been "handcuffed" with stock options.

Up to that point, I'd often wondered how different my life would have been if, at any time, I had chosen another road. I had always turned my back on the path of least resistance, looking for adventure, but the easy path had never been as appealing as my current situation. Yet, here I was again at a crossroads, where I realized that my decision to stay or leave Microsoft would take my life in an opposite direction.

What should I do?

I imagined my life traveling the world. That first vesting of options was just the right amount of money to live a full year of real adventures. The cost was tremendous, though, as I would forfeit all my current unvested portfolio options, all the future ones I'd receive, the best job I had ever had, and the promise of becoming a millionaire. I would never land another job in a position similar to what I built for myself at Microsoft. At best, even if I could find an upper management position in a big American corporation, it would not come with any of the stock options I had already received but not vested.

I would be trading a guaranteed good life for a year of adventure and the certainty that I'd be back working at a lower wage for another company for the rest of my life.

A year of adventure against an early rich retirement.

Then I imagined my life if I stayed at Microsoft for another twenty years. I had already exploited all the learning opportunities the company could offer me, and I saw that as a drawback. My job was still interesting, but it had begun to lose some of its original appeal.

One of the great benefits of working at Microsoft was that the rapid improvement of technology dictated the pace of our work. It required constant changes, and dull moments were nonexistent. After ten more years, I would probably still like my job, but it would certainly transform into just a job, albeit a well-paying one.

I would probably be able to reduce my current twelve-hour days to nine hours and enjoy most of my weekends. Budget would never be an issue when it came to all the mini-adventure holidays I would want to take around the world. My salary would allow me to buy a beautiful house on Lake Washington with a view of Mount Rainier. I could trade my old motorcycle for a fancy sports car. I could even buy a small four-seater plane.

I would be set for life, but the years would fly by more rapidly than I would realize. Would I be happier? After twenty years, I might be too old and out of shape to consider risking my life on a major expedition. Life would be as good as it could be. Life would be so good that even my dad would be impressed and envious.

I would have lived the American Dream for most of my life and been ready to retire early, maybe even richer than my father. But what would I do with my retirement? Maybe Microsoft or the corporate life would have killed my drive for adventure. Maybe I would have killed it myself. A part of me might feel hollow. I'd have all this money, but neither the energy nor the will to do much with it.

Twenty years down the road, somewhere in the back of my mind, I feared I would often be thinking…

What if…?

If I chose to quit Microsoft in two months when I vested the first 25% of my stock options, turning my back on the best opportunity, I wouldn't be set for life, that was for sure. I would be a fool and lose the respect of my family.

But I realized this American Dream had never been mine. Sure, I would live mini-dreams, but I would never feel the freedom of an explorer. A two-week holiday with a bush guide on some ecotours would never offer me the thrill I could have as an adventurer, nor the real human encounters.

I realized that I had escaped from a small world in France to find refuge in another small world in the USA — a much more luxurious world, but a small world nevertheless.

I knew I had to decide quickly. In two months, I would vest enough money to take that one year off, but the longer I stayed after that, the bigger the golden handcuffs would become, with exponential returns added every six months. And like many of my friends, I might never be able to quit Microsoft. Weighing the pros and cons of both lives still wasn't enough for me to clearly choose. To gain more perspective, I dove into my memory, reflecting on my past, trying to understand who I really was.

In 1988, I would have been considered an unemployable loser in most societies. I arrived in the States with less than two hundred dollars, zero understanding of the English language, and having never touched a computer. And I held no degree. I was a high-school dropout with no work experience.

Yet, in less than two years, before turning twenty-four, I had become an international program manager, heading a team of a few dozen computer engineers for one of the world's greatest and most prestigious companies. Over almost four years, I also took a series of courses and earned a license in massage therapy, a private pilot's license, and the highest level of scuba diving instructor license. I had made it. I was no longer a loser. I could stay at Microsoft in a lifelong career filled with security, and I was set to retire wealthy at a young age.

The path of least resistance was obvious — I needed to stay quiet and continue down my road of security.

No question.

It was the right thing to do…

For most people.

Which was why, at the age of twenty-six — fully aware of what I was giving up — in the early spring of 1993, I resigned from my Microsoft career to follow my childhood dreams.

Chapter 50

I, Tarzan

"Owning our story can be hard but not nearly as difficult as spending our lives running from it. Embracing our vulnerabilities is risky but not nearly as dangerous as giving up on love and belonging and joy — the experiences that make us the most vulnerable. Only when we are brave enough to explore the darkness will we discover the infinite power of our light."

— Brené Brown, *The Gifts of Imperfection*, 2010

So, I left. And I left without the fortune I could have made. But I had enough savings to do what I had always dreamed of doing (for a year, at least): explore the Himalayas and far-flung jungles, meeting and learning from Indigenous tribes.

At barely twenty-six, I knew I was in my prime. I didn't want to lose my health, fitness, passion, and drive for adventuring. It was time for me to live my dreams. The world was calling me.

When I told my family I was quitting Microsoft, in their minds I had suddenly fallen lower than I'd ever been before. It was as if I'd committed suicide. I had become an instant failure.

I had failed to set myself up financially when I had the world's best opportunity. No matter my small previous accomplishments, to my father I would forever be a disappointment. All my adventurous dreams were frivolous and would never generate financial success. I would never be able to redeem myself in his eyes.

First a high-school dropout, then a Mountain Commando dropout, I had now become a Microsoft dropout.

In France and in my early months in the USA, most people had judged me based on their preconceived ideas that a diploma was the key to success and that you had to follow the path you'd been told to, without ever trying to realize your own. I understood that these people not only looked down at those whom they judged, but they also minimized themselves and their potential, limiting their own lives in the process.

Life isn't about diplomas and certificates, even if that's what society wants us to believe. These are just small steps that may help individuals in moving forward. Sadly, most people hide behind their diplomas, restricting their own lives to that little cocoon of comfort they've built with their studies, even though it may be light-years away from the real life they've dreamed of living.

All my life, I'd been torn between following my dreams, regardless of what others thought of me, and yet hoping to impress my parents, desperate to receive their recognition and respect. Compromising was achieving neither.

I still can't help but think that with my parents' support I may have had a shot at being an Olympic athlete. When I first moved to the USA, the very first time I went on a rowing machine, I nearly broke the indoor rowing world record. Later, in Japan, within two weeks of learning the basic techniques of cross-country skiing, I placed eleventh in the Sapporo International Ski Marathon in a field of twenty-five hundred skiers.

That same year, after less than three months of cycling, being entirely new to the sport, I won the UCI Asia Road Race Prologue, becoming Japan's amateur national champion and placing third among all the pro teams, even without the proper equipment. No profiled helmet. No aerowheels. No time-trial bike. Just a regular road bike with clip-on aerobars, a standard helmet, and cheap wheels.

With a Sport-Étude, I could have competed at the highest level in rowing, become a track pursuit cyclist, an elite cross-country skier, or even a biathlon champion — all Olympic disciplines. I had the physical abilities, mental edge, and determination for it. I discovered all these sports too late, after I was too old, and I had been resenting my parents for years for their lack of recognition and support.

Both my mother and father are still alive today and may read this memoir in denial, not understanding that they may not have been the supportive parents I had wished for. And maybe they'll also think that they've always been proud of my achievements. If so, that's something they were unable to express to me in any way, which affected me my entire life.

Maybe they didn't think my goals and dreams were realistic, believing they gave me all they could, even though I feel they weren't ready to be parents. Not when I was a kid. Not when I was a teenager. And not when I was a young adult quitting Microsoft.

I could never forget how my parents' behavior affected me, but I slowly understood that I had to try to forgive them, to let things go. Not for them but for me, to be at peace with myself. I couldn't forgive myself until I tried to forgive them — a process that would take years, a lifetime actually. But I had to take that first step into blinding my world from their judgment. I couldn't spend my entire life trying to please my family.

I finally realized that I would probably continue to disappoint them, which still deeply troubled me. I still longed for their recognition, but I understood that our ways of thinking were too different. Their preconceived, encapsulated little world couldn't be more distant from my world, where dreams were a reality without boundaries, a reality we could choose to embrace with all our strength. The day we stop dreaming is the day we stop living. Dreams aren't fantasies to keep in the back of our mind, they are life goals to be pursued. Regardless of the outcome, each step we take toward following our dreams is a full day of life.

I've mentioned before that love wasn't something any of us shared easily. To this day, I have never, not a single time since my childhood, been able to tell my parents that I love them. Not any more than they have ever been able to tell me that they love me. But I always loved them, and I still do, more than they will ever know. I finally understood that love didn't always need to be verbalized. People love in different ways, and I came to realize that my parents loved me in their own way.

I also realized that maybe if they had given me the love and support I craved so much as a child, if they had not tried to prevent me from accomplishing my dreams, and if my life as a kid had been easier...

- Maybe I wouldn't have had the drive to succeed.
- Maybe I wouldn't have joined the Special Forces.
- Maybe I wouldn't have left my native country to live in the USA and work at Microsoft.
- Maybe I wouldn't have realized any of my dreams.

After all, maybe I owed them that much.

We can't choose our parents or our childhood, but we can choose to stop living life in the past. We can choose who we want to be, who are friends are, what our life will be. The future is for us to grab, and it's up to each of us to make it what we want it to be.

I had a choice. I could live the life my family wanted me to live. Or I could live *my* life.

My childhood dream of being an adventurer wouldn't be just a dream. It would be my reality.

Before turning twenty, during mountain rescues, I learned that life was the most precious gift. Yet many people go through it without ever truly living. So instead of taking out a loan and buying a house like most of my friends, I decided to spend my small savings to venture into a world of far-flung places and great adventures. It may be difficult for people to even conceive of leaving a safe and comfortable nest, but it is what adventurers do. Following a dream requires imagination, drive, and perseverance. It took a huge leap of faith for me to leave all the security behind and embrace who I truly was.

I was that boy who grew up reading all the tales of the world's greatest adventurers. I was that boy freediving with sea lions in my bathtub and swinging as Tarzan from the trees in my backyard. The boy who studied maps of Africa and the Himalayas, planning amazing explorations.

Life isn't a straight path from A to B. It's a complex maze with multiple doors, each one taking us in an entirely different direction. Some doors may be wide open, others may be closed or even locked, but we choose the doors we go through, and they will determine the path of our lives.

Friends tell me that I'm lucky because I've always lived a full life. Because I had many opportunities. Because I lived my dreams. A few even tell me they never had a choice or opportunities.

Nothing ever comes easy. Some choices may require more effort or sacrifice than most people are willing to give or can even comprehend. Sometimes opportunities don't exist; we have to create them. But we always have a choice. This is the Maze of Life. This is our life, and it's never set in stone.

The adventure begins as soon as we start dreaming it.

As a kid who fully believed he was Tarzan, there were no barriers between my imaginary world and my real world. To me, they had been one and the same. There were no limits to what I could achieve, and I finally decided to merge those two worlds together again. I became Tarzan. I became Jacques Cousteau. I became the very person they inspired me to be. An explorer. I finally became me.

In April 1993, I booked my one-way plane ticket to Asia, leaving the USA to pursue my own American Dream…

With no guidance, no boundaries, and no limits, I made my dreams a reality, and my life as an adventurer began.

I was finally free.

Jean-Philippe with the Mentawai, 1993 (left) and 2008 (right).

Epilogue

"And then there is the most dangerous risk of all — the risk of spending your life not doing what you want, on the bet you can buy yourself the freedom to do it later."

— Randy Komisar, *The Monk and the Riddle*, 2000

More than two decades later, I can't imagine what my life would have been like if I had stayed at Microsoft. One thing only is certain: it wouldn't have been the adventurous life I'd dreamed about. So many of my friends forfeited their dreams for the comfort of security. I risked everything to live mine. I have come to realize that I gave up financial wealth for another type of richness: an incredible life of adventure, discovery, and human encounters. I have become rich with experience, for I have always lived a full life. My dreams. My life.

Most importantly, I have become rich with love and family. We can experience many incredible things in life, but it's being able to share these moments with loved ones and others that is the biggest achievement.

One of the most considerate, compassionate, and giving people I have ever met — my wife, Yumi — became the bridge between my sister Karine and me. With Yumi's help, Karine and I rediscovered the bond we had lost since early childhood, exchanging our most intimate thoughts about life and sharing the secrets of our very different childhoods. These were moments of understanding and compassion, often deeply emotional, but also of healing.

Throughout my travels and experiences, I was blessed to meet wonderful people. Through these magic encounters and the rediscovered bond with my sister, I was able to reflect on my life. Following Cousteau's words of wisdom: *"When one man, for whatever reason, has the opportunity to lead an extraordinary life, he has no right to keep it to himself,"* I chose to break a long-buried silence and share with others by writing *I, Tarzan*. If we choose to live our true life, no matter the odds, we can all be Tarzan.

Afterword

In 1993, Jean-Philippe left the city behind to travel through the dramatic vistas of the Himalayas and discover the depths of Southeast Asia's rainforests — living out his childhood dream.

After a number of solo adventures through the mountains and jungles, he found his tribe that same year. While exploring some of Asia's most remote mountains and jungles, he was compelled to stay in the thick tropical jungle of Siberut, where he met the Mentawai Indigenous people. He was blessed to be not only welcomed but adopted as a clan member, sharing the life of this hunter-gatherer tribe. Even more fortunate, he was able to witness the entire apprenticeship and daily habits of the man who would become one of the most revered Mentawai shamans and leaders today.

Following his first immersion in the Mentawai clan, Jean-Philippe moved to Japan for four years. During this time, he busied himself teaching French and English, racing XC ski marathons and ultras, and road cycling.

After he left Sapporo in 1998, Jean-Philippe's thirst for adventure and desire for cultural preservation led him to conceive his largest scale and most extreme expedition, an undertaking that had never before been attempted. It's an achievement that remains unique to this day, and one that sets the bar for any adventurers who choose to follow.

His three-year sea kayaking adventure covered three thousand nautical miles through seven countries following the flow of the Atlantic and Pacific coastlines that cut through Central America.

From storms at sea to armed bandit encounters, shark attacks, and bouts of malaria, nothing could stop his determination to conquer an adventure that no one else had done before. This intrepid journey caught the world's attention and was featured in numerous media outlets across North America and beyond.

Dancing with Death: An Inspiring Real-Life Story of Epic Travel Adventure, the winner of four international book awards and an Amazon bestseller, depicts this enlightening and oftentimes grueling journey through a compelling narrative.

After returning to Seattle, Jean-Philippe's amazing encounters with Indigenous peoples along the way inspired him to found the Native Planet Non-Profit Organization, an NGO dedicated to protecting the welfare of some of the world's most fascinating tribes.

Jean-Philippe also worked as a professional travel and culture photographer; his images of Indigenous communities have been published by *National Geographic*, the United Nations, and other prominent publications around the globe.

During the kayak expedition, while visiting a small traditional Maya village in the mountains of Guatemala, he met Yumi, a Japanese woman sharing the same passion for travel, Indigenous cultures, and endurance sports. They got married in Japan at the end of the expedition.

Jean-Philippe and Yumi moved back to Seattle in 2002. He participated in track cycling races, became a USA cycling coach, and with Yumi founded and led a cycling club, organizing cycling fundraising events to finance humanitarian projects to help the Mentawai.

For a full decade, Jean-Philippe returned frequently to meet with the Mentawai people, working on malaria prevention and cultural preservation projects while documenting their culture and lifestyle; he started by capturing photographs and producing texts.

His incredible life-changing adventure with the Mentawai shamans inspired him. He kept his best photos from magazines to unveil in a future project: a photobook of his unique images featuring the lifestyle and culture of the jungle dwellers, which is now in production. (Of note: The photo montage preceding the Epilogue illustrates the time between the end of *I, Tarzan* and the beginning of *Dancing with Death*, which will also be the subject of an upcoming book.)

In 2006, he continued his work on the Mentawai culture by acting as guide, interpreter, and logistics director for a documentary film crew, co-starring alongside famed French actor Patrick Timsit and producer Frederic Lopez. The result was the award-winning *Rendez-vous en Terre Inconnue: Patrick Timsit chez les «Hommes-Fleurs» en Indonésie*, which received critical acclaim and record-breaking viewing numbers.

While leading the Seattle-based cycling club, in 2007 Jean-Philippe organized and led his first Pyrenees crossing tour. It quickly became clear that he wanted to curate something different from other tour operators.

He couldn't get onboard with the idea that something as spectacular and thrilling as cycling the Pyrenees could become a well-worn template for huge commercial conglomerates. He wanted to share one-of-a-kind adventures with cyclists who yearned to see more. He took all that energy and passion for cycling, adventuring, history, culture, and travel and poured it into designing the most unique and incredible cycling tours of Europe.

In 2008, he also worked as interpreter, personal guide, and expedition logistic coordinator for world-famous, multiple award-winning photographer Sebastio Salgado.

At the end of that year, Jean-Philippe and Yumi crossed the Sahara by motorcycle, traveling four months throughout the Sahel countries of Western Africa — a journey he planned not to follow his own dream but to accomplish a dream of his father.

In the spring of 2009, after more than twenty years of travel and adventure, Jean-Philippe moved back to his native French Pyrenees with Yumi and extended his tour repertoire to include Corsica, the Alps (where he had lived and trained as a Mountain Commando), and other awe-inspiring destinations. He rebranded the company as VéloTopo in homage to the cycling destinations he had covered and treasured — from the Pyrenees to the Alps, the island of Corsica, Provence, Dordogne, Asturias-Cantabria, the Dolomites, and the five epic countries of France, Spain, Italy, Switzerland, and Andorra.

In 2016, the year he turned fifty, Jean-Philippe set himself a challenge to cross the entire Pyrenees, cycling over major mountain climbs in less than three days — a challenge that usually takes strong cyclists a full seven days. It was his own half-century celebration, a wink at the solo-run crossing of the Pyrenees he had done thirty years before, a month before leaving his native country.

In 2019, Yumi, also an elite cyclist, suggested they race as a pair in the world's longest and toughest cycling race across Europe. No pair had ever succeeded before, and Yumi wanted them to give it a shot.

They raced unsupported across Europe from North Cape, Norway, to Tarifa, Spain, crossing fifteen countries and covering over 7,800 kilometers with a staggering 80,000 meters[1] of elevation. In spite of losing two days to mechanical incidents, they finished it in thirty-three days, averaging 236 kilometers and over 2,424 meters[2] of elevation daily, to set the record as the first pair to ever finish this race.

This epic adventure is the subject of a book Jean-Philippe is currently writing. It's not a mere record-breaking, bike-racing book. It's a tale of courage that will inspire all to live their dreams. It's a fight against age and adversity to show that even as we're aging, we can continue to accomplish the impossible. If you'd like to be notified of its release, please join the mailing list at www.jpsoule.com.

In 2020, at age fifty-three, Jean-Philippe participated in his first solo ultra-bikepacking race in the Sultanate of Oman, placing twelfth in a field of eighty athletes from forty different countries and taking the first position of any cyclist over fifty years old. He got hooked on ultra-cycling.

1. 4,800 miles with a staggering 262,000 feet of elevation
2. 147 miles and over 8,000 feet

Entering his mid-fifties, Jean-Philippe never stops imagining and planning new expeditions and travels. The adventure continues…

> *"We only feel the weight of age that we allow ourselves to feel."*
> — Jean-Philippe Soulé

I. UNITED STATES OF AMERICA XI.
DEPARTMENT OF TRANSPORTATION — FEDERAL AVIATION ADMINISTRATION
THIS CERTIFIES THAT IV. JEAN-PHILIPPE SOULE
V. 12451 NE 141 ST
KIRKLAND WA 98034

DATE OF BIRTH	HEIGHT	WEIGHT	HAIR	EYES	SEX	NATIONALITY VI.
12-27-66	72 IN	184	BROWN	BROWN	M	FRANCE

IX. HAS BEEN FOUND TO BE PROPERLY QUALIFIED TO EXERCISE THE PRIVILEGES OF
II. PRIVATE PILOT III. CERT. NO. 534157554
RATINGS AND LIMITATIONS
XII. AIRPLANE SINGLE ENGINE LAND<
XIII.
VII.
SIGNATURE OF HOLDER
X. DATE OF ISSUE 07-27-92 XIV. VIII.
ADMINISTRATOR

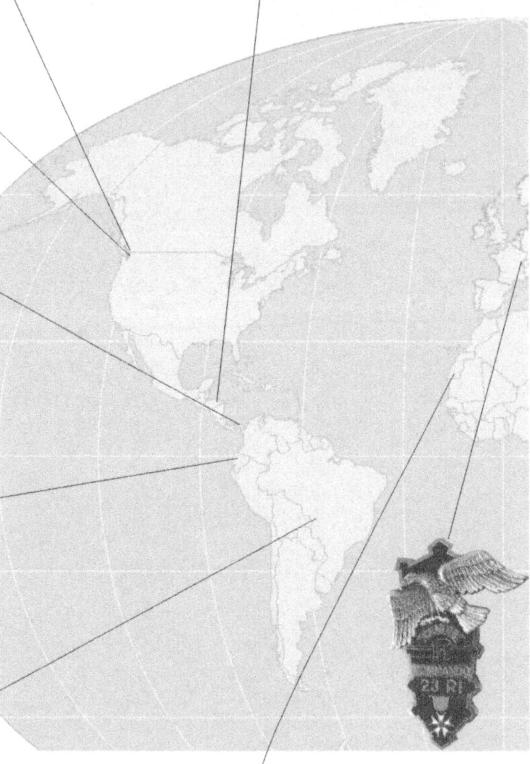

謹賀新年

今年もどうぞよろしくお願いいたします。　平成14年　元旦

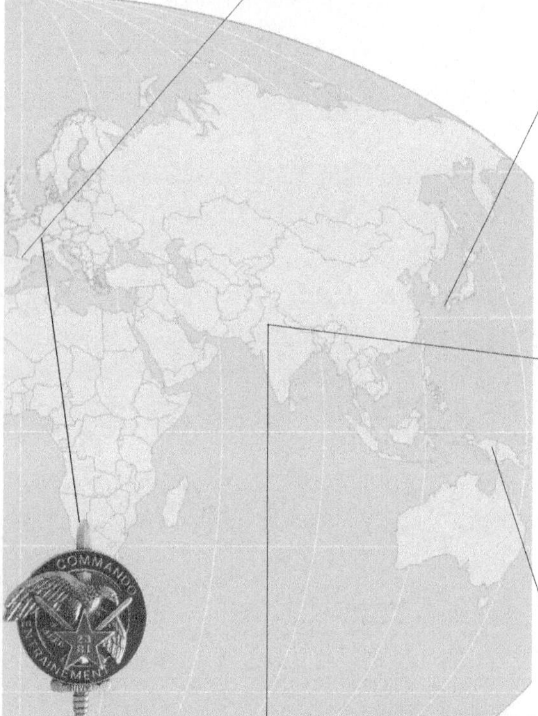

Author's Note

I, Tarzan: Against All Odds describes my first twenty-six years. A rich life of epic adventures followed, including traveling through most of Southeast Asia and the Himalayas, living with the Mentawai jungle shamans (a book in progress), and completing a three-year Central American kayaking expedition just before my thirty-fifth birthday (chronicled in *Dancing with Death*). These inspirational books are all part of my **"*Live Your Adventure* inspirational memoirs series."**

Twenty more years of travels and endurance sports came next. As an endurance athlete, guide, and ultra-cyclist, I'm also writing books about the later years in my life and how I combined extreme endurance sports and travel. These books will inspire you to continue to live your dreams, have beautiful adventures, and maintain good physical health, even after the age of fifty.

I invite you to peruse a sample of photos and to join my mailing list to be informed about future releases at: www.jpsoule.com.

If you've enjoyed *I, Tarzan: Against All Odds*, your honest review can help me continue to write new books. I can't express how grateful I would be if you followed this link to leave a review:

https://mybook.to/reviewtarzan

Thank you,

Jean-Philippe

Your free eBook!

Sign up for alerts about new releases and a free download of *Dining with My Cannibal Friend.*

Dining with My Cannibal Friend

"You are big and white. You have a lot of meat and you look delicious!"

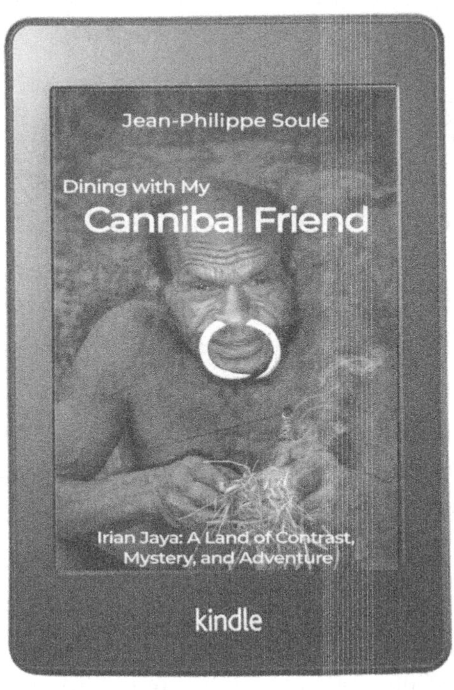

Six thousand words are all it takes for you to join the award-winning author of *Dancing with Death* on a grand travel adventure.

In this short but gripping narration, he will guide you through a world few could imagine—where the inhabitants practice ritual cannibalization. True stories are often better than fiction.

Your free eBook:
https://getbook.at/cannibal

More Books by the Author

DANCING WITH DEATH: An Inspiring Real-Life Story of Epic Travel Adventure

Fans of Jon Krakauer will devour this gripping tale of adventure, survival, and a search for life's deeper meaning.

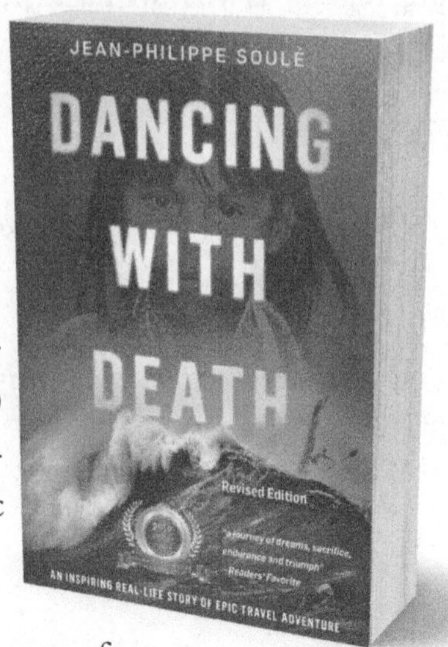

The winner of four international book awards and an Amazon bestseller, *Dancing with Death: An Epic and Inspiring Real-Life Travel Adventure* depicts an enlightening and oftentimes grueling journey as the compelling narrative recounts the author's three-year sea kayaking adventure, covering 3,000 miles through seven countries following the flow of the Atlantic and Pacific coastlines through Central America.

How many of us fantasize of walking away from the daily grind of the American Dream to embark on a grand adventure? That's exactly what former French Special Forces Commando Jean-Philippe Soulé did in real life — abandoning his cushy Microsoft job to launch into a three-year kayaking adventure of unforgettable discovery and life-threatening danger in Central America.

In 1998, Jean-Philippe and his travel partner Luke Shullenberger shed the trappings of comfortable civility to venture into the Central American Sea Kayak Expedition 2000 — an ambitious quest to paddle all the way from California to Panama. The bold expedition would take the two men across 3,000 miles of the remote and wild Central American coastline, spanning three years, seven countries, and countless once-in-a-lifetime experiences.

Now, twenty years later, Jean-Philippe Soulé reflects on this incredible and enlightening journey in *Dancing with Death* — a compelling real-life travel memoir that documents the tales of exploration, endurance, and self-discovery that Soulé and Shullenberger experienced as they kayaked across the world's most exquisite and treacherous waters. Readers of all ages will be inspired as they follow Jean-Philippe and Luke on this extraordinary transformational voyage — testing their limits, exploring new cultures, and learning that life is what we make it, if only we dare to reach for our dreams.

A FEW EDITORIAL REVIEWS:

> *"Thrilling adventure, soulful insights and crisp, fast-paced writing."*
> — IndieReader

> *"What the power of human will can accomplish is inspiring, emotional, and empowering."*
> — The Book Review Directory

> *"A fast-paced story that will grip you and inspire you. Highly recommended."*
> — The Wishing Shelf

FROM THE AUTHOR:

> *Dancing with Death* will take you on the ride of a lifetime. It's a roller-coaster of resilience, rare encounters, and moments that will leave you on the edge of your seat, as well as a fascinating account of adventure, passion, and an insight into our very own lives. I hope reading this book will inspire you to pursue your passions and dreams.
>
> — Jean-Philippe Soulé

Jean-Philippe is currently working on new real-life adventure memoirs. Find out more about Jean-Philippe and all his books and view his award-winning photos at www.jpsoule.com

Made in the USA
Monee, IL
28 July 2021